PRAISE FOR
The Nine Rooms of Happiness

"By helping you find grace in the metaphorical emotional rooms of your life, *The Nine Rooms of Happiness* walks you through the lifelong process of finding joy and health."

— DR. MEHMET OZ,
bestselling author and host of *The Dr. Oz Show*

"You can be happier every day, and this book shows you how. Plus, once you are, you can also be healthier and fitter. Using the strategies within these pages, Lucy stopped stress eating and lost 25 pounds. *The Nine Rooms of Happiness* will help you achieve your most personal goals."

— JILLIAN MICHAELS,
health & wellness expert on *The Biggest Loser*
and the NBC show *Losing It With Jillian*

"In our hectic lives, it's too easy to get bogged down sweating the small stuff and lose track of happy moments. *The Nine Rooms of Happiness* reminds us to focus on the big picture and find simple pleasures every day. I recognized myself in some of those cluttered rooms. Now I'm ready to create my own happier emotional house."

— DEBORAH ROBERTS,
ABC News correspondent

THE NINE ROOMS OF HAPPINESS

THE NINE ROOMS OF HAPPINESS

Loving Yourself, Finding Your Purpose, and
Getting Over Life's Little Imperfections

Lucy Danziger and
Catherine Birndorf, M.D.

voice

Hyperion   New York

The Library of Congress has catalogued the hardcover edition of this book as follows:

Danziger, Lucy S.
    The nine rooms of happiness : loving yourself, finding your purpose, and getting over life's little imperfections / Lucy Danziger and Catherine Birndorf.
        p. cm.
    ISBN 978-1-4013-2335-6
    1. Happiness.   2. Conduct of life.   I. Birndorf, Catherine.   II. Title.
    BF575.H27D37 2010
    158.1—dc22

                                                            2009036537

Paperback ISBN: 978-1-4013-4156-5

Hyperion books are available for special promotions and premiums. For details contact the HarperCollins Special Markets Department in the New York office at 212-207-7528, fax 212-207-7222, or email spsales@harpercollins.com.

FIRST PAPERBACK EDITION

10 9 8 7 6 5 4 3 2 1

To our families and all those who
help us realize how happy we are

CONTENTS

ACKNOWLEDGMENTS

This book, this effort, this process, is dedicated to all those who make me happy and put up with me when I forget to be grateful, content, present, and pleasant. Leading the list is the amazing James Danziger, without whom I couldn't be me, quickly followed by my kids, Josie and Julian, the two most fun and multifaceted people I know. I am also indebted to my brother, Peter, the competitor and all-around nice guy; my mom, Sarah, the creative cheerleader; and my dad, Tony, the supporter and honest critic. (And I can't leave out the WSM, Liz, helpful advisor and publishing maven.) I'd be nowhere without this loving, tight-knit family, which, for the past two decades, has included the Danzigers, especially Gigi (the most glamorous of my relatives) and Danny, an accomplished author himself. Plus my wonderful friends: Andi and Lisa, who listen to it all, tirelessly, and a small group of special women who I adore. And my cadre of talented and dedicated editors at *Self*, who've helped make the magazine great every month, and my bosses who allow a working mom to write a book in her spare time. Thank you also to our patient and positive editor, Gretchen Young, and the talented team at Hyperion's Voice imprint, without whom this book would never have happened. Two special shout-outs go to Mark Reiter, who believed in the idea behind this house metaphor, and my passionate and brilliant, warm and sisterly coauthor, Catherine. Without you I'd still be *suckin' it up, Buttercup!* Now my hope for all you readers is that you let this book change your life for the better, in any room where you are faced with a mess. Happy cleaning.

—Lucy Danziger

First, I want to thank my husband, Dan, who is the most supportive, even-keeled, loving, and sarcastic person I know—and who knows me sometimes better than I know myself. Thanks also to my daughters, Phoebe and Hannah, for always loving and challenging me and tolerating my not being there to put them to bed on nights when I had to work late. Thanks to my parents, Carole and Larry Birndorf, who have always encouraged (but never pressured) me to go after what I wanted; my brother, Steve, my oldest new best friend; my sister-in-law, Susie, the sister I never had; my parents-in-law, Roz and Stan, who welcomed me into the family from day one; and Brian and Steph, my brother- and sister-in-law, who set the bar high. I want to thank all of my friends who've helped shape who I am, especially Sarah, Caitlin, Robin, and Stacy. To Debbie and Carolyn, for peer supervision. Thanks to all my colleagues at Cornell, especially in the Payne Whitney Women's Program, for supporting my endeavors beyond the ivory tower; and Sharone Ornstein, without whom this book couldn't have been written; to the women interviewed here, for sharing your stories; to my patients who have provided me the privilege to care for you; to my agent, Mark Reiter, who took this idea seriously and helped craft its clarity. And to my writing partner and good friend, Lucy Danziger, who helped discover the writer in me: You are the perfect complement to my shrinkiness. And thanks to all the readers out there; I hope you feel validated and enlightened by the stories in these pages, since this book wouldn't have meaning without your participation.

—Catherine Birndorf

I have sometimes thought that a woman's nature is like a great house
full of rooms: there is the hall, through which everyone passes in
going in and out; the drawing-room, where one receives formal visits . . .
and in the innermost room, the holy of holies,
the soul sits alone and waits for a footstep that never comes.

—Edith Wharton,
"The Fulness of Life"

Welcome to Our House . . . and Yours

THE SCENE: my bedroom. The alarm clock goes off at 6:35 A.M. As I reach to press the off button I think: *I should have gotten up earlier.* Sunlight is streaming through the shutters as I get out of bed, being careful not to wake my husband, who is dozing next to me. I walk down the hall and peek into my daughter's room—she's still asleep, her stuffed dog cradled in her arms, her sweet, slender body curled up and cozy. I look in on my son, who has tossed off his covers and is snoozing with arms and legs splayed out, proving once again that sleep can be an aerobic activity. I smile and let these two snapshots set in my memory . . . then I berate myself, thinking, *I don't spend enough time with my kids!*

I pass through our living room, where the dozens of photos covering the bookshelves and end tables remind me that I am blessed in many ways: a tight-knit family, wonderful friends, and a great job. My eyes linger on a picture of our little, gray, shingled bayside weekend house . . . and I think: *Why don't we go there more often?*

Then I see my home office desk in the corner, piled high with unanswered letters and unpaid bills and I groan. *I have to catch up on those!*

I enter my kitchen to start the coffee and watch the morning TV headlines. I avert my eyes from the dishes stacked up in the sink and think: *I should have put them in the dishwasher last night.*

An hour later, after an invigorating jog through Central Park with my dog, I'm still high on endorphins as I head to the bathroom to get ready for work. I feel strong and healthy, energized and optimistic. My husband and kids are awake now, going through their morning rituals, which assures me that all is right with the world. As I step into the shower, I catch a glimpse of myself in the mirror and think, *Oh, yeah. I still hate my hips.*

Do you see a pattern here? By most people's standards I have it all. But even so, on this beautiful morning, I am tormented by a dull ache of dissatisfaction. I sabotage my happiness, as if to tell myself, *I don't deserve all this.* And whenever I do manage to feel good about myself, or my accomplishments, my next thought is: *Who do you think you are?*

I have a name for such thoughts—nega-speak—and I had come to regard them as my constant companions. Taken individually, they are not evil or undermining. In fact, they can serve as essential alarms, sounding off when I'm at risk of becoming a little too pleased with myself. They provide me with necessary smug-proofing.

But collectively, these glass-half-empty-isms are a menace that can shake the foundations of the life I've built with my husband and family. Even in the face of overwhelming evidence that I am lucky and loved, these negative thoughts fill me with feelings of inadequacy, guilt, and stress.

Did I say *me?* I meant *we. All* of us. All women.

We struggle every day to achieve a happy, balanced life, yet we allow the slightest misstep to throw us off balance. And it's usually the little things that knock us sideways, not the major ones. The big problems we face down with courage, forbearance, even grace.

The poisonous mind-set I described above—the negativity, perfectionism, self-sabotage, and dissatisfaction—is the biggest happiness stealer in many women's lives. It's a disease, an emotional cancer that you can, and must, learn to cure. With our help, you will.

In fact, the very process of writing this book with a coauthor who is a gifted and insightful (and uniquely approachable) psychiatrist has almost completely cured me of my bad habits. I say *almost* because self-awareness is an ongoing process that never really ends. The morning scene above was the *old* me; for the most part I have learned to think differently, to be happier every day, and to live with less inner conflict. I have also learned I have to work for my daily doses of happiness, recognize them when I find them, and appreciate those moments when they arrive.

Turns out most of the time I am happier than I think I am. Perhaps you are too. We're here to help you discover this fact for yourself.

Being Happier Is Like Being Fit; You Have to Work at It

As an editor of women's magazines for more than fifteen years—helping women achieve their own personal best and realize their health and well-being goals—I've learned that the little things can be overwhelming for many women, while those circumstances that are devastating on the face of it (illness, loss, divorce, etc.) may actually turn out to be galvanizing (as in, *What doesn't kill me makes me stronger*). The events that most often manage to steal our happiness are the minute details that we allow to get under our skin. How do I know this? Because month after month, in e-mails and letters to the editor, through polls and surveys online, along with questions posed by readers to a lineup of esteemed experts, I hear what's on the minds of 6 million monthly readers of *Self*. Weight issues, friend tensions, family squabbles, money problems, plus conflicts with mothers, brothers, boyfriends, bosses, and even ourselves, result in guilt, regret, longing, insecurity, and the search for perfection in all areas.

Even as the editor in chief of one of the largest well-being lifestyle magazines on the newsstand, I struggle with the need to feel happy and healthy. It's a discipline, like staying in shape or not spending too much money or eating healthfully. And just because you "arrive" at being fit, slim, debt free, or happy doesn't mean you can stay that way without trying. You have to appreciate the perfect moments when they present themselves and understand that not everything has to be perfect for you to appreciate your own happiness. Meanwhile, trying to attain such moments requires a combination of focus and practice, since you can train your brain to adopt a positive mind-set, as well as learn to become a happier person.

At first, it requires you to break bad habits and replace them with good ones. But it gets easier. Like a tennis player who needs to change her grip to make sure her backhand doesn't go into the net, after a while the muscle memory of her powerful swing becomes more natural. Practice it enough, and eventually you just swing for the ball, without having to think your way through the process—your body just knows what to do. The same is true of happier thinking: It may seem foreign at first, but after a while you'll begin to string together more positive moments with ease.

For me, the turning point was one day realizing I needed to change the way I think, and then actually doing it. Once I got my own act (mostly) together I wanted to write a book to help other women do it also. I was eager to team up with the right mental health professional, one who is both a talented clinician and a down-to-earth person you want to tell your life story to, someone who neither passes judgment nor minces words.

I was lucky enough to find the perfect collaborator, Dr. Catherine Birndorf. She is a leading specialist in women's mental health and can help almost anyone find happiness by showing them how to recognize their own participation in their emotional reality. I play the role of "every woman" for the sake of this book, and tell my stories in the first person as a way of illuminating common thought processes, while Catherine stays one step removed as the expert, always referred to by name. What we share is a common philosophy, that women are not victims, but architects of our own emotional destiny.

The first step is to identify patterns that may be trapping you in an unhappy dynamic. The next is to realize that you have a choice, that if something isn't working in your life you have the power to change it. Through self-awareness and understanding how these patterns work, Catherine helps us see that each of us can live a happier life.

Suck It Up, Buttercup! And Other Useless Advice

I never wanted to go to a shrink. I'm from the school of tough love, even for myself. My friends know my motto has always been "Suck it up, Buttercup." When I say it to myself, essentially it means, *Don't whine!* I can usually snap myself out of a bad mood just by telling myself, *Stop complaining—look around and see how good you have it, how lucky you are!*

When I get stressed over being too busy, I remind myself, *You're lucky to have a job, a family, a list of "to-dos" that keep you scheduled to the hilt.* I try not to act spoiled—instead to feel grateful for all that I have, and the blessings I can count daily.

Hate my butt today? I want to rail on myself for such frivolous blather and tell myself: *Think about your friend battling cancer who'd love to be complaining about saddlebags rather than the chemo.*

Too many bills to pay? *Cut up the credit cards, freeze 'em, or just stop the mind-set that allows you your pricey "treats,"* I say to myself.

Cold, wet, rainy morning? *Bundle up and go running anyway! There's no such thing as bad weather, only bad planning. Or bad clothing choices.*

For a long time, tough love worked for me. But then I realized it's no way to solve problems; it's just shoving them down, out of sight. And I was still feeling down on . . . me. Oh, and I *was* "sucking it up" . . . by stress-eating, drinking too much wine, not sleeping well, getting overly tired, getting injured, and suffering from repeat sinus infections. Plus I was carrying an extra twenty-five pounds. I appeared to be happy but I was a walking font of negative thinking. Fortunately, I finally decided to stop sabotaging myself.

Even when women manage to do the right things for their bodies—exercising regularly and eating right—they often don't feel *good* about themselves. I relate, and I have always tried to edit a magazine that held as its central philosophy that being fit and healthy is only one component of well-being; the other half of the equation is how you feel *inside*. But everything seems to come crashing down when you don't feel so good, or think you don't look your best.

Self discovered another amazing fact in a survey: Of all the things that send women to the doctor (allergies, stomachaches, headaches, etc.), the number one complaint is anxiety or related symptoms. I soon realized that happiness—or what I would later understand to be contentment—was the true goal for women, not flat abs, glowing skin, an adoring partner, or a comfortable number on your bank statement (though those can help).

I decided six years ago that *Self* needed a happiness expert. We already had a fitness expert, a sports medicine doctor, two nutritionists, and a handful of other experts writing on topics ranging from beauty to kinesiology. The outer self was covered. I realized that emotional health was the true topic underlying most of the other physical ones, and *Self* needed someone to help our readers with their inner selves.

That same week, I got excited as I watched an interview with a young psychiatrist on the *Today* show talking about women's mental health issues. Dr. Catherine Birndorf was fresh, intelligent, perceptive, and nonjudgmental as she talked about the connection between our physical selves and our emotional selves, and how mental health is a vital component of physical health. I realized that she was talking about me—and every woman I know.

I decided right then that *Self* needed Dr. Birndorf. Pronto! I tracked her down at Weill Cornell Medical Center, where she founded the Payne Whitney Women's Program, and invited her to write a Q&A page on happiness for the magazine. I also started talking to her regularly about why a woman's moments of jubilation or even just self-satisfaction tend to be fleeting, and why the extended periods between those joyful moments are plagued by our inability to appreciate all the good around us.

Not Your Typical Shrink

Catherine and I have always been eager to help people, but we do it in different ways. My close friends tell me I'm "the lifestyle police," always telling everyone what to do! (They're smiling when they say that. Usually.) Catherine is the type of person a tourist might stop on the street to ask directions. She gets asked for advice while in stores, on the bus, on the chairlift. If I'm the editor who shares common complaints but also has access to the experts who can help us, Catherine is the psychiatrist we call for consultation—but an approachable doctor who isn't scary or distant. She is the thoughtful listener, the one who you *want* to tell you what to do; but she won't, because her job, she says, is to help you figure that out for yourself.

She is not your typical shrink, though she hates to hear that, since it seems not only to put down her entire profession, but also to set her apart in a way that makes her feel less serious. However, "despite" her warm personality, she is also an experienced and well-respected expert on women's mental health who has the knowledge, clinical skills, and practical touch that makes her great at her job.

So I'm the tough-love women's magazine editor who wants to empower women to help themselves, and Catherine is the professional who says that first they need to have a little help in order to do that. Our people skills complement each other's.

At the end of the day, our opinions don't matter; what matters is we both want to help women have their own opinions, follow their own inner compass. We come to the same goal from different ends of the spectrum. My approach has been to tell myself, "Get over it," and Catherine's is that first "you have to work through it." This book will help you do both.

Individual Stories, Universal Emotions

We have not, for ethical reasons, used the personal stories from any of Catherine's patients, or the stories that appear in *Self*, but those two platforms inform our expertise. Our nearly thirty years of combined experience addressing issues important to women inform every page of this book, since we recognize universal emotions in the individual anecdotes.

No two women are alike, but we guarantee that you will relate to something in these pages. You'll recognize the emotional quandaries and happiness pitfalls we have illuminated in these stories, each one drawn from hundreds of women across the country we interviewed over nearly two years. For obvious reasons (they talk about sex, money, in-laws, siblings, friendships, and their own body hang-ups) we have disguised some identifying (but insignificant) details of their lives. No one is properly named unless we say so specifically, and you shouldn't try to figure out who these women are. They are generous women willing to share; they could be any of us, and we thank them for telling their stories. If you think you recognize yourself or a patient or pal of the authors', understand that each of them could be anyone—yourself included.

Your Life Is Like a House Full of Rooms

Knowing how good she was at helping the readers of *Self* solve their problems each month, I asked Catherine to write a book with me about how it's the little things that bring us down, and how we internalize conflict rather than deal with it in a healthy way. She got as excited as I was, and together we came up with a model that works.

The idea is to see your life through the metaphor of a house, in which every room corresponds to a different emotional area: The bedroom represents sex and love, the living room is for friendships and your social life, the office represents your career, money, and work life. Being happy in a room is often tricky, since you can physically be in one room and emotionally ruminating about another. One messy room can bring you down, even if the others are neat and tidy. Conversely, one neat room can help bring you up, if you know how to use it.

We are here to teach you how to clean messy rooms and shut doors on others so you can be happier in your entire house, every day. With this metaphor you'll learn not only how to be happier in every emotional room, but also how to live in the moment and enjoy the room you're in, no matter what messes exist elsewhere.

By evaluating the problems that came up in the interviews in the following chapters, we will show you how to solve your problems. The process we have developed works, and I am living proof of that.

Now it's your turn.

1

What's Stressing You Out, When Everything Should Be Great?

Everyone is dealing with *something*, even when everything seems right from the outside. It's a theme in our lives. The very act of worrying keeps us busy, but it can keep us from seeing the bigger issues.

The challenge is to figure out what's really bothering you, what patterns of self-destructive behavior you want to change in order to be happier in every part of your life, in every one of your emotional rooms. Perhaps you'll relate to this lament:

> From the outside, you'd think I have it all: beautiful house, wonderful children, devoted husband. But am I happy? I think so. There's nothing that has gone terribly wrong. There's no reason for me *not* to be happy. But I don't feel happy so much as I feel I'm just going through the motions. Sometimes I have the feeling that there's more and I just haven't found it yet. But what . . . and how dare I want more? Isn't all that I have enough?

Of course it is. And she does have enough. So what is missing? Perspective, for one thing. Once you have put all the little things in perspective you can begin to discover your passion and purpose, and find out how you can make a meaningful contribution to the world.

If you are fixated on all the messes in front of you, it's too easy to get distracted from the bigger picture. Once you figure out the big stuff, doing something as mundane as emptying the dishwasher can be a pleasure, if your head is in the right space. We're not saying you will become mindless. Quite the opposite: Everything you do can have a sense of purpose if you understand yourself better.

Who's Happy? Not Who You'd Expect

As the saying goes, money doesn't buy happiness. Nor do fame, glamour, your own TV show, and all the things you might think would make for a happy life. Dozens of studies have shown that the things we think will bring us happiness—winning the lottery, a new house, etc.—do little to boost our long-term inner satisfaction. They may make for a night of celebrating, but before too long the old you reappears, dissatisfaction and all. The effects are temporary—whether the event is positive (a new job) or negative (losing your job); within a few months people return to the same happiness level they had before. In fact, once your basic needs are taken care of, *more* money, *more* success, a *bigger* house, etc., won't bring lasting happiness.

Studies abound that back this up. In a seventy-two-year longitudinal study at Harvard, research conducted by renowned psychiatrist Dr. George Vaillant looked at what makes men happy over their lifetime and found that happiness entailed having good relationships, particularly with their siblings and friends; adapting to crises; and having a stable marriage. Avoiding smoking and not abusing alcohol, getting regular exercise, and maintaining a healthy weight also added to individual happiness. It's just the latest in a series of studies that all basically come to the same conclusion: Happiness comes from within.

In fact, we may even be born with it. Or at least half of it. Researchers believe each of us has what's called a "set point" for happiness, which determines about 50 percent of your happiness quotient. The other 50 percent is determined by what happens after you're born. Of that half, roughly 10 percent depends on where and how you live, the circumstances of your life. So whether you live on a palm-tree-lined beach or out on the frozen tundra, have ample wealth or just enough money to get by, these details account for only one-tenth of your happiness. That means a whopping 40 percent of your happiness is completely up to you—determined by how you feel, how you react to events, and what your basic coping mechanisms are.

Think about how much 40 percent of *anything* is. How happy would you be if you got a 40 percent raise or were able to add 40 percent more longevity (or about thirty years) to your life? A 40 percent swing is enormous. And that's how much of your happiness you can change with just a little bit of effort. All it takes is a decision on your part to reconsider some basic assumptions and patterns.

First of all, realize you are the sole proprietor of your happiness. You're not a victim or a product of events—you're in charge. This could work the following way in the office of your emotional house: You think the terrible economy is "happening to you," but you have a choice in how you react to anything that comes your way. Imagine that your boss walks into a meeting and says, "The company is in dire straits. We have to downsize." Do you say, "I know this is going to be difficult for everyone, and I will help in any way I can"? Or do you rush to the bathroom to burst into tears and call your significant other as you sob: "I just *know* I'm going to be fired!" Which person do you guess gets the ax?

Or instead of imagining a bad course of events, try thinking of what would happen if all the good things you wished for came true: Let's say you won the lottery and were suddenly in possession of $30 million. What would it change? Everything? Nothing? I would travel more but do it in a socially purposeful way. I'd love to start a foundation to help women around the world live self-directed, meaningful, and healthy lives. Would I quit working altogether? Kick back and eat bonbons? No way! Having more money wouldn't make me happier—it would make me feel more responsibility to give back and be a better person. It might change my job description or even my address by a few blocks, but it wouldn't change my happiness. (Or so I tell myself; the effect makes me feel happier right now.)

What happens to you and around you isn't always in your control; how you react to it is, and once you understand that, you can decide to change your own inner satisfaction meter. Your job is to stop thinking that life events make you happy (or unhappy) and start understanding you're a participant in how happy you are, or aren't, and that's a very good thing.

2

You Have the Key to
Your Own Happiness

Don't believe us? Okay, you're right. It's not one key. It's several keys, a whole ring of them, and in the coming chapters we will explain these keys, which will help you break your self-destructive patterns.

One such key is the Relationship Equation, $A + B = C$, where *you* are A, B is someone you are having trouble getting along with (your mother, your boss, your spouse), and C is the relationship you have with that person. You may never be able to change B, the other person, but that doesn't matter. You have the power to impact the relationship just by changing A, yourself. Being able to alter C, the relationship, is what matters, and you can do it.

Catherine adds that when a patient comes in and complains that her mother is driving her crazy, as she has for the last twenty-five years of her life, she wants to jump up and down and say, "That's such great news because we can solve this problem. To make things better, your mother doesn't have to change. The only person who has to change is you. And since you are here, we already know that you want to make things better. I always say, 'Look, you're my patient, not your mother, and we can definitely help you. And by doing so, we will change the relationship.'"

The keys are in your possession and you decide which one to use to solve each problem that's causing you angst. Knowing you can make your own inner happiness quotient go up is both comforting and a big responsibility, since it means you have the power to change—or not. It's up to you.

About the Rooms Concept
and Where It Came From

Catherine told me about a defining moment during her third year of medical school at Brown. This turned out to be a useful lesson for me as well and was the genesis of the main concept behind this book. Here's her story in her own words.

A med student's third year is traditionally an exciting but challenging one because you're on the ward "trying on" being a doctor in several disciplines. I was on the pediatrics rotation, under the tutelage of a legendary teacher, Dr. Mary Arnold. I went to see her to talk about my career, and she steered the conversation to my personal life. Tapping into decades of bedside intuition, she was pressing me about what was really on my mind.

I started talking about my relationship with the medical student I had been dating seriously for two years. We had so much fun together that I ignored all the ways we were different, and not right for each other in the long term. For women, it's one of the most important questions you can ask yourself: What would my life be like with this person? But it was one I'd avoided thinking about, probably because I knew the answer.

Dr. Arnold took out a pen and drew three circles on a legal pad. Each circle represented an area of my life with my boyfriend: social, romantic, and family. The social circle was where we shared common friends, the family circle represented our backgrounds, and the romantic circle was about the relationship. Next she took her pen and pointed to each circle and at me inquisitively, as if to say, How is it going here, and here, and here?

I didn't even need to answer. Seeing it on paper, it was obvious where my life was good and where it was not working.

She put down her pen and sat back, as if to say: Session over. With one simple drawing, she helped me realize that my romance, for all the fun I was having, didn't integrate well with the rest of my life. If only one area was working well, it was not going to make me happy postgraduation. For most women, having a partner who fits into all three circles is essential to our happiness long-term.

Now when I think of relationships, I often think of a Venn diagram, overlapping circles. In my model each person is a full circle, and the relationship is the middle area, where the circles overlap. Women who are experiencing too much overlap (almost concentric circles) have lost a healthy sense of self, whereas those women who have too little overlap (circles barely touching) lack a sense of connectedness. These types of issues come up a lot in the bedroom.

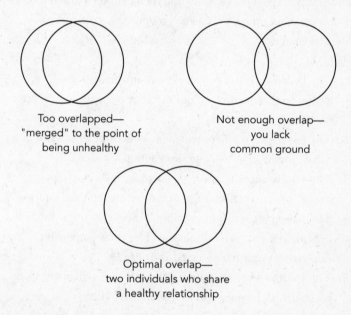

Too overlapped—
"merged" to the point of
being unhealthy

Not enough overlap—
you lack
common ground

Optimal overlap—
two individuals who share
a healthy relationship

Catherine told me this story over lunch one day. She drew the connected circles, and all at once everything clicked—I realized that my life could be described as a series of spaces, and together Catherine and I transformed those spaces into the rooms of a woman's house. An emotional house.

We saw that this house was a compelling metaphor for the way women live and think. We go from room to room all day long, switching roles and needs with ease. And yet we're often not emotionally in the room we are physically in, because we're preoccupied by the mess down the hall. This makes it impossible to enjoy ourselves and be happy in the moment.

The emotional rooms metaphor is illuminating, since we can use it to appreciate the aspects of our lives that are going right, even when there are some spaces that may need a little cleaning.

How to Build Your Emotional House

The first step is to put up some walls and then delineate which feelings and behaviors are appropriate within each room.

Let's take a tour:

1. **The bedroom** is where you explore intimacy—sex, love, desire: our connection to our mate, or our search for a life partner.
2. **The bathroom** is where you face issues of health, well-being, vanity, body image, weight, and aging.
3. **The family room** is where you deal with those you're closest to, such as parents, siblings, and other nearest and dearest.
4. **The basement** is full of childhood memories from your upbringing, your school years, and all those important experiences that have shaped your life.
5. **The living room** is where social connections happen: Here we deal with friendships, neighbors, and all types of peer comparison, such as envy.
6. **The kitchen** is about emotional nourishment and sustenance, sometimes even food. You discuss chores and the division of labor here, at the multifunctional kitchen table.
7. **The child's room** is all about parenting, as well as the question of whether or not to have children.
8. **The office** is your job, career, and other meaningful work. It's also where you grapple with money and financial security.

9. **The attic** in this house holds emotional heirlooms: expectations of your ancestors—where you came from and where they want you to go.

This is how we constructed our house. There are many other ways to do it. You may decide you have a different number of rooms. Or your rooms may be used for other purposes. Whatever suits you. You will get a chance to draw an emotional house that works for your life.

And what house would be complete without an add-on? That's why we are including a tenth room, where you go to get away, to think or dream, to contemplate or vegetate, to do whatever you love, or do nothing but enjoy the solitude. But it's not a place for you to self-destruct with alcohol, drugs, or Oreos. It's a productive, positive space where you can think about your passion and perhaps even find your purpose, the pursuit that is most meaningful to you.

You need to visit this tenth room regularly. It can be an almost spiritual place, since it's where you will get back to your true self, the person you are when no one else is around. This tenth room may not even be a room—it could be an activity such as jogging or walking, reading or meditating, cooking, folding laundry or knitting—but it is a mental space where you can think.

The tenth room is where you get to work on you and truly become the architect of your own life. But first we need to get the other rooms in order.

How Many of Your Rooms Are Neat? Just One? That's Enough!

This is a very important point: You don't need to have *nine* tidy rooms to be happy. Nobody ever has all of her rooms neat at the same time. In fact, one key process is to be okay with conflict, which helps you learn how to be happy even when things *aren't* going right in all parts of your life. This is essential, since you may need to close the door on that messy room and come back to it later, when you have the time and inclination to clean it up.

The good news: There are probably more clean rooms in your house than you realize. The bad? You are often in the wrong room and have to go to the source of the problem before returning. The best news is that once you've done the heavy lifting, you don't have to do it again. Your rooms will stay neat enough so that some light dusting or tidying up will let you feel happy and stress-free for a long time to come.

Say It Loud: I'm in the Wrong Room!

You often don't realize it, but you are sabotaging your relationships and your happiness by letting thoughts from one messy room dictate your behavior in others.

Here's an example: not having enough sex? You two love each other, but after a standoff, or a bout of the silent treatment, coming back together isn't easy. Your fights are always over the same things: You're tired, and he's not making enough of an effort around the house. And the cash isn't flowing the way it used to since he had to take a less well-paying job. If he'd help more around the house at least that would even things out a bit in your mind, and give you a moment to relax, sit, and put your feet up after dinner, and who knows? If he loaded the dishes in the dishwasher and gave you a little shoulder rub, things might start warming up. So the problem isn't in the bedroom at all; it may start in the office, where the bills are paid, or the kitchen, where you divvy up the household chores.

Can't allay your anxiety in the office because the *real* problem is a philosophical difference between you and your mate about spending and saving? You may need to visit the basement to explore childhood memories of family money woes. But the conversation should start at the kitchen table, not in the bedroom. When you finally do return to bed, hopefully you're a bit enlightened and feeling closer. One thing is for certain: Withholding sex won't solve household tension; it will only cause more fights.

We are always aware of the things going on (and wrong) in other rooms: bills to pay, children misbehaving, job tension, etc. And it can make it near impossible to just be happy in the moment, even in bed. And therein lies the problem. You may need to learn to close some doors.

We Clean Our Actual House,
but Rarely Our Inner House

Women are caregivers by nature, often helping those around them before they help themselves. Most women focus their free time on their outer world, the parts of their life that exist in their actual house: relationships, children, job, extended family, and the rest of it. We clean and cook and do the laundry and go to work and then chauffeur the kids around on weekends, and when we do have a little spare time to spend on ourselves it's usually the outer self that gets the attention: We focus (happily, most of the time) on getting dressed, doing our hair, looking our best, going to the gym. And while it is worthwhile, even enjoyable, to present a polished persona to the world, it's not the same as taking care of the *inner* self.

At times the divide between the outer self and the inner self can get so big that there is no connection between the you projected to the world and the you that you recognize as the best version of yourself. One day you wake up and don't like either the inner or the outer you and think: What *happened* to me?

This Isn't a Weight-Loss Book . . .
but I Lost Twenty-five Pounds Writing It

What do *you* want to lose? What bad habit or self-destructive behavior do you want to change? Do you repeat the same pattern over and over (for years) and not evolve?

Applying the concepts in this book helped me see how I'd linked my happiness to body image, how I used sugar to treat my anxiety and wine to douse what I called my "stress fires." By working with Catherine on my family room and other messes, I was able to see that I'd fallen into self-destructive habits (I was internalizing all the stress, friction, and conflict with people I love). And just by changing my emotional inner life I was able to shed unwanted pounds without going on a specific diet (I *hate* diets!). I just didn't need as much food to feel satisfied, since now I was eating for pleasure and sustenance, and not to feel better or self-soothe.

This is not a weight-loss book; it is a life-solutions book. You can obsess about the one thing in your life that's going wrong, or you can learn to let the things that are going right become catalysts, building on the good and minimizing the bad in a positive chain reaction, where you let one good event become the spark for more positivity. When you do that, suddenly it's "all good." Or at least it's *good enough*.

The wonderful irony here is that if you take better care of your inner self, your outer self will look and feel better as a result. I didn't set out to change my body, but by getting my inner house in order, I changed everything: inner self, outer self, and how I relate to the world. The keys are here for you to do it too. Get ready to get happy.

3

You're Happier Than You Think You Are

Once upon a time Catherine and I thought the only truly enlightened people were those who'd had a near-death experience or lost a loved one. We thought those life-changing experiences made the survivors grateful and wise forevermore.

We thought wrong.

Such shattering experiences can change your life . . . but only, it seems, for a while. Then you go back to the old you, for better or worse.

While working on the annual Women's Cancer Handbook at *Self*, which cofounded the Pink Ribbon for Breast Cancer Awareness back in 1992, I have met many women who have faced such life-threatening challenges—diagnosed with advanced-stage breast cancer or, equally threatening, ovarian cancer or metastatic melanoma—and they have survived. Most of these courageous women say the same thing: The hard lessons learned when facing death become less front-of-mind over time. Just as your hair grows back after chemo, once you are "cured" you largely revert to the same personality traits and behavioral patterns you had before. No one knows whether this is part of our survival mechanism or if it's simply our happiness set point reasserting itself.

Michelle, a Los Angeles–based working mother, now in her midforties, who survived a life-threatening bout with colon cancer ten years ago, explains it this way:

You know you're cured and healthy and things are back to normal when you blow up at the little things. It's like a blessing, a welcome back to the land of the living. Because if I can get pissed off at my twelve-year-old son for not making his bed, we both know we're back to normal. I'm just Mom, I'm not Cancer Mom, who could be dying soon. I'd love to tell people you embrace a lighter, brighter way of living once you go through something like that, but the truth is, ultimately you're just you again.

She adds that you do gain a new, bigger perspective, which puts the irritations in context, and it's all just part of a normal, happy life. Michelle says that she tries to remember not to stress out, but adds: "There's nothing wrong with the ups and downs, the silly aggravations. I know I'm lucky and grateful, but it doesn't mean I have to feel that way every second." So the lesson seems to be that "normal" means having ups and downs. The gift is to appreciate both.

It is possible to learn to love your life and the people in it without having a brush with death. Consider the poignant contrasts in Catherine's life and marriage. Catherine and her husband, Dan Labow, both went to medical school but chose different paths to helping people—Dan is a renowned surgical oncologist specializing in one of the deadliest of cancers: pancreatic; Catherine is a respected psychiatrist treating women grappling with problems ranging from relationship crises and depression, to managing family and career, including pregnancy, infertility, and motherhood.

When Dan meets a new patient, someone recently diagnosed with pancreatic cancer, he is greeting someone who may have more hope than time, while Catherine's new patients may arrive with more time than hope.

Imagine that their new patients could switch places for even a day. How would their outlook change if they thought they could possibly die within a year or two? Would they abandon their daily rituals? Change everything? Change nothing? If you could imagine for just one minute that today is one of the last ones you'll spend on the planet, would you appreciate the little things or disdain them? What would you feel most? If we had to predict your answer, it would be: gratitude, overwhelming love, empathy, and appreciation. But you couldn't sustain it every minute (for even that one day!), since that would be impossible. It's simply not the human condition.

This idea is poignantly dramatized in my favorite play, Thornton Wilder's *Our Town*, where the mundane takes on extra meaning after the naive young character Emily has died, but gets to relive one day of her life. She chooses her twelfth birthday, since it was such a typical yet joy-filled day. She doesn't want to choose a significant day, such as when she got married or learned she was pregnant. At one point she asks the Stage Manager (the play's narrator) if human beings ever appreciate "every, every minute." He answers: Saints and poets, some moments only. It's impossible to appreciate "every, every minute," but if we're lucky we can appreciate some moments.

In my life, I try to identify these moments whenever I'm able. I call these "perfect moments" because they make it possible for me to see that my life is full of blessings. All of ours are. For me, the easiest time to identify a perfect moment is when I'm at the water's edge with loved ones and I see glistening sunlight sparkling on the water, and I can take a mental snapshot of this beautiful scene and tell myself, this is it, a perfect moment. And I feel that my life is lucky, blessed, and full. And then, just like that, the moment is gone. Something interrupts it and I can't get it back.

Learning not to let little things bring you down and to appreciate the "perfect moments" in the ordinary day is a life's work, but there are a few tricks that will help you reframe your nega-speak and self-defeating habits into positive behavior, if you choose to.

Let's Be Real—There Are Serious Things to Feel Down About

We won't pretend this book can help someone cope with the stress and fear they experience when dealing with life-and-death situations or the trauma of divorce or total financial ruin. We call those A, B, C problems. This book addresses the X, Y, Z problems, the little ones that should come at the end of any "What's bothering me?" list but tend to push their way to the front of women's minds. When X, Y, Z problems persist they can grow into A, B, C issues quickly, since, for example, a bored woman who seeks excitement may be tempted to have an affair, and then what started as a little problem (lack of stimulation) quickly grows into a big one (finding herself tempted to leave her marriage). So if we're not happy, even when everything is okay in our world, we may blame our spouse or our circumstances, instead of looking inward for the answers. If we don't address them, the X, Y, Z problems in this book can become A, B, C problems before you know it. It's within your control to make sure the X, Y, Zs stay at the end of the alphabet, and focus on what really matters in your life.

Even when there is no reason to be anxious, women create reasons, and often we ruminate on the wrong things, according to a study in *Clinical Psychology & Psychotherapy*, which found that 85 percent of the things women worry about happening never come to pass. Plus, we'd add, women spend an inordinate amount of time fretting over things they can't control. Yet such thoughts plague us day and night. Worry in general seems to be a female epidemic. See if any of these laments sound familiar:

- Whenever there's a cash crunch in our family, I turn it into a doomsday scenario. We're broke. We'll lose everything! Will I ever feel secure?
- When I look in my mirror, I compare myself to friends who look ten years younger. Why don't I look as young as other women? Or as pretty?
- My husband is much more patient with the kids than I am. Why can't I be more like him? I just go off the handle. I need a break.
- Why did I waste time watching that stupid movie last night when I could have been reading, working out, paying bills, sleeping? I have so much to do!
- I constantly catch a view of myself in a window and think I look fat. What do others think? If I were my honey, I wouldn't want to sleep with me!
- If I ask my boss for a raise, she'll laugh—or fire me. I don't understand how to get ahead. I work harder than anyone, but I am not appreciated.

- I worry that my life is just passing me by. If I were rich or famous, I'd be happier. Plus, I could make a more meaningful contribution to the world.

Catherine has heard all of these negative thoughts and many more from her patients, friends, and every woman she knows—this inner monologue is like elevator music for too many of us, constantly playing in the background of our lives. If you don't have an effective strategy for dealing with these minor problems, they can become the big problems. This is why women need to rethink and shift the paradigm.

Your Memory Wants You to Remember the Good Times

Memory is a filter, editing our past like a scrapbook computer program. You go on a trip, and the pictures that make it into the album all show you smiling, enjoying yourself, sharing good times. A picture of frowning children or getting caught in the rain doesn't make it, nor do other unflattering shots for that matter. The overall positive events linger, and we even manage to take an embarrassing childhood anecdote and make it palatable in hindsight. A truly upsetting memory may remain intact in order to protect us against future injury, since if we hurt ourselves we need to remember not to do that again.

But the filter is selective, and Catherine explains this as the "childbirth" effect: If you actually remembered all the pain you went through giving birth, you'd never do it again. Perhaps this is one reason our minds soften the bad parts, leaving us to believe that our past was full of mostly positive memories, or at least that the pain "wasn't that bad."

When I was growing up, my family used to drive from Manhattan to southern Vermont for weekend ski jaunts. I enjoyed the long hours in the dark car with my brother, counting Christmas lights or playing license-plate bingo. Once there, we would sleep all piled into bunk beds in a family friend's condo, then wake early to spend long freezing days on icy runs, where I'd chase my faster pals down the slopes and career dangerously close to chairlift poles. I recall loving every minute of it, so when my kids were old enough to ski, I packed them into our car and drove four-plus hours on a dark Friday night to try to re-create that fun family-bonding experience. It was, to say the least, harder than I remembered.

In today's version of the ski weekend, it became an endurance test that left me wiped out: I'd carry skis (the kids were little); park the car in a far-off lot. We'd finally get through the ticket line (paying a small ransom for the privilege of waiting in another line, for the lift) and then get onto the slope, where everyone immediately started shivering. One child or another would need to go to the bathroom, or get cold, want hot chocolate, or be impatient and not want to wait and go ski off ahead. By late afternoon, we'd trudge back to the car, exhausted, return to the house to watch TV, make dinner, and go to sleep early. Before bedtime, the phone would ring.

It was my nonskiing spouse, calling to check in on how our day went.

"Great!" I'd exclaim, and in that retelling, the sun was shining, the kids were exhilarated. My son loved snowboarding in the half-pipe, my daughter fell off the Poma lift three times (okay, so she cried, but we all thought it was high comedy, and now even she can laugh about it!). Suddenly all was whitewashed; even I started to believe we all had had a grand time. But if someone, a scientist, using what's called the Experience Sampling Method, had beeped me randomly during the day, asked me to rate my happiness, on a scale from 1 to 10 at that moment, I'd have rated it a 3 or lower. Yet if I'd been asked at the end of the trip how it had all turned out, I'd probably have given it a 7 or higher. These are the tricks the brain plays. It is human nature. And this exact experiment has been done, showing memory is a filter that sees things in a positive light.

The interim scores were always lower than the final one, which led researchers to conclude that we are our own best editors when it comes to remembering how we felt in the past. (Ask someone if they are happy in the moment—while shivering on a cold chairlift, for example—and they'll likely tell you they are not. Ask at the end of the trip if they had fun, and they'll say yes.)

The question is, to what end? Why does our memory play tricks on us?

Many talented and respected psychologists, psychiatrists, neurologists, and others have spent decades researching just this question.

The father of positive psychology himself, Martin Seligman of the University of Pennsylvania, has written that the quality of our overall happiness depends more on how we remember things than on how we experience them. Seligman stresses that the spin our memories put on things is more important than how we feel in the moment. By contrast other leading positive psychologists, such as Daniel Kahneman of Princeton University, emphasize the importance of the "experiencing self" as a measure of happiness more than the "remembering self." Kahneman says it's the moment, the actual experience, that matters. Clearly, researchers are grappling with the question of whether the memory of an event is more important to our happiness than the actual experience of the event.

I know that I look back at my life and see it through rose-colored goggles: I'm a sentimental optimist. If I had fun skiing once, I assume I'll have fun skiing again. Seligman believes this makes sense, since happiness isn't how you feel in the moment, it's comprised of three essential components over a lifetime of experiences: pleasure, engagement, and meaning.

I would add that in my years of editing well-being features of, about, and for women, I've found that most of us *want* to be happy. From the point of view of my remembering cold ski weekends, there may have been many miserable moments on the mountain, but in my mind, the lines are shorter, the hot chocolate warmer and creamier, and the frigid wind just a gentle breeze. Despite the long trudge through the parking lot while schlepping little skis, I tell myself it was fun. I want to see the glass as half full. And I want to be rewarded for my natural optimism. So long as I'm pursuing happiness, I like to tell myself I'm on the right track.

Here is the truth about our memory: Looking back, the little niggling annoyances fade away, and we believe we were happy. So if we ask ourselves if we're happy right now, we'd find reasons to downgrade the present from, say, a great day to an only okay day. Ask ourselves in the future to look back at the moment we are living presently and we'd say we were happy then (meaning now) and realize it was actually pretty great. The key is to have that perspective *as we live our lives.*

Think ahead, two weeks, two months, two years, any time frame, and say to yourself a sentence that characterizes what is happening in your life right now, and how you feel about it. Mine would be something like this: "Those were good times! Writing that book, editing *Self* magazine, running triathlons, enjoying my happy marriage, raising two bright teenaged kids, all of it!" The day-to-day stresses, like the bills, the squabbles over homework to be done, my own deadlines at the office, the few pounds that come and go, and all the rest, would just fade to the background and not matter. So why can't we feel that way *right now*, when the stresses are front and center in our minds?

Like editing images for the family album, your job is to try to realize that despite the snapshots that need omitting you are living a happy life. If you find a way to understand that everything that isn't bad is good, you can understand this: You are in fact happier than you think you are *this moment*.

So if your memory wants you to remember the *now* as a happy moment, why fight it? The more relevant question is: How do we help it along?

No One Can Make You Happy.
Well, *Almost* No One . . .

In Bhutan, the king proclaimed that he wanted the people of his country to think not about the Gross Domestic Product but about the "Gross National Happiness" in a measurable way. He made it an official mandate to produce happiness.

By this measure, one reason we westerners have gone awry is that we've made the number one pursuit the GDP, prioritizing all things material. The GNH is an emotional measure of success, and by the Bhutanese way of thinking, if you pursue happiness, you'll be more productive too. We applaud this as a concept, but the trouble is no one agrees on how to measure this type of success, or even if we're using the right term for it.

Happiness is a tricky word because it is not a destination you arrive at or a sustainable state of being. It's a feeling that you experience, just like any other, and it comes and goes. You can generate it, but you can't keep it; you can make it, but not necessarily hold on to it.

Catherine and I don't even think *happiness* is necessarily the right word for what we're pursuing. We joke that it's "the H word" because it can be a negative if women think it's the Holy Grail. Instead of pursuing "happiness" as some permanent state, we want you to appreciate the moments when it eludes you, as well as those when you experience it.

My word for *happiness* is *gratitude*, as in *I am grateful for all of the gifts, tangible and intangible, bestowed upon me*. When I'm not feeling grateful for all that I have, I realize that I'm being childish or spoiled. For Catherine the word is *contentment*. She tries to appreciate and be present in the flow of life, in everyday moments. When she's able to do that, not being *un*happy is enough. Being okay with how things are is the real gift, the mind-set that brings us to a higher place and purpose.

Feeling appreciative of the good things you have is what leads to experiencing more of *whatever* you want to call it: contentment, gratitude or—okay—happiness. It's the general feeling of a positive emotion we are going for here, not the label you use to describe it. The goal isn't necessarily to be happy, but to feel happier no matter what else may be going wrong.

Any author who writes a book claiming to be able to make the reader *happy, happier*, or able to find *happiness* is setting herself up for failure. We are not actually going to make you happy, since the only person who can *make* you do anything is you. Catherine tells her favorite shrink joke here: How many shrinks does it take to change a lightbulb? Only one, but the lightbulb has to want to change.

So we want to come clean right now: We are not going to make you happy. Only you can do that.

If the unexamined life isn't worth living, and the examined life is full of foibles, the most evolved woman examines her life, sees the flaws, and can put them into perspective. I love this bit of wisdom: "The fool thinks he's a genius and the genius thinks he's a fool."

Our corollary: The unhappy woman believes she should be happy all the time. The happy woman believes that there will be times when she is unhappy.

Which woman are you?

4

Draw Your Emotional House

The first step in figuring out your inner architecture is to draw your emotional house. You can do this in your head, or with a pen and paper. We've always loved markers and sketch pads, so we encourage you to commit to a piece of paper for this project. (We promise it'll be fun.) One note: Over time, you may need to redraw the walls, since as you evolve so will your house.

The most useful model may be a cross section where all the rooms are exposed at once, like a dollhouse. We like to draw a three-story house with nine rooms. In our house, the basement and attic lie below and above the other rooms, and on the first floor you'll find the family room, living room, kitchen, and office, since those are the most public spaces. Upstairs lie the master bedroom, the bathroom, and the child's room, since those are more intimately connected.

Neither Catherine nor I live in houses with many stories and nine rooms. We live in New York City apartments, and you know how cramped those are! But trust us, you need a room for every area of your emotional life, and this drawing doesn't necessarily reflect your actual abode.

Now make a list of all the rooms that will be in your house—include the basics (bathroom, kitchen, etc.) and your specifics (kid's room or office), each corresponding to an area of your life. You may add or subtract a room, depending on your stage right now. So if you know you don't want kids, the second bedroom could be a guest room or a place you sew, paint, or write. Once you decide you are including a room, the relevant question is, how big should it be? And that is directly correlated to how much time and emotional energy you invest there and how important that topic is to your overall happiness.

For me, the bathroom was always large because I was preoccupied with weight, fitness, and health in a way that took my attention from other thoughts, and even when I wasn't in the bathroom these distractions followed me into every other room. I would walk into a party and think, *Do I look fat?* instead of, *Oh, there is so-and-so I want to talk to!*

Many women's bathrooms are the largest in their house, since it's where we scrutinize the number on the scale, the bags under our eyes, and all nature of self-criticism. It's also where we need to love ourselves and take care of ourselves (doing a mole check, indulging in a bubble bath, or remembering to floss). The bathroom connects to the bedroom, since feeling fat can torpedo libido faster than you can say *Not tonight, honey!* It connects to the kitchen if you are dieting, and your child's room if you don't like the way your tummy sags after popping out a couple of babies.

Meanwhile, you may think that my kitchen is tiny because I don't cook much. (No domestic goddess here!) But most women's kitchens are fairly large, whether they cook or not, because the kitchen isn't just about meal prep or eating or dishes; it's about all the household chores, responsibilities, and upkeep. We all have to divide up who does what, and if we are married and have families, there is usually a conversation about who will pick up the child at soccer, or take her to the dentist afterward, or any number of other little details that you deal with in the course of a normal day. This is why the kitchen is a multipurpose room, a place where you cook and clean, yes, but also discuss all the household matters at the kitchen table. It is literally the hub of the house.

For each room, think about the big issues you struggle with there, as well as the little ones. If you are constantly aggravated in one room, it has to be larger than the others, because you will spend more time cleaning it up. A room can also be oversize if it brings you an enormous amount of joy, like that newborn in your child's room. If you can't stop thinking about your dwindling cash reserves, for example, that makes your office bigger than most.

Your Emotional House Will
Harken Back to Your Childhood

My emotional house always has a strong nostalgic element—and to this day my family room is huge because I have a close relationship with my brother and his kids. In fact, because he and I played together for long hours growing up (zinging each other with balled-up socks before video games made it possible to "kill" your sibling without actually inflicting pain), we still compete, now in triathlons and skiing and each other's children's accomplishments. This sibling rivalry is both a pleasure and a pain, but mostly a joy, since no one can "zing" at me like my brother, but he is also my first call on all matters family-related. Ever since our parents split up, we've been in it together, through thick and thin, and always will be. So my family room and basement are connected, and both are relatively large.

Catherine explains that the memories we carry through life become an important, even essential, part of the happiness picture as we consider our adult relationships and our patterns of behavior. The basement turns out to be the largest room, since it is the foundation of our house, and those memories (both painful and joy-filled) serve as the blueprint for our emotional architecture.

The Tenth Room Isn't Always a Space,
but You Can Disappear There

An important place for me when I was a child was my personal space—a little bedroom eight feet wide, rarely used, at the back of our prewar apartment, where I would go to disappear. Everyone needs such a place. I would sometimes slip away to that forgotten little room behind the laundry area, near the back door. My parents called it "the dog's room," because that was where the family mutt would curl up to find quiet.

It was a place where I could pat the dog and read and write and avoid scrutiny. Not every house has one and not everyone has the luxury of slipping away in the middle of the day, but the idea is to create some kind of a sanctuary. It's wherever you go to think and contemplate your day, your life, your authentic self. You can do it on a walk, while swimming laps, or wherever you can be alone with your thoughts. For some women it's the solitude of folding laundry; for others it's a long shower or just lying in bed with a book.

It's critical that you go there daily, if only for twenty minutes, especially now that so many of us live on top of one another in our busy, stressed-out lives. I think of it as a "mouse hole," since you can basically disappear into this space and no one can find you or bother you there.

Kids are great at finding mouse holes, since they are better at closing out the world when they need to get away from the noise and the demands of school and family. It's why Harry Potter's little nook under the stairs appeals to children of all ages; it may be small, but it's *his* and he can get away from the dreaded Dursleys when he goes there. We all have our version of the Dursleys, and we all need a space under the stairs, a mouse hole, even if it's only a room in our minds.

Now You're Done and Can Take a Breath, or Even a Walk

Once you've drawn your house and have learned to move from room to room, you will have more control over yourself and your emotions in every room. Then you'll be able to leave your house and see the bigger world—and your role in it—without having your thoughts and feelings about it distorted because you are constantly worrying about those messy rooms. Just by changing the dynamic within your emotional house, you can finally get to the point where you can go out and experience the world from a new perspective: a happier, more confident, and meaningful place.

And You Get to Furnish It!

You have a floor plan, so now it's time to place the big defining pieces for each room—a bed in the bedroom, TV in the family room, table in the kitchen, mirror in the bathroom, etc. The goal here is to take notice of the ways you spend time in each room. For some women, a beautiful bed and luxurious sheets are the key to their bedroom. Perhaps for someone else a futon on the floor is fine, or they have a gorgeous view or tons of sunlight streaming in every morning, or a comfy chair to read in. (Or great, carefree sex, no matter what their bedding preferences.)

As much as I wish everyone in my family sat in the family room playing Scrabble every night, that just isn't the case. I've had to come to terms with the reality of my family room: my husband, James, is on his laptop, writing his blog about photography; my son is using his computer to look up musical chords and teaching himself to play guitar, strumming and singing and entertaining everyone with silly songs; and my daughter is "i-chatting" with pals. It may not be the perfect Norman Rockwell family portrait, but at least we all congregate there, and that makes all of us calm, relaxed, and content. Sometimes, I've decided, sharing the same air is enough.

That's it. Now you're done sketching. You have your emotional house. Next you need to decide which rooms are neat enough and which ones you want to work on.

Where do you want to spend your emotional energy cleaning up a mess? That's where to head first.

5

Pearls and Other
Bits of Portable Wisdom

Each time you are in a messy situation, you have a choice to make: Either shut the door behind you (promise yourself you will clean it up later . . . when you have time, energy, or the right head space), or dive right in. Ready to go? We're providing you with an array of problem solvers here, to break the old negative patterns and replace them with positive thinking (not happy thoughts but productive ones). We call these *key processes*, since you use them to work through the problem and get to a new understanding. You'll then gain a little sound bite of wisdom, called a "pearl," to take away with you and use the next time the issue comes up.

By learning to think differently and reframe the problem, you'll be able to break the patterns that make you (and those around you) unhappy in each room. First you have to recognize the pattern, then decide to change it. The key processes are like arrows in your quiver, and you get to use whichever one works best in that situation.

A Key Process Is Useful; a Pearl Is Forever

A pearl is a tiny little takeaway reward that you can keep in your pocket and think about any time a similar issue comes up. It's like a worry bead because it helps you by reminding you of previous conflicts and how you solved them. It's a shortcut or token that you can pull out whenever needed, and it's easy to remember. The idea of calling these insights pearls originated with Catherine, who recalls being on rounds in med school and trying to diagnose cases.

She and her fellow students held in their heads copious amounts of information about rare diseases, uncommon symptoms, and all nature of medical conditions with names that you could hardly pronounce. But the best doctors also kept in mind the simple truths about unusual or complex cases, and these they called pearls. A pearl was a little bit of wisdom that helped them treat patients who usually had straightforward problems. "If it looks like a duck and quacks like a duck, it's probably a duck." This will remind you that you can overcomplicate things and not see obvious problems staring you in the face.

Or you can blame your state of unhappiness on all the wrong things, and miss the obvious one—you. It's up to *you* to make the changes that will bring you more happiness (or at least less discontent) in every room of your house.

Cleaning Up Your Messy Room

Catherine explains that the first step is learning to identify the patterns of behavior that are causing you trouble and creating the messes in your rooms. These patterns are often defense mechanisms, which we use to protect ourselves from emotional pain. They include things like regression (you revert to childish behavior), displacement (you shift your emotions about one person onto another), reaction formation (you act the opposite of how you feel), etc. These self-defeating, self-destructive patterns often repeat for years before some precipitating event causes you to want to change them once and for all.

You may not even realize why you're unhappy, since these defense mechanisms can work for you until they start to work against you. Your stubborn and persistent nature can take you up the corporate ladder pretty far, until one day you find yourself stalled and realize you have to learn to be more cooperative to make the next step. You've been resisting the suggestions of others, and now it's costing you the next big promotion; it's time to do something about it.

Or in your personal life, your mom may drive you nuts every time you're on the phone with her (wanting to know when you're next getting together) and so you simply stop calling her back. That just makes her more determined to reach you and tell you some annoying detail or how to live your life. The pattern devolves into a lack of communication and your connection suffers until the two of you are basically dysfunctional. Now what? Believe it or not, you have the power to change this dynamic and make it work for you.

But how? Catherine says it takes desire, work, and a true commitment. Plus you need a couple of handy tools. Sometimes you may need to try more than one. Luckily we have a full lineup, and on the following two pages is a simple chart to refer back to any time you're having a problem.

These are just nine of our favorite key processes to use in any given situation where they can help you think differently. Some are what we call kitchen science and others spring from the annals of psychology and psychiatry but with a friendly, layman's spin. You will find them in every chapter, explained more fully.

The chart also includes pearls, which relate to each key process. There are nine listed here, but you can add others, from anywhere and any source that speaks to you—a song, a play, a poem, or your grandmother's favorite expression: "There's no time like the present." Pearls are so precious you'll want to collect and keep them for the rest of your life.

This Chart Is Your "Cheat Sheet."
Refer Back to It

KEY PROCESSES	PEARLS!
1. Screening. Replaying childhood memories like a movie. Freud wrote that we see today's events through the "screen" of this past memory, so it's a significant experience, or scene, relevant today. You bring this filter or perspective to every room, but it originates in the basement, with all your other memories.	**You can't live in the past. Now is it.**
2. Pinging. Also called mirroring, as defined by Heinz Kohut, an influential psychoanalyst. It's the feedback from loved ones you trust. You use these little sonar-like signals to "ping" your way like a dolphin through the shoals to open water and finally reach a point where you can follow your inner compass. You ping most in the family room.	**Be authentic, be true to you.**
3. A + B = C. This relationship equation applies to every close tie you have, but it is especially relevant wherever you have conflict with someone you love—in the bedroom, family room, and kid's room. If you want to change the outcome, it's simple—change A, yourself.	**You can't change them. You can change yourself.**
4. Venn diagramming. Overlapping circles show two people coming together in a healthy relationship. The diagram is useful to illustrate how much you and your partner are connected: too much, too little, or just right. (Note: These were shown on page 15.) It is used more in the bedroom, and you want overlap, but not a total merging of the circles. Sorry, all you *Jerry Maguire* fans, but "You complete me" isn't the goal. No one can complete you, they complement you. You're each a whole circle.	**We don't complete each other. We overlap.**
5. Self-involvement. Also called narcissism. You can be overly involved in yourself, positively or negatively, but either way it affects relationships in every room of the	**It's not all about you.**

house. Self-involvement originates in the bathroom, where the mirror is found, but you may not like what you see. We say walk away from the reflection to have a fuller, happier, more meaningful life.

6. It's not either/or . . . it's both/and. The idea is to give up the all-or-nothing mentality and realize you can have two contrasting ideas be true at once. You can be both furious at someone and love that person. Disagree but be respectful. Most useful at the kitchen table or in the child's room. The key is not letting these personal battles get the best of you. Learn to tolerate emotional discomfort.

Conflict can be okay.

7. Acting out. When you can't express yourself you act it out instead (such as being late when you're angry at someone). It happens in every room of the house, especially with people you have trouble expressing yourself with, like a respected elder or your boss at work. You act badly rather than tell someone how you really feel, since it could be damaging to your current relationships or even to your future. It won't make up for an imbalance of power.

Actions speak louder than words.

8. Too much of a good thing is a bad thing. Being too nice or too giving allows others' needs to suck the life out of you. This occurs so often in the living room that we call it "the giving room." You also commonly see it in the kid's room and the family room. The airlines have it right when they tell you to put your own oxygen mask on first. Take care of yourself. It's not selfish; it's self-preservation.

Know your limits. Be strong to help others.

9. Not to decide is to decide. If you are putting off a major decision and you think it will wait, the delaying is a form of action in itself. To delay is to act, even if it's passive. By missing the boat, you may experience regret about not moving ahead in your life. It's like the old saying: Nothing ventured, nothing gained. But it's also something lost.

Go (along with the status quo) or grow.

How a Typical Scenario Works
(from the Family Room)

Your older sister, who knows you have already booked your vacation, says: "I don't think you should blow off Mom's birthday and go on your vacation!" Normally this would lead to guilt and conflict with your controlling older sister, as it has for decades. But here is a new way of thinking about this situation:

- **First, identify the problem.** In this case it's the conflict between you and your sister over what should be done for your mother on her birthday. Consider her message (she may be right), then the messenger (she may be jealous of your fun plans), and then your own feelings (you've thought long and hard about this trip and it was the only time you could go).

- **Next step? Figure out the source of the mess.** Catherine calls this recognizing the "unconscious process"—a pattern of behavior that may once have worked but is now tripping you up. Catherine calls what the two of you are doing "repetition compulsion," since you have been in this pattern for so long, it's like an old familiar dance and each of you knows your part. It's how you two sisters relate.

- **Third step: Decide if you are in the right room.** If these problems started elsewhere, you may be in the wrong room. For you and your sister, the family room is closely connected to the basement, since your father died young and you both feel compelled to be your mother's surrogate spouse and take care of her, especially on her birthday, and all other holidays.

- **Fourth step: Break the pattern.** Find the key process to clean up the room. Here, the key is learning to live with conflict. Catherine often tells patients, "It's not either/or, but both/and," which basically means you can have two opposing emotions at the same time. Going back to our example, you, the sister who's going to miss her mother's birthday, would tell yourself: "I know Mom will be disappointed and Sis is annoyed, but my vacation is important to me and it's the only time I can take it." The conflicting emotions are something you can live with. It's not guilt versus pleasure, it's guilt and pleasure. Catherine says your thought process doesn't have to be "Submit and feel angry," or "Go and feel guilty." Rather, you should find a compromise you can live with. Perhaps an early birthday dinner before you leave? There will always be conflict, but that is something you can live with, once you know how to handle it. Then you should enjoy the vacation and not let big sis strip your buzz.

- **Finally, see that you've earned a pearl of wisdom.** You can keep this pearl in your pocket to help you sidestep these patterns in the future. In this case the insight is that conflict is part of every relationship, and it's okay. It doesn't have to make you unhappy. Think: "We may not always agree, but I can live with that. We still love each other!" It may even strengthen your bond, since you've related authentically instead of repeating the old pattern. One way to think about this is that you can tolerate the discomfort of your sister's attempt to heap guilt on you, and you may even want to tell her off for doing so. Then tell yourself *I can live with this conflict and enjoy my vacation.* It's not an either/or situation. You can be *both* annoyed at your sister *and* have a great time on the beach. As you toast with your umbrella drink, repeat after us: Conflict can be okay.

Now Add *Your* Own Pearls to the List

If you have a favorite pearl, feel free to use it, share it, add it to the "string of pearls" in this book. It can be a song lyric or a motto or a mantra. I have theme songs. A recent favorite of mine: "Miss Independent" by Ne-Yo, about a woman who has her own thing (that's why her man loves her). I also love Beyoncé's "If I *Were* a Boy," since it's about a woman's desire to live in a way that is true to herself, and not one that conforms to social norms. Another empowering anthem is "The Climb" by Miley Cyrus, with that great line about there always being another mountain to move. (I relate, since I never seem to take the easy path.) Many positive messages speak to me in music, I listen to my headphones while I run, and it helps to remind me that even when I feel down, I need to try to use the little things to pick myself up and help others, too. So for me, music provides pearls on a regular basis.

You can use any kind of reminder that works, such as a movie line, a passage from a poem, or a quote from a favorite novel. It could even be a photograph. It doesn't matter what it is, as long as it works for you.

Using these thinking processes and the shorter pearls will help you in each room of your house. Let's start—enter a room, any room. Since we have to start somewhere in this house, we will bring you to the basement first, that dark and scary place, where all your memories are stored and have the power to make you unhappy today.

But only if you let them.

6

The Basement

Where the Memories
Are Stored

The basement is sometimes a dreary, musty space, but it can be instructive to go down those creaky stairs, pry open the boxes, and rummage around in your memories. You may be surprised to learn where your aversions and preferences really come from. Perhaps you are scared of the dark and remember that night when you were a kid walking along a country road in the dark, far from home, and your sister, brother, and cousins scared you by jumping out from behind the bushes, making you scream in terror.

Okay, that happened to *me*. And to this day, I have had to grapple with a fear of country lanes on quiet starless nights, and the idea that someone or something is going to jump out from behind a bush and try to hurt me. All because of a stupid hoax when I was nine.

The basement is where all your memories get stored. (Don't confuse the scrapbooks of your childhood with the family heirlooms in the attic; those belonged to your grandma, and for our purposes, the attic is where your ancestral expectations are kept.) The basement is where all your childhood hurts and torments are stowed away in cabinets and under the stairs. You would rather not revisit them, but you have to in order to understand how you think and feel today.

The basement is the biggest room in the house because it's the footprint of your emotional architecture; those memories are the precursors to all else. Of course, some memories are more important than others.

I like to say that everyone is always getting over something, their "Rosebud." In *Citizen Kane*, a great and powerful newspaperman utters "Rosebud," as his last word, sending an intrepid reporter on a search for the meaning of the wealthy magnate's life. Rosebud, we learn in the last scene of the movie, was the name of the sled Kane had when he was young and happy. (The sled is a symbol of his innocence, his last moments of being carefree.) In a flashback you see him sledding when he finds out his mother is sending him away to be raised by an uncaring banker, who arrives out of the blue.

In each of our lives Rosebud may not be so dramatic or so easy to pinpoint, but there is something—an insult or an emotional bruising—that each of us will never forget and that rests close to our consciousness. Like a scar, it never goes away. We may not realize it, but we are reacting to it in some way for the rest of our lives.

Think about it: What is your emotional hot button, the event that is "the key" to your past, which explains some part of your motivations and your pursuit of adult happiness?

These defining moments can be big (a divorce) or small (a teacher who tells you, "You'll never be good at math"), and then you spend the rest of your life reacting to that by either becoming an engineer or by not being able to balance a checkbook. Either way the memories are significant because they influence how you think and act today, affecting every relationship you have and creating conflict in every room.

Imagine that you are in your daughter's room, arguing with your eleven-year-old because she refuses to write a thank-you note to her grandmother, your mother. She wants to shoot off an e-mail, but you insist that a handwritten card is the only proper response. You are in a stalemate until you realize that this "battle" is an echo from your past, that you fought with your mother when she made *you* write thank-you notes to your grandmother. Now you're not sure if it's your voice or your mother's in your head as you push your daughter to pick up the pen.

This isn't about you and your daughter, even though you might think you're in your (emotional) kid's room. You suddenly have a clear image of yourself sitting weeping at the kitchen table, being told you had to write a note before you could go out and play. You remember now that your own grandmother always appreciated—as in "quietly demanded"—such notes.

That's called a "screen memory" because not only is it still as clear as a movie for you, but you are still "screening" your behavior and perceptions through it. You need to understand that your actions today—including this argument with your daughter—are distorted by that memory. Writing notes was a painful ritual for you because your grandmother corrected your spelling and grammar in red ink and sent the notes back to you, like homework. One year, you rebelled and thanked her for her present on the phone. You later learned that she was so upset about not getting a thank-you note that she punished you by not sending you a birthday check!

Tell your daughter the story of your painful memories—red-inked notes and the embargoed birthday check—and see if that moves her or at least helps you both understand where you're coming from. Your goal is not to win this argument; your goal is to connect with your daughter and see if you can find common ground.

Why Are Some Memories as Vivid as a Movie Scene?

Freud coined the term *screen memory*, but we are co-opting it here to express the idea that your childhood memories are like home movies. What didn't make the final cut is not as significant as what did, since that is the one you replay now, decades later.

So much of our adult life is filtered through what we remember from childhood. The screen memory may not even have been real, that is, what actually happened, but it is real to *you* . . . and may be bringing you down, in ways you don't even realize.

These memories are a critical part of who you are and how you act and think, since they play an important role in every room. A typical screen memory can be a childhood hurt, a harsh criticism you'll never forget. You continue to see things through that screen, so if someone makes fun of you for being a bad speller or horrible cook, you overreact, by becoming an editor or a top chef. Or you shut down to avoid further hurt. Either way you're doing what we call "screening."

Fear Lives in the Basement

The basement can be the seat of powerful fears, but for me, it is also a source of powerful motivation. Here's just one example: As a young girl, I was always scared of monsters—monsters in the closet, monsters under the bed—but thanks to Steven Spielberg and *Jaws*, that fear morphed into a lifelong phobia of sharks. I grew up going to Martha's Vineyard and watched them making that movie, then went to see it the first chance I got. I was young enough to be traumatized (but old enough to know better) by that scene in the beginning in which the young woman is torn apart by a shark and pulled under. That scene was filmed on my beach and is forever etched in my memory, as if it had happened to me! The fear may be irrational, but it's still real, imprinted on my brain as readily as a real event.

One of the most liberating achievements of my adult life was forcing myself to get beyond my fear of sharks and my fear of swimming in open water. I told myself I just had to get over it, but as Catherine would say, first I had to get through it. Before I could do that, I had to recognize that I was stuck, that my fear of sharks was preventing me from realizing my long-held dream of completing a triathlon.

Catherine says that what I was doing is called "counterphobia," where you do exactly what you fear the most. Some people learn to fly, even get their pilot's license, because they are afraid of getting on a plane. Counterphobia could be considered your body's way of trying to overcome what it rationally knows it shouldn't be scared of. Ultimately, though, it's a form of reacting, as opposed to acting. By integrating your new experience you can change how you feel about an event and even how you feel about fear in general. Which is to say that it is something you can master.

I had no idea how this fear was holding me back in other areas as well—it was as if the fear of one thing was spilling into other "rooms" and causing me to be fearful in ways big and small. The litany of fears was

long: scared of the dark, scared of failure, scared of looking stupid or vulnerable or asking for help. But once I started to conquer this shark fear, I
found it was easier to be brave in every part of my life. As in, "If I can do
this . . . then why not all those other things?"

Getting over it, and through it, was a long process. I got a little help
from the natural world when another fin-related event helped me do
what Catherine calls "remetabolize" my fear of sharks. (She means I had a
chance to churn through it and get a new perspective on it.) Years ago, I
saw dolphins playing near the beach in South Carolina and thought: *Not
every fin is scary. They are welcoming me to come swim, come play, get in the
water!* Once I finally did go in the water, I slowly but surely began to enjoy
swimming in the open sea. I was then able to complete a triathlon, a sport
I had been eager to try for years before I'd gathered my courage.

Catherine explains that fear is paralyzing, but every emotion related
to the basement can also be paralyzing, since it's where we get "stuck" in
the patterns of our past. You can be trapped in a guilty pattern, an angry
pattern, and any of the emotions that stem from childhood hurts.

Living with the Past Means Storing
It in Boxes, Where It Belongs

We all have memories that make us cringe, that we wish we could put in
a box somewhere and never take out. Some are painful, others merely
embarrassing, even humorous (now). For most women, the worst memories include men we wish we had not slept with or moments of humilia-
tion in high school, when the "mean girls" attacked us for being un-cool
or nonconformist. For some women, these memories are painful enough
to be traumatic, and everyday decisions are still affected by them years,
even decades, later.

But you don't have to be trapped by your memories. They are yours,
and yours to change. Catherine tells us that everyone has to make peace
with her past, but this involves delving into it, since you have to bring it
up, think about it, and understand it differently, in a new way. You may
still feel embarrassed or fearful from time to time, but you'll know where

the feeling is coming from, and that diffuses its power. Then you can change the impact of those memories, and in doing so, you can also change your life.

That is the beauty of the basement—it may be the largest room in the house, but it's also not *in* the house; it's under it. That means you can always climb the stairs, turn out the light, and go to any room you choose without taking the baggage with you.

ALL I WANT IS A LITTLE TOGETHERNESS!

"I feel my kids growing up and slipping away from me. I want to organize our family weekends so that we're together more often—just like when I was a kid and we all had long days at the beach. But my kids are always fighting me. All I want is for us to be together, share some quality family time. It feels like it's impossible!"

—Judith, 43; Brooklyn, New York

Judith is a successful lawyer with a private practice that gives her reasonable control of her time. She's married with two daughters and a son, ages nine to fourteen. When Judith thinks about the happiest time in her life, she always goes back to summer days on a beach in Nantucket. The memory is so powerful that she gets happy every time she smells salty sea air.

Those summer days—which, she is quick to point out, were spent in a shabby cabin that didn't have a working telephone—reside in her memory as a golden, uncomplicated time when Judith and her brother were always in or near the water. Her father was reading books and newspapers, propped up on an elbow on a striped beach towel until the flood of words exhausted him and he would snooze. Her mom was either chatting with a friend or walking along the beach, looking for sea glass. Judith recalls her mother being happy all the time, whether she was watching the kids play or fixing up the house or handing out tuna sandwiches and potato chips. For Judith, this was a time when her family was relaxed and secure.

At least that's how Judith remembers it. But dig a bit, and she'll admit that it was a mirage. When Judith was thirteen, her parents' marriage fell apart, and they stopped going to the little shack by the water. Two decades later, she took her husband and very young children back to that cabin to show them around. It was a bittersweet visit—Judith was still enthralled by the place, but she realized that the beach there was the source of both her happiest memories and her unhappiest because it was where her idealized world imploded. This trip as an adult helped her see that her memory was deceptive. None of her beach recollections were really about togetherness. The beach, she now realized, was a place where no one in her family communicated. All the parallel activity was a way of avoiding intimacy and honesty. As Judith puts it, "We were constantly on top of each other but didn't connect. The beach itself was a natural sanitarium—so beautiful, peaceful, and remote that any unhappiness or anguish could be put on pause, if only for the month of August."

Yet despite her recently acquired perspective about what really was going on in her parents' marriage and how it cast a shadow on everything that happened at the beach, Judith is *still* trying to get back there.

For the past fifteen years, Judith saved all her discretionary income and used it to buy her own beach house. She was determined to re-create her treasured years for her children. But they don't want to go to the beach every weekend—they have friends to hang out with, sports to play, parties to attend.

But Judith insists on dragging them to her precious weekend retreat anyway. As a result, an activity designed to bring everyone together has become the source of temper tantrums, recriminations, and tears. The kids are angry and miserable, since they don't want to go. And Judith is unhappy and confused—why isn't it fun?

The problem, according to Catherine, is that Judith isn't in the family room, as she wants to be, but in her own little memory-filled basement, where she is trying to re-create the past and this time get it right. It's as if, in her mind, the beach was perfect but the family was broken and she wants to repair it now, all these years later.

The unconscious process, explains Catherine, is that Judith isn't over her injury and she is trying to master the trauma. She's stuck there, because it was a traumatizing experience, and now she wants to move forward, but first she has to start back at the beginning. She is going to repeat it until she gets it right, like a scene in *Groundhog Day*, where the Bill Murray character has to replay the same day over and over until he gets every detail the way he wants it.

Judith already knows (though she hasn't fully accepted it) that her memories are distorted. But she also needs to see that there is a disconnect between what she wants to achieve—a connection with her kids—and what she is doing—driving them away. Judith wants her family to be together, but she isn't creating togetherness; she's merely forcing her own flawed fantasy down the throats of her children.

When Judith is pressed to be more specific about her beach memories—How did it look, feel, smell? Who was there, what was everyone doing?—she begins to understands that her screen memory is so vivid because it was her last-ditch effort to see her family as a unit before it got torn apart by divorce. She knows rationally that everyone was off in his or her own private world—her mom talking with friends, her dad reading or snoozing. Judith and her brother were playing by themselves, blissfully ignorant of any marital tension—or perhaps escaping it. This version of her family was what she wanted, not what she had. She must acknowledge that *what she wants* (a family connected and communicating) won't happen precisely because of *what she is doing* (forcing them to spend their weekends at the beach). Once she does, she can get out of the basement and back to her family room in the present, where connections happen.

If Judith can hear what her children are asking for, she may very well end up getting what she really wants: quality time with them. After a quick negotiation, maybe at the kitchen table, they may agree that they will do alternate weekends at the beach, and her kids can bring friends if they want to. Everyone gets what he or she wants, and everyone is more attuned to one another's different notions of leisure time. That is the real *connection* Judith is seeking.

In Judith's case, taking the journey to the basement makes her wiser about her entire house. "It took being a totally misguided parent to make me understand my childhood," she says. "Exploring my basement made me confront the fallacy in my memories. I learned that you can be sitting on a beach towel in the most beautiful setting next to someone you love—and not be connecting."

So by facing the mess in the basement, Judith now has created a cleaned-up family room with people who are talking, smiling, and laughing. It may not be at the beach; it may be at the mall or in line at the movies, but she should be happy that she is connecting with them anywhere. Connect, don't control. The goal is to connect everywhere and anywhere—in the car, an elevator, while walking the dog. Even while sitting in your cramped family room.

I WAS THE BAD SEED GROWING UP

"My mother always 'joked' that I nearly killed her when she gave birth to me. But it wasn't a joke to me, and after a while it became part of my role in the family—the bad seed. She and my dad and older brothers and sisters always told me they all felt that I was trouble from the day I was born. Sometimes we'd make light of it—as in, 'What else do you expect from her?' but I can honestly say that it became the vision of myself that I couldn't get away from, even as an adult."

—Arianna, 35; Deerfield, Massachusetts

Arianna is a makeup artist who believes in the transformative power of makeup and hair styling to help you be whoever you want to be every day. And yet she doesn't allow herself that luxury, at least not on the inside. All her life she has felt like the black sheep who could never do the right thing, never make the grades, and certainly not live up to her mother's version of being the perfect daughter.

In high school she skipped class, hung out with all the wrong people, and got into drugs and an alternative rock scene. One day she jumped on a bus for New York City and started doing makeup for bands there, and she never went home again. "I thought, fine! I might as well rebel, since that's how they see me anyhow." Her sisters and brothers (all older, since she was the last baby her mother would ever have) all made good, worked in the local community, and raised families. But Arianna stayed single and, in her mind, was forever the rebellious teenager.

But now she wants to grow up and move on and have kids. "I'm thirty-five and it occurs to me that it's now or never, and though I'm happy, I think I could be happier if I started a family. I have the kind of business that would be ideal for a working mother. So how do I get to the 'mother' part of the picture? My mom and I don't really talk anymore."

It's clear she is stuck in her childhood and needs to stop reacting to what her mother told her all those years. Catherine says that as long as she believes she is that teenage "black sheep" she will be stuck. It's a self-fulfilling prophecy, but she can stop it at any time.

First she needs to recognize the unconscious patterns and look carefully at the screen memory playing over and over in her head. Arianna is feeling both angry and guilty and no longer wants to let these memories define her role in the family or the world at large.

There are several ways for Arianna to tackle this issue. Perhaps she could consider her mother's perspective and what it was like to nearly die. Her mother's fear and inability to cope with that scare may be why she kept "joking" about it, unwittingly hurting Arianna's feelings. Or perhaps, on some level, her mother did blame Arianna.

But what happened was *not* Arianna's fault, and she needs to believe that. One method to reprocess this traumatic experience is called rescripting, giving new language to old events in order to make sense of them. She can tell herself, "What happened was not my fault. I was a newborn baby and I didn't mean to hurt my mother." Additionally, Arianna has to stop trying to change her mother's view of her as "the problem child" and focus on why she allowed others to define her this way. As she thinks about it, she needs to realize that guilt played a major part in this family dynamic. And rebelling completed the picture.

Arianna's key process is the relationship equation: $A + B = C$. She has to realize she'll never change her mother but she can change herself, thereby changing the outcome.

Catherine explains that although Arianna was just a baby when this trauma occurred, she has taken on the responsibility for what happened to her mother. Once she decides to move on, she can pack away those memories and get out of the basement. Arianna, like every woman, gets to define or transform herself, be who she wants to be, and make her life her own. Her challenge will be to figure out who that person is and what makes her happy.

NO MAN IS THE BOSS OF ME!

"I watched my father be so demeaning to my mother that I will never forget it and as a result I won't let any man be the boss of me. I knew I had to be financially independent and never cared if I got married, though I want to be in a loving relationship. Actually, any man (teacher, coach, boss) who tells me what to do makes me want to do the opposite. I know this is holding me back, but I can't seem to change."

—Maxine, 30; Philadelphia, Pennsylvania

Always a tomboy and fiercely independent, Maxine grew up thinking that she never wanted to play the traditional role of wife and mother. Her mother was never appreciated by her dad, who bullied her. He ordered everyone in the family around; the only person who ever stood up to him was "Max," since she was the oldest and felt like her job was to protect her mom and little brother and sister from big bad dad.

But as she grew up, being stubborn and willful cost her, in terms of relationships, success at her jobs, and also her happiness. She knows she wants to change but doesn't know how. "I trust no one as much as myself, and I don't want to—as I say in my own childlike way—let anyone be the boss of me!" The screen memory she will never forget is when her dad came at her mom in a rage and Max flew to her mother's defense and stood up to him. "I swear to God he would have hit her had I not been standing there. It was like he knew I was as tough as he was." From that moment, Max decided that being tough was a good thing.

But she never lets herself be vulnerable, and she's sick of not moving ahead in her relationships. She knows she could have a family and feel better in all aspects of her life if she could allow other people to take the lead occasionally and really listen to their advice. Instead she tunes them out. With her, it's *my way or the highway*, and eventually her love interests choose the highway.

Catherine says Max is stuck in the basement, and all her other rooms, especially the bedroom and the office, are affected because she can't have a relationship and gets in trouble at work for not playing office politics artfully.

Her unconscious process may be that in her screen memory she has now traded places with her dad, which is clinically known as "identifying with the aggressor." She has inadvertently and unconsciously become the intimidator, and she is now trapped in her own pattern of trying to be as tough as she perceives the men around her to be. She wrongly feels she has to bully back, in order to be "equal," but now she's jousting imaginary foes because the people around her are not trying to fight or hurt her.

Maxine needs to get out of her basement and into the bedroom, where she can begin to have a healthy, adult relationship. She has already recognized the source of her behavior. Once she realizes that she is constantly reacting to old memories, Maxine can short-circuit that behavior and tell herself to "act, not react." First she can ask: What is the best way to be the authentic me? She can start fresh and decide to change her future, even if she can't change her past. Screening, it turns out, does not have to be defining. Catherine would tell her that she can evolve, once she makes the decision to do so. "Go or grow" is her pearl, meaning she can go along as is, not changing, or she can grow and evolve and see her life improve. Once she is aware of the choice, it's clear what she needs to do.

FEAR RULES MY LIFE

"I'm scared of everything! I need to stop being afraid of the dark when I have to leave my house, or thinking I'm going to be raped any time I am alone in a strange place. I feel fearful before I do anything new, but then when I actually do it, I'm fine. I don't want my kids to know I think like this. But I do!"

—Georgia, 38; Norfolk, Virginia

It turns out that Georgia's mom was nervous too. "We called her 'nervous Nelly' and would laugh about her crazy antics, like calling our friend's house if we were five minutes late, and standing on the porch with her arms crossed, looking angry when we pulled in. When I learned to drive, I thought she was going to blow a gasket waiting for me to bring the car home . . . as if I would surely have died! It made me nuts, but I love her."

Georgia's family has a long history of people feeling anxious, and no one thinks twice about it. But she knows she got this from her mom, even if she spent her twenties doing daredevil things like hiking in Nepal, biking across the United States with her girlfriends the summer after college, and riding on the back of her boyfriend's motorcycle.

As Georgia thinks about it, her nervousness really came to light when she had her own babies. "I remember thinking that my newborn baby girl was so precious and fragile that I wouldn't let anyone hold her for weeks. Even my husband couldn't do it right, and I would never leave her with a babysitter. I was nervous about everything: SIDS, vaccines, even someone reaching into the stroller and kidnapping her. Then as she got older it was swine flu and the like. As she leaves to go to school I now worry about abductors and rapists, and realize I have become my mother, despite all my efforts not to. What happened to the world-traveling motorcycle-riding twentysomething that I was? Then on some level I think that worry equals love, and I know I love my daughter so much because I worry about her. Well, that's what I tell myself."

Georgia is feeling bad about her anxiety and is worried that her daughter will pick up on it. Now that her daughter is six it's getting harder to hide these neurotic tendencies, or to keep them in check. "I feel like Debbie Downer because when Mia tells me she wants to go swimming, my first comment is, 'Never dive in unless you know how deep the water is!'"

Catherine says it's common for women, and especially mothers, to do what's called "catastrophizing," jumping to the worst thing that can happen, almost as a defense against the actual danger involved. So a mom will hear "skateboard" and think broken arm. Many mothers have these fleeting thoughts and worries, but they typically don't paralyze them or ruin their relationship with their kids. (If they do cause distress and significantly interfere with your daily activities, then there may be a bigger problem to treat.) But for Georgia and most women, she can have these thoughts and still go ahead with her plans—the key is to learn to enjoy them without catastrophizing.

To break the pattern she has to get out of the basement and into the kid's room, or suffer the consequences. At the playground she hovers, and she won't let Mia go on a class trip to a water park unless she goes along. Catherine says Georgia doesn't want to do to her daughter what her mother did to her. But anxiety runs in the family, so she may be working against her own DNA. That's called "genetic loading," a term for when traits are passed down through generations. Anxiety tends to have a heritable component, just as depression does, and despite your best efforts you can't always will it away.

Georgia is going to have to act the part of relaxed parent, even if she doesn't feel that way. Sometimes this is enough to unlock new paths of thinking, and other times Catherine asks a patient to do what is called cognitive behavioral therapy (CBT), which basically means trying to change how you feel by changing how you think. You learn to rescript, by identifying automatic thoughts (*Something bad could happen!*) and replacing them with new, more constructive phrases (*She's gone out with her friends before and she was okay then, so she will be okay this time. Plus I need to let her do this!*). Georgia might say, "Be careful, honey!" but at least she can manage to make sure they're not the first words out of her mouth.

Georgia was smart enough to go to a CBT therapist and learn new strategies to calm down. So now she's in her daughter's room and enjoying their relationship more, knowing that she can let her daughter grow up and not suffocate her. The key process was to separate her own fearful thoughts from her daughter's potential experience. Remember the Venn diagram? Georgia was overlapping too much with Mia, not letting her have any independence. She had to back off to help her daughter grow and experience life fully and safely.

Once you've weighed the risks and benefits, you need to understand that not letting your child do something is as much a risk (to their development) as letting them do it is to their safety. Being a concerned parent is a good thing, but being overbearing and overprotective is not.

One final thought on the basement, which is the source of so many of our behaviors: The past should inform the present, but you don't want to get stuck in it. You can't steer the car by looking in the rearview mirror without crashing. To go forward, focus on what's ahead of you in the road, not what you've passed. A glimpse in the mirror can be helpful, but your future lies in front of you. Look ahead.

7

The Family Room

Where the People You Love
Drive You Crazy

When I was young, my brother and I loved to play together and compete, and to this day we still act like overgrown puppies, going out for jogs and bike rides and sprinting to the finish with the same fierce competitiveness that we had when I was in seventh grade and he was in ninth. We race each other down ski slopes and compete over who called Mom last and who has paid off their mortgage (okay, he wins in most of these categories). Catherine says we still act like adolescents all these decades later because that was the age we were when we last lived under the same roof. The model you had as a kid is the one you tend to replay, over and over as adults. And that is where the conflict comes in—with your mom, dad, siblings, aunts, uncles, and anyone else you have known forever and still spend a lot of time with. You're not a kid anymore, but they still treat you like one.

The family room is where you spend time with the people you love the most but who have the unique ability to get under your skin. How you define your family is up to you—it can include a best friend or a favorite aunt, or it can include second cousins you grew up with who feel like siblings. The defining term here is nearest and dearest. That closeness means you are going to snap at one another, maybe even yell at each other, but you know the love will always be there. You can wear your pj's and put your feet up, you can belch and not have brushed your teeth and still feel comfortable with these people because they're family. You have to love them no matter what—but you don't always have to like them.

Since no one is ever on their best behavior in the family room—by definition that would take you to the less casual living room—you often revisit patterns of childish behavior that are not always healthy as an adult. You can "revert to type," which is Catherine's way of describing how siblings start to interact as if they were still at the age when they last lived together as a family, before going off to college and careers, or other cities. It's the childhood closeness that brings you back together no matter how far-flung you've been for how long; a good jab about how your sibling is starting to act just like crazy (insert nutty relative name here) cuts the distance and years to nil. You know you could make each other laugh that way once, and it's reassuring to know you can still do it now, as if nothing has actually come between you, nothing important anyway.

You like the familiarity and keep replaying it, even when it may be less appropriate or productive to forging adult relationships that are based in the here and now. The fact is if everyone's happy acting like nine-year-olds again, you're probably not feeling any conflict. But more often one or the other sibling decides it's time to grow up, or a precipitating factor forces them into the adult reality world (a lost job, a foreclosure, a sick parent, or some other grown-up-level crisis), and suddenly one person wants the rest of the family to snap out of it. But something weird happens: Sometimes they can't. They know only one way of interacting, and they're stuck, like a broken record, replaying the same stupid dynamic that seemed fun in the good times but is downright annoying when you need an actual grown-up sibling by your side.

The shrinks call it "repetition compulsion," since you continually and unwittingly repeat patterns of behavior unless you've identified them and decided to change them. Think about it: Aren't you and your sister or brother still replaying the years when you both lived at home? That can be fine, and fun, until it stops working for one of you.

Keeping It Real. Sometimes Real Painful!

There are ways those old patterns help "keep it real," since you can rely on those who love you the most to tell it like it is. And they rarely spare your feelings, which is why the family room is both pleasurable and painful, like tickling till it hurts.

For me, coming home after being the boss all day is refreshingly real. I tell my teenage son that the people in my last meeting of the day thought my joke was funny. I try out the joke on him and wait for his response, and he deadpans: "They only laughed because you pay them." Then he looks up at me and smiles, like "gotcha," and goes back to his Facebook pals. I know he loves me and he shows it by never giving me a false compliment. In most families, no matter if you're the boss or the worker bee, when you get home you're just you, and you still have to take your turn loading the dishwasher and hauling out the garbage. No one has to be nice to you for the wrong reasons, and this is a wonderful thing, because it guarantees that you have healthy counterbalances in your life.

To be emotionally well-rounded, you need to be treated normally by people who don't identify you as the outside world does. Catherine gets that normalcy from her ten-year-old, who authoritatively tells her, "Mom, you can't wear *that* to work!" I have what I call my "kitchen cabinet"—my daughter, my son, and my husband. They are the trusted ones who will tell me exactly what they think of my latest TV appearance— that I repeated myself or my hair looked poofy. (Thanks, gang. Duly noted.)

Feedback Is Critical. We Call It "Pinging."

We measure ourselves and get feedback minute to minute from the first day we are old enough to communicate and understand others, which is to say from the minute we're born. In psychological terms the process children use to gauge such feedback is called mirroring—they see what gets "reflected" back to them by parents, teachers, coaches, and other adults and learn from it.

As an adult moving through your day you seek out feedback that is helpful in navigating choppy waters. (How am I doing at work? Did I disappoint my dad on his birthday? Do I spend enough time with my kids?) We call this "pinging," since it's as if you send out little sonarlike signals to the people around you, and the pings come bouncing back, either posi-tively or negatively, and you learn to read them and gauge how your behavior is perceived. Like a dolphin, you need to send out the signals constantly and read them accurately in order to steer away from the shoals and out toward open sea.

That's how you eventually learn to know yourself, and what your own internal pings tell you. Over time, these pings help you become self-aware, so that you can follow your own inner compass toward a direction of your own choosing. Some extremely self-aware people seem to have an easier time of finding their authentic inner voice, but for most of us, it can take practice, work, and a lifetime of pinging to get to the point where follow-ing our inner voice comes naturally. The goal is to listen to your own in-ner pings, but that can take practice and some real and helpful feedback from people you trust.

There are true pings and false pings, and eventually you learn to dif-ferentiate. Here is an example of how we learn to tell the difference at an early age:

A while back Catherine's daughter proudly showed her a drawing she'd done of a horse. "It's the best drawing I've ever seen!" Catherine told her. Hannah, smart six-year-old that she was, didn't buy it. "You're just saying that because you're my mother," she said. "Well, I *am* your mother," Cath-erine said, sensing she was in trouble now, "but it's *still* a good drawing." Hannah took another piece of paper and a crayon and scribbled a tangle of lines and said, "How do you like *this* horse?" She was testing her feed-back system: Could her mother be trusted to tell her the truth? "Well, I will always love something *because* it's yours," Catherine said, "but that's a scribble mark, not a horse."

Hannah was satisfied. She'd found a "true" ping, which meant that she could trust her mother to tell her the truth.

Pinging Is Your Inner GPS

Early feedback is critical in molding your personality. Of course, nature plays an enormous role as well, but patterns of behavior and relationships are largely learned from those around you at a young age. Pinging is one of the methods by which you learn who to trust. It's also how you ultimately learn to trust yourself.

It starts from your earliest thoughts and actions—a baby's cries are a way of putting forth her needs. Is she hungry, wet, sleepy? How her caregiver responds to these signals contributes to how she will relate to others in the future. As extreme examples, the anxious mother may pick up her baby all the time, because any cry makes her worried. Though well intended, this hyper-attention to the baby's needs may lead to the child feeling overly dependent, or smothered, or needing to rebel to get out from under the overbearing mother. On the other hand, the depressed mother, who is unable to motivate and respond appropriately to her child's needs, may not be able to soothe her infant. If this disconnection continues for months or years, that baby may learn that her needs and desires won't be satisfied by others, and in the future expect very little from her mom, or spend the rest of her life trying to elicit a response from her mother, who was so unavailable and aloof. This same individual may grow up to be overly solicitous of those around her, in reaction to her early parental deficit.

The point is that a healthy amount of connection, attention, and feedback are what we're after, not too much or too little, when raising our kids. Both nature and nurture are at work here (though there is nothing you can do about your DNA), but how we were nurtured and how we choose to nurture account for an enormous part of who we are. If we can understand our own pinging experiences, we actually have a chance to change our patterns of behavior and our interactions with those we love.

Catherine explains that this early feedback helps determine your character traits (needy versus secure, outwardly seeking approval versus able to reassure yourself). You also develop your sense of self-esteem, since pinging is one way of seeing where you're headed (reading the sonar) and where you are on the grid, like some GPS of the personal self. Are you funny? Smart? Athletic? Creative? Musical? True pings let you know for real, which is why it's so shocking when an obviously terrible singer shows up on *American Idol* and makes a fool of herself. One wonders, has no one ever told this person she can't sing? These nonperformers are often a little out of touch, and observers can't help but think, have they never had true pings? Is it possible they aren't able to see themselves as we see them, because the mirroring in their life has been distorted?

I am the product of an overly positive mom and a loving yet scrutinizing dad. There are times when my mom thinks I hung the moon and I know this can't be the case, but I appreciate the love she is trying to show me. So today a compliment that comes too easily I swat away and don't internalize. But the same is true at the opposite end of the feedback spectrum because all my life I had to brace myself for the honest assessment from my dad, who despite his best efforts to be supportive always delivered the untarnished truth about my performance (*pretty good* has always been high praise in his book).

I now find I'm often defensive, and expect criticism even before it's delivered. While I value constructive or critical feedback more than an easy compliment or flattery, it's also true that I get defensive even when the person doesn't intend to be critical. My "preemptive" move is to sometimes be overly critical of myself before anyone else can level a harsh remark, as a way of being self-deprecating and trying to defuse a situation. Or I'll lob an offensive comment at the other person when I anticipate criticism coming my way.

This combination of warm, intuitive mom and critical, intellectual dad meant I had to find my own way through their extreme pings and figure out what was real for me. Now I'm grateful for both of their approaches, since it means I can pretty much figure out what's real, what's flattery, and what's vitriol; today I listen to my own calibrated inner compass, and that serves me well most of the time.

A saying that I learned long ago, "You're not as good as your best days, and you're not as bad as your worst days," has gotten me through the ups and downs of running a magazine. Another favorite is "Don't believe the hype." Meaning you can get a great review or win a big award one day, and then get berated by a blogger another, but you still have to get to work and do your best every day, earn your next success. Working hard and surrounding myself with people who willingly and liberally disagree with me—in almost every meeting—has helped too. (Pinging like true family members!) But then I still have to make the call, make the final decision and move ahead, for better or worse, following my gut.

How do you do that? Part of it is mastering the type of thinking described in this chapter. First you have to understand where those outside critical pings are coming from, then you modify those ideas with your own notions about what's right for you and what's someone else's baggage that you don't need to carry.

Catherine reminds us that pinging is always complicated because every ping comes from an individual who brings to it their own experiences. A tough parent may have had his own tough parents or could be the product of softies and is reacting against that. A pushover parent may be reacting against a strict upbringing and trying to be the kind of parent he wished he'd had. Either way the pingers usually mean no harm, and the sooner you figure that out, the easier it is not to let a ping sting. But don't forget to listen, because most pings have a little bit of helpful information embedded in the message.

Pinging Goes Both Ways

We also ping, giving out feedback to those around us. We send pings to those we love, and hopefully make sure they're authentic. Let's say your child refuses to practice the piano but wants you to tell her she's playing well enough for the recital next week. You ping, "Well, if you want to play better, you have to practice more! You get better every time you play that piece!" If she practices plenty but still misses notes, your ping can be more forgiving but still honest. "You sound great, honey. There were a couple spots that need smoothing but you'll get it together by next week." Even if you want to say something sarcastic, like, "I could have read a book in the time it took you to find that note!" you have to bite your tongue and rephrase it in a loving way. The best pings are when you manage to both keep it supportive and keep it real.

Imagine your child doesn't do well in a baseball game . . . three strikeouts and he drops a fly ball. You are disappointed but must keep your feelings out of it. Saying "Better luck next time" or "Good try" is supportive. What's not? Saying "You should have caught that! You're not keeping your eye on the ball!" Your pings matter more than his actual performance . . . or lack thereof. They are what the child will remember, not the bad game. Your *reaction* to the failure could last a lifetime. Not everyone is born to be a musician or an athlete—the key is to help your little Beethoven or Derek Jeter find his authentic self.

Helping your loved ones find their own way means you can compliment them for being gifted, but the minute those gifts look less than Olympian, you don't say, "What happened? You used to be so great!" Depending on the goal (fitness or sportsmanship or scholarship) your job is to say, "What do *you* think is going on?" or step back and tell them, "As long as you enjoy it, do it." Best is to help them figure it out for themselves. If you get upset, suddenly they will be reacting to your emotions, not theirs.

The minute they aren't achieving they need to know you love them anyway; you're the parent, not the coach or the scout. At that point in the game, it either becomes their passion, or they can move on to something else. Your opinion shouldn't be a factor. This is how they will find their authentic self: when they aren't doing it for the positive ping but doing it because they choose to, not because you want them to.

Your whole life is ping! ping! ping! ping! From your first breath to your last gasp, you will ping and be pinged. The best pings will be those that are neither hurtful ("That song made my ears bleed!") nor fake ("You're the best!"), since your integrity as a pinger gets tarnished. The point of pinging is to be as authentic as you can be, but empathetic too.

We are all seeking what is authentic, in ourselves and in others. We don't believe feedback that is either too effusive or too harsh, which is why we value some reviewers above others. The family room is where we first get this sense of whom in our lives we can trust to tell us the real deal.

So let's get into it. Here are stories from real women experiencing what we all feel in the family room: the stings of those who love us most.

TOO BIG FOR YOUR BRITCHES

"My mother always told me that other people, especially women, won't like you if you are too successful or have it all. If you're thin, fit, and pretty or, back in high school, the fastest runner on the track team or the class president or head cheerleader, people will think you're full of yourself. She was constantly saying, 'Don't get too big for your britches!'"

—Jean, 45; Chicago, Illinois

Jean is still hearing these words in her head all these years later and has allowed them to put the brakes on her potential. A mother of two living in an affluent Chicago suburb, about five miles from where she grew up, Jean has her MBA and used to work in management consultancy, but when she was pregnant with her first child, she decided to stay home with the kids while they were little.

Jean manages to raise her children, run the house, and do plenty else as well. Her kids are now in middle school and thriving, and she does fund-raising for two children's organizations, cochairs the school auction to fund financial aid, and loves to entertain—and is amazingly good at making it all look easy.

Although Jean describes herself as blessed, she feels guilty all the time, "and not just because I'm Irish Catholic, but because sometimes I'm not sure I deserve all the good things that have come my way." Jean was very successful at her job, rising to the top of her work group and making a bundle of money. She has a very comfortable life, a handsome, supportive husband, and two great kids, plus a beautiful home and nice vacations every year. "I'm a lucky person, really I am." So why the guilt?

From Jean's perspective, she and her mother are very close. They talk on the phone several times a day, and see each other several times a week. But it's not entirely loving. Jean's mother torments her, dropping little comments like "Who do you think you are?" when Jean pulls off one of her dazzling holiday fetes or gets a community service award for her fund-raising efforts. Jean thinks these little jabs have to do with the fact that "Mom feels insecure. She never got to go to college—she raised us four kids and was at her husband's beck and call and feels competitive with me and more than a little jealous." Jean says her mom almost boasts about the sacrifices she made for her family. "I had everything I needed right here at home with you kids and Dad," she's told Jean too many times.

But Jean never totally bought her mother's line about being satisfied with what she had. She sensed her mother's resentment at not having the same kind of opportunities. As much as she always says she's proud of Jean, she has acted in ways that have eroded Jean's confidence and made it hard for her to enjoy her successes. Even in high school, when Jean ran cross-country, her mother would smile when her team won the city championships but later tell Jean she should be careful not to look or act too successful since "people will talk."

Jean seems to feel guilty about her own success in contrast to her mother's many sacrifices. But Jean is sick of the conflict and all the bitterness.

Here, as in most cases, it is important to recognize that there is an unconscious process at work. Jean appears to be stuck, perhaps because she hasn't adequately "separated" from her mother, emotionally speaking, and become her own individual adult. In other words, she still cares too much about what her mother thinks, even now that she herself is a mother in her forties. When this kind of overinvolvement happens, it often means you haven't fully completed the developmental process called "separation/individuation," a concept coined by Margaret Mahler, a renowned child psychoanalyst and childhood development specialist. Some children have trouble with this phase of development, often because the mother may have anxiety issues of her own, and consequently, she and the child became enmeshed and have difficulty separating.

Now Jean wants to break the pattern, for her own happiness, and it's a struggle to step out of the dance she and her mother have done for years. Jean has to explore the basement—her childhood memories—to better understand where her feelings come from. She remembers a moment when she ran fastest at the state championships and her mother, before congratulating her, said, "You know, people are going to hate you for being Little Miss Perfect." Shortly thereafter Jean started to eat more and slowed down and stopped winning track medals, as if to be more likeable in her mother's eyes and in the eyes of other women.

Which takes us to the bathroom, to get her healthy body back. Over the years, Jean allowed the little stinging comments and her mother's simmering bitterness to chip away at her self-respect. But a year ago something clicked and she decided to stop letting someone else determine what she would look like. It happened on a family trip to the Bahamas. Jean was about twenty-five pounds overweight, was perpetually tired, and had no sex drive. And she felt guilty and unable to enjoy staying at a luxury hotel in a gorgeous location with her beautiful family.

She decided it was time to make some real changes to her lifestyle.

"I can't go through the next half of my life feeling like this," she said. "I have to do something." Jean started running on the beach and limiting her cocktails. She soon started feeling more energetic, more interested in sex, and was, without tremendous effort, shedding some pounds. She felt proud, and her kids and husband noticed the transformation and complimented her.

But her success was bittersweet; her transformation initiated a new spate of bitterness from her mother. Still, it made her choice clear. "I was not going to go back to being fat in order for her to love me more, so I decided to be who I wanted to be despite what other people, including my mom, might think. So when Mom says those nasty things I tell her, 'You know what? I'm happy.' And that shuts her up."

"Don't get too big for your britches" feels dated, like something she can return to the basement and put in a box marked TRASH, since it no longer holds the same power over her.

Now Jean may get irritated by her mother, but it doesn't penetrate the same way or cause the old harmful guilt. "I've made a decision to value myself, take care of myself again after a lot of years of focusing only on others, and this is the source of my strength."

So her key process for cleaning up her family room was to stop allowing the negative pings from her mother to affect everything—her weight, her tiredness, and her stress level. Jean realizes she can shrug off the bad pings.

Jean has things squared away in the bathroom as well. "I look in the mirror and feel proud of my body and what I've accomplished, and I think: *You're not too big for your britches, you're just the right size.*" We'd tell her to think about this as her own personal victory, one that doesn't reflect on anyone else or their personal baggage or shortcomings. Her body and healthy lifestyle are things to be proud of, to cherish and take care of, and she has accomplished a new level of health, fitness, and total well-being. She can help others by inspiring them, but letting them bring her down helps no one in the end. She can go back to the family room, where the zingers still fly, but now she can say: "Be true to yourself" and don't let the pings bring you down. Be authentic, and be your best self.

EVERYBODY LOVES ME! WHY NOT MY IN-LAWS?

"I can't take it—his family hates me. I can't do anything right by them, especially my mother-in-law and my sister-in-law. Yet when I bring this up to my husband, he acts like I'm making it all up and refuses to even acknowledge it's happening."

—Joanna, 38; Bernardsville, New Jersey

Joanna, a vibrant, optimistic, and whip-smart mother of two, is fed up with her in-laws and tries to explain to Rick, her husband of twelve years, how miserable his family makes her. He knows Joanna feels excluded and put down by his family, but he doesn't see how bad they make her feel. Or he doesn't *want* to see it.

In fact, when Joanna and Rick visit his family in Massachusetts, everything seems fine while he's around. It's when he goes off to play golf with his dad and Joanna is left with her mother-in-law that things go south. Joanna is usually able to hold it together, but on their five-hour drive back home to New Jersey, Joanna confesses that she feels humiliated and disparaged, especially by Rick's sister, and that his mother does nothing to stop it. His family adores Rick and has always felt that Joanna was not good enough for him. She had hoped that becoming the mother of his children would turn the tide and make them at least accept her, but they just make her feel bad about her parenting skills—even mocking what she feeds her children (organic food, tofu hot dogs, vegetarian entrees). "They hate everything about me, and it's just not fair because I try so hard."

Rick is in denial. He listens to Joanna, but he doesn't really acknowledge any of her grievances. In the past, he just told her to fight back, dish it right back to his sister. (It works for him!) "Why can't you just let it roll off you?" he says. "You're tougher than that." He tells her that the tension has more to do with Joanna's need to be loved and to always do the right thing than any egregious behavior on the part of his sister or mom. "Don't take them so seriously."

Joanna says, "I am not going to get down in the mud with them. I could easily spar with them, but then I'd be as bad as they are. I could tell them their kids always need a bath, or something equally stupid, but that's not who I want to be. I want to be respectful of my in-laws, and I need his help. He has to get them to stop picking on me."

It kills Joanna that she can't win over the in-laws, since most people find her an affable woman. She has done everything she can think of to please her husband's family, such as always arriving with a gift, and remaking the bed with clean sheets when she leaves. She even gives Rick plenty of time alone with his dad on their visits. She believes most of the tension comes from the fact that her in-laws think she should quit her job and spend all her time making her husband dinner and doting on their children.

"Rather than see me as someone who makes him happy," she says, "they see me as an interloper, taking away their beloved boy. I always have to defend myself. They forget that Rick is half of our parenting team and is part of all the decisions we make."

Joanna would quit making these trips altogether except that she treasures the great relationships her kids have with their cousins and grandparents, but she always feels like "an unwanted outsider."

.   .   .

Catherine points out that Joanna is focusing on the wrong person. Her problem isn't with her in-laws; it's actually with Rick. Joanna feels Rick doesn't stand up for her, and Rick feels Joanna is too sensitive. They need to look closely at their dynamic and acknowledge that there are issues pulling them apart when they visit with Rick's family. He starts to relate more to his sister and mom, leaving less overlap with Joanna. So suddenly, the Venn diagram of their marriage is thrown out of whack and they fail to connect on parenting and all other issues that aren't so scrutinized at home. If Joanna and Rick realize they are disconnected from each other in this scenario, they can begin to see that a dysfunctional pattern emerges whenever they go to his family home. They just can't figure out how to relate to each other when they are overwhelmed by the strong bonds back on Rick's turf.

The key process here is to reconnect the circles of their Venn diagram, which means Rick and Joanna have to find some common ground when they are with his family. The way they interact is the critical piece of the puzzle, since if Rick is loving and protective and stands with Joanna, the in-laws will follow his lead and treat her with more respect. Once they are more connected, and she feels less left on her own, the dynamic will change.

We would tell Joanna to think about how she contributes to the disconnecting circles. Is she actually encouraging Rick to disappear with his dad but feeling resentful in the end? Is she standing on ceremony with her usual rituals and not being flexible about fitting in with his family? Maybe she can lighten up on the strict diet, or figure out a way to better connect, even if it's just over the kids. The point isn't to "win" or occupy the high moral ground; the point is to overlap.

WHO IS GOING TO BE NICE TO HIM IF I'M NOT?

"I feel extremely responsible for my brother Teddy. I'm his sister and I want him to feel loved, but he is both aggressive and manipulative and always has been. There are times when

I just want to hang up on him, except I feel guilty when I think about how bad he'll feel, so I put up with his harangu-ing. He just makes me crazy sometimes."

—Sarah, 37; Palo Alto, California

Sarah fights with her older brother almost every day, and his abusive phone calls are wearing her out. Yes, they love each other, but they are still having the same fight they've been having their entire lives, which is about his need to run every aspect of her life. She puts up with it because she feels responsible for him. "Teddy is antisocial and angry and I'm the only person who puts up with him. He's single, brilliant, acerbic, and funny, but he's a tech geek and he spends most of his waking hours alone and not connecting with people in a meaningful way." She says she has put up with his abuse because "How else is he going to feel loved?"

Consequently, she regularly gets phone calls during which he yells at her when she doesn't do exactly what he says, about everything from her landlord situation to her relationship with her husband and anything else he might have an opinion about. She hangs up the phone and wants to cry. She wants him to butt out, but she can't break the cycle.

Their parents stay out of it because they're older and have their own issues with Teddy, since he was always a difficult child who got straight As but was impossible to be with. Sarah feels she is the only one who can save him from total isolation.

The sibling dynamic is one of the most complicated ones we deal with as adults because both parties are constantly evolving, yet both get stuck in the past. Whether you are the "oldest" or "youngest," the "smart one" or the "athlete," the "pleaser" or the "problem child," Mom's favorite or Daddy's Little Princess, the role you had in your family while growing up is nearly impossible to shake.

The problem here: They're mired in the past. Catherine calls this being "fossilized." The unconscious process is once again "repetition compul-sion." The question is, what purpose is this pattern serving now? Is this behavior somehow soothing or protecting you? Who benefits and who is allowing it to happen? There may be some emotional benefit, but it's also keeping you down. Ask yourself: What is this costing you and how is it affecting your happiness?

For the answer you have to consider the memories in your basement. Catherine says you replicate patterns of how you communicated love as a child, and if you grew up in a house where bickering is a form of connecting, then you perceive that as love. You can't bicker with your friends or work colleagues or even spouse, since they will read it as a negative emotion. But your sibling understands that bickering is just "our way" and it will be comforting because it is familiar, just like your mom's beef stew . . . even if the meat was overcooked and the vegetables were mushy.

No matter how unhealthy the relationship with a sibling is, you stay "fossilized" as long as you both get something out of it, Catherine says. Often the benefit is the reassuring ping coming back to you, even if it's a negative one. Perversely, here in the family room, familiarity breeds contentment.

At some point, though, you have to ask yourself, Are we going to be like this all our lives? Watching Will Ferrell and John C. Reilly in *Step Brothers* or any of the Judd Apatow movies where the adults act like preadolescents, we all laugh because we can relate to them on so many levels. It's funny and painful at the same time.

A physical therapist and "soother" by nature, Sarah wants to "fix" hurts and help others feel better. She doesn't have kids, so Teddy is like her only child. She is gratified by their relationship, except when he gets nasty. She needs to figure out how to get off the phone whenever he gets abusive and tell him, "Teddy, I need to go now, but I will call you later," and when she does, she can start to turn their conversations in a different direction and stay away from the topics that get him going.

How can Sarah change the dynamic and set limits when needed? $A + B = C$. She is A, her brother Teddy is B, and C is the current relationship. She can't control his behavior, Catherine points out, but she can change their dynamic by pulling back and engaging less, including getting off the phone earlier. She doesn't need to actually hang up on him, just tell him she has to go now, in a civil way, and then hang up. As long as she is trying to fix him—or letting him upset her—she will be stuck in the same cycle of dependency and never change things.

Sarah needs to understand that she is Teddy's sister, not his mother, and that is enough. Only then can they return to a healthy sibling relationship. Sarah needs to know that she can be needed without it costing her so much.

Her key process is: "too much of a good thing is a bad thing," meaning that while she thinks she is being the super sister, always nice and loving, she is doing a disservice to herself and to her brother. Even adults need limits. Placing limits on our relationships is healthy and necessary for safety, boundaries, and comfort. Catherine adds that we have to remember: Limits are a form of love. We all need them. Our happiness depends on it.

STRINGS ATTACHED

"My parents pay for things like a new car every couple of years, or help with my tuition, and then expect that I'll do everything they want, including going on some cruise to Alaska, when I really don't want to go along. I wish I could tell them no—to the money and the control—and yet I love the things they help me afford to do. But I need to be able to live my own life."

—Nancy, 25; Scarsdale, New York

Nancy is making enough money to live in a tiny Manhattan apartment on her banking salary and is thrilled to be living away from home, even if it's just a quick train ride from her parents' house, where she spends Sunday dinner and brings her laundry with her. Vacations would be local or supercheap without the help her parents give her, and she'd probably not even own a car, much less a new one. Her budget is so tight that she accepts the help even though she hates the fact that it means her parents still have a say in *everything* she does, to the point that she thinks: *What will they say about this guy?* when she meets a new potential boyfriend in a bar. She filters all her thoughts through the same mind-set she had years ago, when she was a teenager living at home. It's as if she has her parents looking over her shoulder, even though she's old enough to make her own decisions.

"They have input on where I live, who I date, what I do with my time . . . even my wardrobe choices! But I like the lifestyle their help affords me. I hate this bind I'm caught in."

Her parents enjoy having total input into what she does and perpetuate this dynamic by giving her money. Before Nancy can be happy in the family room she has to get to a few other places in the house and clean them up. Let's start with the basement, where memories are stored. By her own admission, Nancy enjoys the cozy, comfortable feeling of being taken care of by her parents, such as getting money from her dad to go shopping with her friends. The first time she held out her hand and her dad put a stack of bills in it, she thought, *That was easy.*

Little did she know her dad would later ask to see what she bought. She soon learned that if he didn't approve of her purchases he got tighter with the cash or asked her to return the offending items, like that one time he made her take back a low-cut top and she was humiliated because she knew the salesgirl at the store. The next time she bought a miniskirt she shoved it into her purse so he wouldn't see it and showed him the more conservative choices instead. She's still doing it, rebelling by wearing clothes she knows her parents would never approve of, all these years later.

Catherine says the process at work here is acting out, and Nancy has to ask herself why she continues to behave like a child. In her heart she knows that she would be better off in a sensible dress that didn't make her look overly sexy, but she wears the skirt her dad wouldn't approve of into the bar as a way of reacting, as opposed to acting.

The problem: She doesn't want to be controlled, so she is reacting to her father's voice in her head rather than making her own decisions. But at what cost? She is failing to move ahead and grow up and think: How do I want to represent myself in the world?

She's "infantilized," stuck in the role of the child. Catherine says Nancy has to be honest with herself about the fact that she is materially driven and then decide to either accept her parents' money and constraints, or live a different and less expensive life on her own terms.

Nancy has to get out of the basement. We'd say: Get to the office and start making your own money, and then live within your means. Grad school can wait, and you can pay for your own life now and live it the way you choose.

So Nancy's key to cleaning up her family room and being happy there is to think about her life going forward—growing up and untying the parental strings—as a way of leaving the past behind. If she is really invested in breaking this cycle, she has to take responsibility for her behavior and make some changes. (Get a roommate to share the monthly nut? Live without a car?) She can't expect that her parents will change their desire to control her—which they see as loving—but her own choices can have a real effect on the relationship.

Whenever a pattern of relating ends up frustrating you, think of the relationship equation $A + B = C$. If Nancy is A and she focuses on a few lifestyle shifts, her overall relationship will change, even if her parents don't. Nancy needs to pull away slightly, to be more of an individual. She can pull back a little or a lot, but she needs to do it in a way that is appropriate (for example, don't tear up the check and say, Take this money and shove it!). She should simply tell her parents what she is doing so they understand it's not meant in an unloving way, just a healthy one. It's up to her to decide if she wants to go with the status quo or grow up.

The pearl for Nancy is "Go or grow"—she can go along with the flow of her family and their rules or grow by stepping out of the pattern and being her own woman. This is an example of the adult decision making that comes with leaving the family room and the nest, financially and emotionally.

I FEEL LIKE I'M MARRIED TO MY SIBLING!

"My sister and I are so close it's crazy. We spend all our vacations together, we run together before work, and she is the first one I call whenever something happens to me. In fact, if my husband and my sister were drowning, I'd definitely save her first. I couldn't live without her. It's like we're twins. Still, I can't help but think it's holding me back in some ways."

—Stephanie, 34; Philadelphia, Pennsylvania

Stephanie is an investment banker who wants to pack as much into her day as she possibly can, starting with a run along the Schuylkill (with her sister Elizabeth), until she goes out after work to meet friends for drinks (with her sister, of course). In between she spends long hours at work, but texts and phones her sister several times a day. "I don't even talk to my husband that often, so I know it's weird. But on the other hand, he and I don't have to check in that much because we don't have that much to talk about. With Elizabeth it's like we're in lockstep. I know I should branch out and meet new people, but I just don't want to. And whenever I do go off and do my own thing it's not as much fun without her."

The sisters take every vacation together, and Stephanie's husband is resigned to it. He knew, going into the relationship, that he was getting a "two-fer," but since he and Elizabeth get along great, it works. Sometimes she's the tiebreaker and a useful ally when he needs one. But Stephanie is now afraid that she's stuck in her childhood and won't even want to have kids until her sister is married and having them also.

Catherine refers to this as twinning, a concept first described by Heinz Kohut, M.D., which is when you so connect with a best friend, a sibling, or a work pal that you are overidentified. You want to be alike in order to build strength, feel safe, have a positive pinger right next to you all the time. It's your built-in security blanket. Twinning can happen in ways big and small, like on a sports team, when you find someone you always pass the ball to, or with a college roommate you only will go to the dining hall with. Later it can be someone you love to socialize with, since you have the same taste in movies and theater, restaurants and bars.

But rarely do you have such a "twin" from cradle to grave; that is when the twin can become an impediment. You move away from the roommate once you graduate, and you might change jobs and be separated from the work pal. With a sister, it's harder to get the right amount of separation, since the relationship lasts a lifetime. The twin relationship may get in the way of personal growth. Stephanie, newly married, isn't bonding with her husband, Sam, the way newlyweds do, while Elizabeth, who's not seeing anyone, spends nights with her sister and brother-in-law watching TV, and not meeting anyone new, including a potential mate.

The two young marrieds are not figuring out their own way to resolve conflict, and this may later blow up in their faces. All marriages hit bumps. How you deal with them and communicate is the key to whether you get through the inevitable stresses. If Sam and Stephanie never learn to connect, then Stephanie will forever feel "married to" her sister, and her actual marriage may not survive in the long term.

Sam and Stephanie can get to the bedroom and the kitchen table and try to work on their relationship, but Stephanie also needs to separate more from Elizabeth.

The key process here: You need to learn to separate and become an individual, with your own schedule and priorities and personal growth. This is a three-way Venn diagram, since Elizabeth and Stephanie are very overlapped and Sam has only a sliver of overlap with his wife, and his circle touches the outer line of Elizabeth's, since they are pals. But the biggest overlap is between the sisters, and until Stephanie stops merging with Elizabeth the marriage doesn't stand a chance to grow. She has to be a whole circle, apart from her sister, in order to have a healthy and mature relationship with her husband.

It's possible for Stephanie to be close to her sister *and* her new husband— and anyone else she chooses to be friends with. She can stay connected to her sibling, but not so close that it prevents her from moving forward. In other words, she has to feel married to her husband, not her sister.

I HATE MY AGING PARENTS!

"I am such a bad daughter. I hate being with my aging parents because it reminds me that I'm getting older too. I wish I could say I love being with them, savored every moment we had together, but the opposite is true: I avoid them because not only are they getting frail, they're also becoming more negative. I am upset when I'm around them, because they're getting old."

—Claire, 47; New Rochelle, New York

Claire is definitely feeling the pinch of being in the Sandwich Generation, living between the children she's raising and is almost "done" parenting, and her parents, who are, at eighty, just entering the time of their lives when they will need to depend on her as they become more frail. She sees her future as a grim one nursing two ailing parents. It's coming at her like a runaway train, and she wants to be more independent, especially after fifteen years of being the "supermom." "It's like now that I am free to travel and live my own life and explore all these different parts of my personality I'm going to have to hang around and be there for my parents, and I know how selfish this sounds, so I'm not proud of myself for even saying it out loud."

The problem here is that Claire is suffering from some pretty strong narcissism, since she not only sees her parents as a burden but also as the "future" self that she is trying to avoid. Aging is her Achilles' heel, and she is looking into a bathroom mirror that is playing tricks on her—when she looks at her mother she sees herself in thirty years.

Claire's unconscious process, projecting her own aging issues onto them, is preventing her from being the good daughter, since it's not her parents that she hates, it's herself, her own future aging self-image. The minute she understands that she is taking this out on them she can start to be nicer and more caring to them, not the petulant or selfish daughter she feels she has become.

"My mother was so beautiful—like Audrey Hepburn—long and lean and chic, and now she's graying and hunched and wrinkled," Claire explains. "It's depressing because I know aging is inevitable, but I wish I could always remember my mother at the height of her beauty, not now as an old lady."

The same is true of her dad, who she will always remember walking too fast for her to keep up as he escorted her to school in his spiffy business suit, attaché case in hand. He was so handsome, she says, like Cary Grant, and he'd always tell her funny stories that would make her feel good about herself and their special bond. And now he hobbles, and she laments that all those fun things they did together, like sailing and fishing and jogging, are in the past.

Claire says it's not only that they are physically aging but that they are also acting like the negative people they always cautioned her not to become. "They act like their own worst selves, like the version of them that isn't nice or loving, since they are constantly in bad moods."

Claire needs to understand that her feelings are related to the fact that her parents haven't taken care of themselves in recent years, and that watching them deteriorate from their former height of health and vitality has been painful. It makes her that much more determined to live healthfully, eat well, and exercise, as if she wants to stop the clock in her own life.

But Catherine points out this isn't about her. It's about them and how she can be more helpful and loving and supportive to them. Her attention is so inwardly focused on not aging herself, which is impossible, that she is unable to see that her parents are still wonderful people and appreciate the fact that they continue to have a lot to offer, and life to live, even if they no longer look or act like movie stars. She is mourning the loss of her image of her parents rather than seeing the opportunity to continue to share experiences together.

"I feel like I'm the living version of that movie *On Golden Pond*, where the real relationship problem is with me, as Jane Fonda, and not the crotchety old dad. I need to be a better daughter, a more loving and understanding person, and cut them some slack. They probably don't even feel well most of the time and yet I rarely think about that."

Our key process here is to get Claire out of the bathroom and ask her to stop looking in the mirror. She can decide to live in the present and understand that her parents won't always be around. The trick is to learn to appreciate the time she has with them now. She needs to get outside herself and remember that it's not all about her. At least not right now.

DISTANT SISTERS, IN AGE AND AREA CODE

"Having a sister nearly six years younger than me was almost like growing up an only child. I barely noticed her existence, except if she invaded my space. It wasn't until we were in our thirties that we actually got to know each other. She was a stranger to me, and I hated that. I realized I wanted a close relationship with my only sibling."

—Ava, 37; Chevy Chase, Maryland

Ava is a successful social worker in the guidance office at a high school, a career choice clearly related to the fact that she grew up in a home where everything looked normal, but where she never felt fully secure with her parents, who were sometimes checked out. "They were babies when they had me, right out of college. They smoked pot with their hippie friends and probably weren't ready to be responsible adults and have a kid when they did. I caught them smoking once, when I was around ten, and I was horrified, not exactly sure what was going on—but knowing it wasn't right. I remember getting on my bike and going to a neighbor's house to feel safe and in a structured environment. That may be my biggest memory: catching my parents doing drugs and thinking—*this is not a safe place for me; who's looking after us kids? I have to take care of myself.* That day, I emotionally left and never came back. It was up to me to make sure my life turned out okay. I never had a curfew. My parents were so lenient that I set my own limits. I feel like I raised myself.

"I had little patience for Eleanor, the annoying little sister in my house, since I thought the most important thing was to get good grades and get into a good college so I could be independent and leave that chaotic household behind."

It wasn't until Ava was a senior in college and Eleanor was a junior in high school that she thought it might be nice to have a relationship with her younger sister. But by then, Ellie had decided Ava didn't matter to her, never seemed to care about her, and that she was fine without her.

"After college, Ellie and I had a nasty blowup while on a family vacation," says Ava. "I tried to get her to talk to me, to tell me what she was thinking—anything at all—and she started screaming at me, 'Why do you care now? You don't give a shit about me!' For so many years that had been true, but now I was ready to start caring. But that didn't mean she was ready.

"She made me grovel for years, trying to win her over, and then I'd get angry because that wasn't nice and she made me feel guilty for not being there for her all those years. The truth is, we were both so angry at each other, and at our parents for not noticing that their children had no connection to each other.

"Most people would have unhappily gone along as they were, not really trying to make the connection, but once my sister and I finally decided we wanted a better relationship, it was as if we had to have every childhood fight we'd never had, to 'catch up.' I felt like we had to be kids again and then finally grow up into the adults we wanted to be, *together*." That went on for years.

In dealing with her much younger sister, Ava is in the basement, grappling with a childhood that left her feeling anxious. Whether parents drink, gamble, or stay out late, Catherine says, a child can feel like the only adult in the household, and when that happens they become "parentified"—the kid has to act like a parent. That leaves the child feeling insecure, so she overcompensates and tries to help all those around her and be perfect, never needing anything or anyone. "Don't worry about me" becomes her mantra. When Ava got married and finally opened up emotionally to her husband, she realized one of the things she had been missing was her sibling, the one she had abandoned back when they were kids and that she had "left" emotionally when she found refuge at her friend's house.

Ava understands why her parents were so checked out—they were reacting to their overbearing parents. Both of them had wanted more freedom growing up, so they gave Ava and Ellie too much of it. The girls, in turn, needed more input, or pinging, from their parents, so they sought it elsewhere—from teachers, neighbors, and finally spouses. Eventually Ava ended up in therapy and became a social worker; she now jokes with her sister, saying, "I had to go to graduate school to learn how to connect with other people the way most people learn at home."

The unconscious process here for Ava is about guilt that she is feeling for disregarding her sister. Despite the fact that Ava is now ready for a relationship, Ellie is not, and she is acting out by fighting and resisting Ava's overtures.

They may be in the right room but in the wrong way, and they need to go back in time to their childhood and hash out their conflicts. Fighting can be constructive for them, since it's a way of connecting and working through their years of not having a relationship. The arguments will continue until they exhaust each other and work through all the bad feelings. Once that happens, they can break the pattern and move ahead in time, to the current day.

The key process to making things better for these two is for them to realize that they are regressing, and that if they want to move ahead they have to begin again as adults and put all these childhood emotions in the past. Close the door on the basement and move into the present part of the house. Something usually happens that jolts siblings into the present day, where they act as adults, at last no longer children themselves.

"What finally got it going for us was the birth of my first baby," Ava recalls. "I had a great life—a good marriage, a new son, and a wonderful job; and I felt like Ellie needed to be an aunt to this new little person, so I reached out to her again. She'd moved to Santa Fe, and we hadn't spoken in a while, but my baby meant she *had* to come visit. I called her and basically begged her to fly out and meet her nephew, and it worked. She brought her boyfriend, who said, 'I am so excited to meet you! I've heard so much about you!' That was the first time it occurred to me that I mattered to her. It took time and many conversations and blowups to knit our family back together."

The two sisters finally created a new relationship, and they cemented that bond recently when Ellie suffered a medical emergency and called Ava, who flew to her side.

"The real turning point for us came when she needed me and I was there for her. She had a health scare—she found a tumor and thought it was cancer—and I put her in touch with a doctor and reassured her that she would probably be fine.

Fast-forward several years: Ava now has an amazingly close relationship with her sister. They talk nearly every day. They—and their spouses—spend a lot of time together. Though they live in different parts of the country, they get together often. Ellie is the first person Ava calls when their mother pulls a typical stunt, or her husband is pissing her off. Ava and Ellie are now related . . . for real.

In the family room, the people there know you the best; which means they know where you've come from, but they may not always know where you want to go (or even who you are today). They continue to see you as the "kid sister" or "daughter," which will always be true, but it's only part of the picture. You need to let them see you grow and evolve, but that doesn't mean leaving them behind. You can still be part of the family in a new way, one that reflects your contemporary self. And happier too.

8

The Living Room

Friends Are the
Family You Choose

There are many kinds of friends: casual acquaintances you've met through common activities, such as tennis, book clubs, or your kid's playdates, or through other friends. Another type is the good friend you talk honestly to about personal topics—money and relationships, work and feelings. Then there are the best friends, who know you intimately and love you despite your faults. These are the inner circle, the family that you choose. The impact of friendships on happiness has been well established, since studies have shown people with close and meaningful ties are healthier, happier, and live longer than those without.

Sadly, the number of close friends most of us have is dwindling, from an average of three twenty years ago to just two in recent years. The reason, according to a study done by sociologists at the University of Arizona and Duke, is that many of us are spending too much time at work. Another scary stat: One in four Americans have no close friends, and the friendships we do have these days are shallower, and often maintained online through social networking sites or cell phones, IM-ing, etc. Most of those online "friends" are not really friends—they're just the familiar faces of people we can't be bothered to call. So you sit in your house, tapping on keys, and think you are being social, but in fact you are more isolated than ever.

If it were a medical epidemic, the loss of actual (as opposed to virtual) friendships would be a front-page headline. But because it's subtle and emotional in nature it makes news only in places like Catherine's office. Still, for women, it has real health implications, especially when it comes to our happiness. But if friends can help you live longer, isolation has the opposite effect; it is a mental-health hazard.

Friendship is so powerful that even being in a "cluster" of happy people is enough to make you happier, according to twenty years of data from the Framingham Heart Study. In academic circles, this phenomenon is called "social contagion," and it can get passed around like a viral e-mail joke.

At times your closest friends may have a bigger impact on your happiness than your spouse, which makes sense, since they can bring you joy and distraction even if your spouse may be bringing you down. Catherine points out that the inherent nature of these types of relationships is different, since the spouse is there 24/7 whereas your friends may live many miles away. In other words, you choose to invite your friends over (when you feel like it), but your spouse is there even when neither of you is in a social mood. Which explains why you often have more "fun" with your friends. But don't confuse fun and frivolity. Friendships are serious business.

Bottom line? Research backs up what we already knew in our hearts: When the events of life turn against you, your female friends are your lifesavers.

Let's hear from some women whose emotional living rooms are a mess.

MY GIRLFRIENDS ARE LIKE MY SISTERS

"I feel like being a good friend is a pillar of who I am. I am a great friend, and I have girlfriends who are so close that they are like my sisters. We will do anything for each other, so if I have a problem with a friend it is devastating to me."

—Charlotte, 27; Austin, Texas

Charlotte is a gorgeous redhead with a wide smile who draws friends to her easily, since she is kind and sweet and funny. She proudly describes herself as a good friend. "If I let my friends down, I feel like a bad person.

I become completely consumed and internalize it. Nothing else bothers me as much—missing a credit card payment or having a messy apartment or anything else."

This "good friend" badge is an issue for her because she has just started seeing a former boyfriend of an old friend of hers, and while they had clearly broken up before Charlotte got involved with him, she feels like it's a big problem, especially since she recently discovered that her friend still has feelings for this guy. He, on the other hand, told Charlotte it was "so over."

Now Charlotte feels bad because she really likes this guy but wants to come clean with her friend. "When I found out there was more to it on her end than I'd realized, I started to play it over and over in my head and then it became a source of unhappiness. I've been thinking: What if this was the love of her life and I ruined her happiness? I'd never do anything to hurt a friend. I'd rather lose the guy than the friend. If someone is upset with me, it's just too painful."

Charlotte thinks she is being sensitive and compassionate, but she's overwrought and it's interfering with a friendship and even her own self-image as a superfriend. Charlotte is questioning if she is actually the "pillar" of friendship she once thought she was.

The fact is that her family room is connected to her living room. Part of the reason is that Charlotte is an only child, and she creates sisterlike bonds with her friends to fill out her "family," something she's done all her life. "I definitely try to build a lot of strong bonds with women. I don't have a lot of second-tier friends. I only have very close friends."

Unlike sisters, though, friends can drop you. And Charlotte says she lost a close friend recently, when she blew up over canceled plans. When she thinks about it, she realizes that she precipitated this "blowup," and it's not the first time. She says, "I think it's like some kind of a loyalty test: If I can lose my temper at these people and they stick around, then they are with me forever." She swears that these confrontations aren't planned. "You'd never know it to meet me, but I have a really terrible temper, and I always end up losing it with the people I love the most." She thinks this is a normal way of finding out who loves her.

"Once we get to that point, it's like I have a 'no divorce' policy with these women, and we are going to be friends until we die. I love knowing that I have that strong bond. It's a great feeling, like growing your family."

But Charlotte knows her friends are starting to lose their patience with her. She also realizes that it's inappropriate for a grown woman to act so childishly and to be abusive to her friends.

Her problem is that she wants her friends to be her siblings, and they aren't. When Charlotte was a child, her parents would scream and yell at each other one minute and would be smiling the next, so Charlotte figures that is a good test of true love: You can act your worst and still have someone love you! But to her closest friends, she is just coming off as a hothead, and she has to change. She's acting out, instead of saying: Will you be my friend no matter what?

She thinks she is creating siblings, but she is actually reproducing her own upbringing as an only child who was envious of all her friends with sisters. They could fight, but they were always there for each other. Charlotte has to recognize her destructive patterns if she hopes to have friends who will love her—and respect her—forever, as true sister substitutes.

Catherine says that Charlotte is displaying what's called "transference." She is putting her friends in the role of missing siblings, and they don't always like it, especially when she tests their devotion. The unconscious process of melding friends and family sends her back to the family room, which she is trying to populate to make herself feel less alone. To change this destructive behavior, she has to get back to the right room, the living room, where a formality or at least civility will require Charlotte to act more maturely—and appropriately—with her friends. It will save her untold tension, since these "blowups" are not providing the security she wants. Instead, they are a source of stress.

Her pattern of making her friends into her family is not working. Charlotte is not the "great" friend she defines herself as being, since her gal pals can't understand why she flies off the handle at them. She's expecting them to inhabit her family room, and needs to understand that they are more comfortable in the role of friend, not sister. Charlotte's key process is to draw the Venn diagram and see that she is too overlapped with her friends, who don't share her need for a surrogate family. If she lets go a little, they will feel less trapped by her neediness and actually want to overlap more, instead of pulling away.

Think of close friendships as you would any healthy relationship: You should complement each other, not complete or try to control each other. This is another case of "connect, don't control." The more you try to control people, the less you will connect with them.

The pearl for Charlotte: Controlling isn't the goal; connecting is.

I'M A TERRIBLE LISTENER AND IT MAKES ME FEEL LIKE A BAD FRIEND

"I'm so self-centered. I get bored listening to my friends talk about their problems, so I end up telling them about my own experiences instead. It's like 'Enough about you, let's talk about me!' Then I feel bad about it. I feel like I'm missing the girlfriend chip!"

—Mary, 42; Los Angeles, California

Mary values her female friends and the fun times they share but feels that she is constantly letting them down. Every time they listen patiently to one of her seemingly endless dramas she is amazed that they truly "get" her and support her and know what she is going through: work triumphs, relationship ups and downs, financial woes, weight issues. She can open up to them about almost anything, and they listen. But when it comes time for her to listen to them, she starts yawning.

She has tried to change, but it's hard for her, and she wonders: "Why can't I do this? I simply glaze over. I think about the fact that I've already had a kid go through the terrible twos, and I can offer advice, but I'm not that stimulated by hearing stories that resemble what I've already lived through. I have to suppress the thought bubble that says, *Been there, done that.* Am I a terrible person? A narcissist? Do I lack empathy?"

Despite this, Mary, a clothing designer living in LA, has kept a couple of close friends for decades; they are like her sisters. They might not even know that Mary feels she's a bad friend, since she hides her lack of empathy well. In fact she is quick to offer advice when she knows the answer. But when she doesn't know how to respond, she feels inadequate and checks out. "One friend had a late miscarriage, and her husband blamed her for overexercising. And, since I felt I couldn't offer any useful advice, other than to be tempted to tell her to leave him, I clammed up. I know she needed me to say something meaningful, but I didn't know what to say. I'm a great problem solver for things I understand. But when I'm in over my head, I feel I don't know what to do, like I'm failing to be a good friend. I just want to tell them what to do. And that's not being a good listener, and that's what they need."

Catherine points out that Mary's obviously very smart and somewhat self-aware, but it's telling that she always wants to feel like the expert. Her overbearing personality is getting in the way of her friendships. When she has the answer, she likes to give it. When she doesn't know the answer, she feels insecure and bad about herself, causing her to shut down and pull away from her friend in need. She feels useless, which is the worst feeling she can have. Mary wants to be helpful and needed, so she offers advice almost before it's even asked for.

We suggest Mary get to the bathroom, look in the mirror, and think about why she needs to be listened to but isn't able to be a listener herself. She's overly self-involved, and it may not be because she's full of herself—it's likely because she has too little self-esteem. She overcompensates by acting more confident than she feels.

Mary's lack of empathy goes back to her childhood. When her family moved to Atlanta for her father's job she felt that no one listened to her request that she be allowed to finish junior high school with her friends. She was very upset and became impervious to hurt. She concluded that showing her strong emotions didn't get her anywhere, and she had to shut down part of her vulnerability to survive those years.

But now it's getting her in trouble with friends who need her to be sympathetic. They have learned not to turn to her for anything deeper than a game of tennis or a movie night, and that is holding her back from intimate and lasting bonds.

To be a good friend, Mary doesn't have to know the right answer—and she doesn't have to feel that her friends need advice. They just need to talk, and for her to listen. If she wants to be a better friend, she needs to be quiet and not try to offer advice and "solve" every problem. Nor is it helpful to offer "That happened to me!" Mary needs to understand that to be a good listener you have to work at it. If she has a reaction to a point being made, she has to learn to hold the thought that's bubbling up. She can start by telling herself it's not all about her. Most important, it's about her friend, who she loves. The pearl: It's not all about you, it's about you being quiet.

I ALWAYS FEEL LIKE I HAVE TO RESCUE MY FRIENDS

"My oldest friend is so needy and down, and whenever she calls I end up spending hours on the phone with her, or having to go out with her, but I have a lot going on myself. I feel like she's sucking the life out of me."

—Cyndi, 28; New York, New York

Cyndi says her four girlfriends from college are her best friends. "Three of us live in New York City and hang out a lot. Another girl lives in California, and our fifth friend is back in Atlanta, where she grew up." The "Fab Five," as they sometimes refer to themselves, are diligent about getting together at least once a year. They know everything about one another, have been through numerous boyfriend breakups, the divorces of a couple of parents, the suicide of one sibling, as well as the more quotidian experiences of finding jobs, getting into (or rejected from) grad school, and what to wear on a first date.

Currently, however, Cyndi is not enjoying her relationship with Gwen, who lost her job at an investment banking firm a few months ago and is depressed. She complains endlessly to Cyndi, who has always considered herself a great listener. But all the listening in the world hasn't helped Gwen, and Cyndi is starting to wonder, What's the point of trying to help someone who won't take advice or try to help themselves?

Every time Gwen calls Cyndi or they get together for dinner (two or three times a week), Cyndi gets a stomachache. "I always get butterflies when I'm nervous, but this is different. Worse. I'm starting to feel like I have an ulcer when I see how upset Gwen is. I've suggested she see a therapist, but she isn't interested and doesn't have the money, so I end up being her sounding board, and it's killing me—and my stomach."

Cyndi realizes that the role she has fallen into with Gwen is a lot like her role in her own family. Cyndi was the "golden girl" growing up, and her younger sister, Emily, constantly struggled with her grades and fought all the time with their parents. "It was my job to smooth it all out, make sure everyone was getting along (or at least not screaming at each other). At the same time I was feeling guilty about what a hard time Emily was having in school. Things were so volatile between Emily and our parents that she couldn't get much help from them. I spent a ton of time going over her homework, helping her prepare for her exams and finish projects. I worried a lot about her when I left for college, but it was also a huge relief to just have to take care of myself."

Catherine interjects: It's clear that her friendship with Gwen has left the living room and has moved down the hall, to the family room. Cyndi has transferred her feelings about her troubled younger sister onto Gwen, and is relating to Gwen as if she were Emily, who she had to save whenever there was a problem. But she's not able to help Gwen, and all of this angst and drama is taking a toll on her. Rather than Cyndi pulling Gwen out of her hole, Gwen is yanking so hard that she's pulling Cyndi down with her. Cyndi's stomachaches are a sure sign that she has to take better care of herself.

Cyndi needs to get to the bathroom and take a look in the mirror. She's not being a good listener—or a good friend—if Gwen's problems are making her reach for the Maalox. She has to take care of herself first, something she never really did growing up with her own little sister.

The key process here is "too much of a good thing is a bad thing," since Cyndi is being "too good" of a friend to Gwen, and it is compromising her own health and well-being (not to mention her ability to help Gwen).

When Cyndi went off to college, she broke away from being her sister's caretaker and became her own person (needs and all). She has to do that again. Just as the lifeguard can't allow the drowning swimmer to pull her under, Cyndi must figure out how to be helpful without sacrificing her health and happiness. It's true in friendships and in a family and in every other part of your life. Her pearl: You have to be strong to help others.

WOMEN SCARE ME.
MY HUSBAND IS MY BEST FRIEND.

"I don't really have many close friends that I tell the deep, dark stuff to. One or two, maybe. Mostly I count on my husband for company and closeness. I mean, is female friendship really that important?"

—Jenna, 32; Evanston, Illinois

Jenna has been married for five years to Sean, a prosecutor with the district attorney's office. She knows she should work harder at maintaining friendships with other women but is reluctant to share too much. "I've been burned. In high school, I told a good friend some very personal stuff and it got around the school. I was so humiliated. Needless to say, that was the end of our friendship." She is happy that she can talk about anything with her husband, but she is feeling some stress these days because her husband isn't always available, because he's extra busy with a case. "It bums me out. I don't like talking to him for the first time in the day when he walks through our apartment door."

Jenna has a few casual friends—a neighbor in her apartment building, a fellow artist she sometimes shares space with, and a girlfriend from college who lives nearby—but she doesn't find them particularly compelling. She rarely makes dates with them, and when she does, she feels pretty "blah" about the experience. "We just don't have that much to talk about. My girlfriend from college keeps up with our old sorority sisters, and it makes me feel kind of nauseated to hear from her what everyone's up to. I liked them okay then, but I hated the gossiping, the one-upmanships, and the feeling that you had to fit in or you were a loser. I'm fine doing my own thing now, minding my own business." Jenna is thinking of inviting her neighbor over for coffee but is afraid that if they don't click it will be awkward whenever they pass each other in the hallway.

Clearly, Jenna hasn't had many positive experiences with female friends. She is too dependent on her husband, who can't always meet her every need in this part of her life—and shouldn't be expected to. When pushed, Jenna admits to feeling jealous of her friend from college who has loads of female friends. She marvels at this friend's ability to have intense conversations, share personal stories, and just have fun "with the girls." Jenna will, reluctantly, admit that she'd like to have more friends, but she doesn't have a clue about how to do that. So when Sean's working late, she ends up alone at home with their two cats, feeling sorry for herself.

Jenna believes she has reason to be wary of sharing intimate details with a friend, but her basement full of painful memories is now keeping her from trusting all women, and she is missing out. Even going through old yearbooks and cheerleading paraphernalia brings her nothing but pain. She can't help but relive those last weeks of school when rumors about her boyfriend cheating on her with her best friend spread, and she was so humiliated she hasn't been to a reunion since.

Jenna's patterns keep repeating themselves, since she is stuck in a time when her friendships didn't work out. Her basement is rife with painful memories of gossipy or mean girls, and so that is all she ever thinks about when she tries to have women friends. But the truth is she is so insecure that when she meets a new female friend she herself starts to dish, in order to try to connect. So she ends up driving away any friendships because she comes off as a gossip herself.

Catherine calls this "identification with the aggressor," and it happens especially when a young person is raised in an abusive household. In

Jenna's case, her mother is fairly harsh, competitive, and doesn't give an inch to her daughter, and never has. "I remember her telling me, 'You're not an athlete, you're just like me.' She always competed with me, whether it was over how to cook the turkey at Thanksgiving or even how to cut the strawberries for a fruit plate. She never has anything nice to say, and my husband tells me, 'Stop beating your head against the wall. Can't you see that she will never change? Don't let her get to you.' But she does, every time, and it tears me up."

Jenna is in the wrong room and needs to go to the family room and "clean up" the mess of identifying with her tough mother, before she returns to the living room and tries to have supportive female friendships. She has to acknowledge that she can't change her critical mom. She has to change how she reacts to her mom if she wants to alter the outcome of their interactions.

The key to cleaning it up is the equation $A + B = C$, where her mom is B and Jenna can decide, as A, not to let her mother get to her. Only then will the outcome, and their relationship, evolve.

She also needs to stop dragging all of her issues into the bedroom by making her spouse deal with them. He may not be telling her this, but he needs her to talk about other things (like how *his* day went). He's her husband, not her shrink, and she must find a better way to relate to him. She needs to find a few girl pals she can go to for perspective and companionship. She's going to feel vulnerable at first, but she can learn to do it, and *must* do it.

The takeaway from this: You can only change yourself, and that is a good thing, because the power lies within your control. Jenna has to learn to be more open and trusting with women. "I found a great husband, so obviously I have the capacity for closeness and I have to learn to let myself trust women the same way I trust him." This will entail figuring out how to relate to women in a whole new way, and not relying on petty gossip as her currency. She needs to expose something about herself and be willing to share her own life details, not those of others. She needs to realize she's been holding herself back from female relationships. Her pearl: Go or grow, and take a risk. It may not be so scary after all.

I'M SICK OF BEING THE TOUR DIRECTOR!

"I am always the one everyone relies on to make plans, to entertain them, to get tickets, to be the tour director. I jokingly call
myself Julie McCoy, from *The Love Boat*, but the truth is I wish
I had someone to depend on. But it never works out that way."

—Linda, 33; Los Angeles, California

Linda is a gregarious, blond, and fun theatrical producer who is "connected" to everyone in the industry. She has a huge group of friends and
relies on them for emotional support, since both her parents are deceased
and she has no siblings. Her extended family of friends is always there for
her—on holidays and during busy weekends of fun activities, and evenings full of movie screenings and dinners in her apartment, where she
loves to cook.

So it's no wonder that her friends turn to her for their entertainment.
They'll call her up and ask what's doing over the weekend, and suddenly
she feels the pressure to produce a full itinerary of events that will stimulate and surprise them. "They'll say things like, 'We really should get
tickets for that new play everyone's talking about.' And I know they mean
I should get them because I can, and because I will get better seats. And
guess what? I do it! Then they'll say, 'Why haven't we seen that new show
at the Getty?' and I know I need to start planning. And for the most part,
I don't mind at all."

Though Linda does get amazing perks through her job, and loves to
organize and entertain, she sometimes feels that her friends are taking
advantage of her. "If I call them and say, 'Let's go to dinner,' they say,
'Great—set it up.' It's like I work for them. Now, I don't mind, but I don't
always want to be in the position of *having* to arrange those fun evenings.
I'm not Santa, and I'm not Julie McCoy. I want someone to take care of
things for me, for once."

The story makes us want to hug Linda . . . and cringe. The problem is she thinks these surrogate family members will abandon her if the tickets and fun stop flowing. But she is giving to the point of resentment and feels like no one is taking care of her. Because Linda has no family, she feels she has to continuously please her friends, or they might leave her.

The unconscious process here? Catherine explains that Linda is exhibiting a common defense that shrinks call "reaction formation," which basically means doing the opposite of what you actually want. So if what you want is to be taken care of but feel that is unacceptable, or you're scared to express that, you take care of everyone around you. It's like you are hoping to get back what you give. But usually the opposite ends up happening, and you feel used and depleted instead of cared for.

Catherine says that Linda is overly solicitous of her friends' whims and needs. Her ability to plan events should not mean that she has to do so in order to keep her relationships. Sometimes she should say no or suggest that *they* make the plans. Linda is so used to being the tour director that it's hard to stop, even though she is feeling resentful. The key to cleaning up this room: Too much of a good thing is a bad thing. She doesn't have to be at work all the time. She can close the door on the office and ask her friends to pour her a glass of wine, put her feet up, and let someone else plan the evening for once.

By doing so, she will be shifting the dynamic—she has to understand that if she sets some limits and doesn't always procure the tickets, her friends will have to step up. This may feel uncomfortable at first, but the subtle change will alter the outcome—and she will start to feel cared for. Remember, too much of a good thing is a bad thing here. The giving room can give back.

I CAN'T STAND IT WHEN
MY FRIENDS BECOME FRIENDS!

"Whenever I introduce one of my good friends to another one of my close friends, I get excited at first, thinking that it will be so much fun to have my favorite people get to know each other and maybe we can even hang out as a group sometime. And then if I hear that they are getting together and I wasn't around (even if I was invited), I become jealous and territorial and think, wait a minute, I introduced these two, and now I hate the fact that I feel left out. I start having this horrible tension in my stomach and feel sick, wishing I'd never introduced them."

—Danielle, 27; Tampa, Florida

As a college event planner for one of the smaller universities in her hometown, Danielle, a successful woman who loves to be social and made this trait into a career, considers herself "the ultimate people person" who regularly puts large groups together. She is always planning events, such as a dinner for the college president and his visitors, or the convocation or graduation, or preparing for next month's open house for prospective students and families.

"I love my job. I am a natural at it, and it is very fulfilling to get to do what I really enjoy for a living. Which is why I tend to forget that when one of my best friends from college is coming to town for vacation and I introduce her to one of my closest friends who lives locally, I am always disappointed—and more to the point, jealous—when they hit it off so well that I suddenly feel like a third wheel! I hate myself for feeling this way. It's so sixth grade, but it's true. Like now I'm on the outside looking in. I think: *What have I done?*

"And then all my insecurities from grade school come rushing back: I'm not the cool one, or I'm not the smart, witty one, or the pretty one. I'm just everybody's best friend who they all depend on and who is there for them. I love that role, but weirdly I feel lonely and left out when others get together without me. I mean, what did I do to make them not want me around? Is it normal to feel this way now, as a grown-up? I feel like high school just never ends. What's that expression? Life is like high school with money. I think that's so true.

"I feel like I'm right back at the time of my life when I'm insecure and I wish I could be more mature and not care what others are doing or thinking. Take a hiking trip or just go off and do my own thing. But then I wish someone would come with me and there I am, right back at the planning again: Let's all go on a hiking trip! I feel like I am so predictable and I'm sick of myself. I'd leave me out too."

Danielle is quite embarrassed by this little "secret" of hers. She hasn't told anyone but her fiancé about it because she thinks it makes her seem so pathetic and immature. "It's ridiculous, I know, but every single time one of my friends starts to get chummy with another person that I introduced them to, I get crazy jealous."

Catherine says that feeling jealous when friends become close is completely normal—to a point—but that Danielle is hypersensitive about this because of her sister dynamic, which to this day continues to plague her relationships with other women. When she was growing up as the middle sister, it hurt her that her older and younger sisters seemed closer, since it felt logical to her that she should be the glue, being the middle child in age. But her sisters shared sports and a love of all things competitive (even though they were four years apart in age, they might as well have been twins, and she even called them "the ponytail twins") and she was more the cheerleader type. It was easy for them to bond over soccer and tennis and their favorite football players on the Tampa Bay Buccaneers, but whenever she tried to do anything to get between them, even just sitting on the couch during a TV show, they would scoff at her hairdo or her makeup or her short skirt and make fun of her to the point that she had to leave the room in order not to cry. So now her sisters are grown up and still close as can be and she feels left out. Her sensitivity to being pushed aside is like an old wound that is easy to bruise or reopen.

When Danielle assigns these roles to her friends she is displacing her disappointment about not being an integrated sister in the sibling lineup onto her friends. Then she gives up too easily, as if she already is resigned to an outcome where she is not included.

Catherine says that she participates in the way things play out, since in some way she is perpetuating this dynamic. She basically gives up and walks away, since she expects that eventually she'll feel bad, so on some level she accelerates the process. It becomes a self-fulfilling prophecy.

Whether Danielle is in the basement (memories of the ponytail twins) or the family room (where the present day means it's still hard to be with them) or the living room (where she sabotages herself by projecting this dynamic onto her female friends), she has to recognize the pattern and decide to break it. The process is a form of acting out, since if she expressed herself and simply explained that she was sensitive to this issue, her friends might make sure to be sensitive to her. From their perspective, they likely don't even notice it's happening. They can't read her mind, so she has to learn to communicate her feelings openly and not be scared of getting hurt.

Her pearl is to be direct, not to act out by checking out: Be honest with yourself and those around you in order to be a better friend, to yourself and others.

I WANT ALL NEW FRIENDS!

"I need new friends. I'm so sick of talking about the same old stuff. Now that we are a little older, they've started talking about wills and funeral plots! I'm not ready to call it quits yet; why can't we talk about our next adventure?"

—Joelle, 56; Rochester, New York

Joelle has always had tons of friends. "Growing up, my friends were everything to me. And when my husband and I moved to a new town, it was very important to us that we made new, good friends, and we did. Over the past fifteen years in Rochester, we have celebrated many birthdays and important events, and we always found time on weekends to have brunch or get families together. It was great."

Lately, however, Joelle has been feeling disenchanted with her friends. "It's like they are still talking about the same stuff. Last week at a barbecue, everyone started talking about their burial plans. I was horrified. I wanted to run from the room and find new friends! I wanted to throw the munchies on the floor and scream, What is wrong with you people? Aren't you bored with yourselves?" That is when Joelle knew she had reached a critical moment in her life.

Though Vin, her husband, wasn't involved in the funeral plot conversation, he agrees with Joelle that their friends are becoming bores. "Vin and I recently did some really interesting volunteer work overseas and I feel invigorated," Joelle says. "It's like I have a renewed sense of purpose. But our friends don't really seem too interested in that. Sure they came over for dinner and a slide show, but then it was forgotten, and we went back to the usual conversations. Which are getting more and more dreadful."

The problem is that Joelle is not feeling as old as her friends feel. She can look in the mirror and figure out that she's not aging as fast as they are, which is a good thing, but it's causing tension. She is exhibiting some narcissistic traits here, since she thinks: *You all may be dying but I am better than you because I am refusing to age.* She believes her way is the right way, and while delaying the aging process is fine, she doesn't need to hate her friends for the fact that they are acknowledging aging, even embracing the phase of life they are entering.

Joelle is also doing what is called "displacement," which is redirecting feelings about one thing (her aging, the fact that her parents recently died, her own mortality) onto another (her friends and their preoccupation with topics related to growing older and even death). Joelle can try to stay young forever, but she cannot force these feelings onto her friends or resent them for how they are acting.

She should also realize that her friends think she is in denial, that not to plan for the inevitability of death or aging is foolish. It's admirable that Joelle feels vital and healthy and wants to stay that way by surrounding herself with young and active people. "I know I'm getting older," Joelle says, "but do I have to act like an old lady before I am one?"

She wants to grow and evolve, but to toss over her old pals would be a mistake. The solution for her is to find new friends who are in sync with this phase of her life. She can still appreciate the shared history she has with her old friends while she has exciting adventures with her new ones.

Here's her key process for cleaning up the living room: It's not either/or; it's both/and. Joelle can have her old friends and her new ones, although she probably can't expect them to meld. These two groups represent parts of her life—her future (new pals) and her past (old pals)—and she can appreciate the time she spends with each, in the present. The pearl: Conflict is okay. In this case, that means you can have different friends for different aspects of your life.

I FLIRT WITH MY FRIEND'S HUSBAND

"Every time I get together with a certain group of friends there is one couple that makes me think, *I wish I'd married him.* Then I get a little drunk and start to flirt with him, and I am so embarrassed the next day because I wonder if everyone noticed and then I worry I have been unkind to my own husband and my friend. But I love flirting with her husband . . . it makes me feel like if I'd married him my life would have been different—freer and better."

—Diane, 42; San Diego, California

Diane has it all: a great husband, a successful sports marketing firm, two teenage kids, and a great life. She's active, pretty, slender, and a fun, upbeat woman. But after a glass or two of wine she becomes flirtatious, though she would never do anything unfaithful or cross the line. It's as if in these moments, she needs more attention, especially from the men in the room. At parties, this often takes the form of flirting with Nick, the husband of one of her old friends, Kathy. Diane and Nick knew each other in college and have always had a little—but unspoken—thing for each other. However, the little spark between Diane and Nick still seems to be there, and it bothers Diane, because when the four of them are together she and Nick talk more than they should, and she doesn't feel like this is nice to either her own husband or her friend Kathy, who always pretends not to notice.

"I know that he thinks I'm fun, and he makes me feel really good about myself, and I think he's a great guy, but at the end of the night I'm glad to be going home with Tom. I know I made a good decision in marrying him. So why do I spend the entire evening soliciting Nick's attention and getting him to laugh at my jokes? It's kind of embarrassing. I really hate myself, feel guilty, and vow never to do it again. And then I *do*."

Catherine says Diane is struggling with self-esteem issues and probably isn't interested in Nick as much as she is in how his attention makes her feel: young, pretty, smart, funny, etc. Diane isn't so much competing with Kathy or jealous of her marriage, but looking for male attention where she can feel safe getting it.

Diane needs positive affirmation from outside her marriage because she is feeling bad about herself—about aging (especially her looks) and what she offers the world. She appears to have it all, but from where she sits her star is waning and she needs to know she's still "got it." This is an expression of narcissism, since it's a form of overinvolvement with the self, even though she is actually lapping up the attention of someone else. It's a reflected admiration, because her own self-love is not enough and she needs to feel it from everyone around her.

Catherine reminds us that there is such a thing as healthy narcissism. We all need to love ourselves; it's essential and self-preserving. But it can cross over into a pattern that can damage our relationships and hurt us. Tom tells Diane she is pretty and smart and winning, and yet she needs to seek the same feedback elsewhere, as if his compliments are not enough. Diane sees Tom as an extension of herself, and since she doesn't always believe her own pings, she doesn't trust his either.

For Diane, the combination of self-love (thinking she's attractive) is combined with self-loathing (feeling old). Whether you feel overly positive or overly negative about yourself can be a problem. Any kind of overin-volvement in the self is considered unhealthy narcissism. Thinking you are hot stuff or thinking you are a piece of dog doo is equally narcissistic, Catherine explains. So when Diane berates herself the next morning for bad behavior, this extreme mood swing becomes part of what's causing her trouble. She needs to understand that rather than feel overly special or overly terrible, she can just be herself.

Diane has to move to another room, since she is spending too much time in the bathroom, scrutinizing herself in the mirror. Her bathroom is tied too closely to the rest of her house, in particular her living room. She needs to find satisfaction and develop other parts of her personality.

Diane is defining herself as others see her, rather than defining herself from the inside out. The solution is to spend more time in what we call the Tenth Room, where she can organize her value system and stop allow-ing the pings of others to define her. To do this she has to value herself in a healthy and productive way. First, she must find her authentic inner self and then develop that person. She has to learn to believe she is attractive without anyone telling her. If she can depend on her own feedback with-out needing it from others, then she can be the best version of herself, not someone seeking or needing that self reflected back at her from others.

Catherine says narcissists often get into patterns called idealization/devaluation, where they flip-flop between polar opposite emotions about themselves so that they either love themselves or hate themselves. One minute they think they're super great, or superior to others, and the next they are down on themselves to the same extreme. The truth is, all of us are a mix of positive and negative traits and behaviors; all relationships contain good and bad behavior, and everything in between. You can like yourself and also accept that you have flaws and, like everyone else, you make mistakes.

For the narcissist, the goal is to recognize that you have both likeable traits and those you have to learn to live with. The key is to learn to love and accept yourself, warts and all. Only then can you truly be open to the lives of others. The more you connect with others, the happier you will be. Get outside your own head, move away from the mirror and back to the living room, where all the interesting people are waiting to get to know the real you.

So the final thought for the living room is that it's about connecting and evolving and listening, not competing. The expression "keeping up with the Joneses" was based on Edith Wharton's father's family, who were wealthy and social but not necessarily happy, as her stories illustrate. It's an expression that is still relevant now, all these decades later, because it is human nature to compare ourselves to others and see how we measure up. Whenever I wish I had the affluence I see around me, I remind myself that I have made my own choices and I am happy with my life, my kids, husband, and job. At the end of the day I wouldn't trade places with anyone, even those with "more." The living room is not a place to harbor envy, or measure yourself against your friends, or "give" too much of yourself. It's a place to enjoy the company of others, offer support, empathy, and friendship, and accept the same in return.

9

The Office

You Earn Your Paycheck
. . . and Your Stress

Welcome to your office, where you handle issues related to whatever it is you define as your work, whether it's in the home or at a place of business. The emotional office in your house is where worries about money and career and purpose all need to be dealt with. It's where you work on your "work," but what you do there is hopefully personally rewarding.

Stress Is Our Perpetual State of Being

Most women feel they are "crazy busy" all the time but always want to do more. The minute I get an open slot in my jam-packed schedule I add a project, whether it's a redesign at the magazine, a new workout schedule, or co-writing this book. It sounds crazy, but I love having too much to do and too little time to do it all. What would I give up? Not my family, not my job, and not my athletic pursuits. I run or bike or swim in the morning so that I can focus for the rest of the day without the itchy feeling of wanting to get up and walk around. That attitude helps me feel like I am getting the most out of myself, and my life, but it can sometimes backfire, like when I get down on myself. That's when I have to fight off the stress of feeling like I could always do everything better.

Most of us say we either have too much to do, or that too little of what we do—other than our family duties—has meaning. Women want to make an impact. They also try to balance their needs and the needs of others. Over and over Catherine and I hear women say, "I can't say no" because they don't want to disappoint anyone. They have a boss, a husband, kids, parents, and friends who all want a piece of them. The question is, how can you have it all—the family and the job, the time for yourself, and the time for others—and not feel like you are shortchanging yourself in any of those parts of your life?

I Do It All . . . Just a Lot Less Perfectly Than I'd Like

When someone tells me, "I don't know how you do it!" it's like a red cape to a bull. I want to ask right back, "What do you mean? Are you saying that I can't possibly do a good job on so many things at once?" The implication that I must be shirking some of my responsibilities as a mother, wife, or working person is embedded in the remark. I know it's often said in admiration, but part of me hears it as a judgment against the working mom, and so I try to disarm the situation by saying, "It's easy—I just do it all badly." Or, if it's about parenting, I'll shoot back, "My children were raised by wolves." Or the dog. Or simply that they raised themselves.

I figure that if I can laugh at myself, my inquisitor will laugh too. But then I ask myself, *Is that how I really feel? Why am I doing so much?* And the truth is, I sometimes think I could be there more for my daughter, or for my husband, who once again has to pick up our dinner on his way home from work. When I was feeling overwhelmed like that, I used to reach for a glass of wine to chill out and douse the sparks of stress in my brain. Now I go for a swim or a run. It's a healthier way to cope with stress, and I often come upon a solution while plowing through the repetitive motions of swimming or jogging that puts my brain on "dimmer" and allows creativity to flow.

Catherine says another key is to tell yourself you are doing your best today, and to forgive yourself for some of the things you don't accomplish. You must be willing to believe that "good enough" is truly good enough.

Whatever your daily responsibilities, the universal emotion seems to be stress about not doing it all well enough. To reduce your feelings of inadequacy about this, you need to figure out when you're in your emotional office, and when you're in another room, feeling guilty, for example, about missing your child's violin recital or lacrosse game.

"The Bad Compromise" and Other Conflicts

The bad compromise is a phrase I coined several years ago when my then ten-year-old son, Julian, was competing in the sprints at his school's "field day" and was so nervous about wanting to do well he was ill the night before. But I was the newly minted editor of a major magazine and didn't want to let either work or family down that morning. It was a disaster in the making.

I went downtown for a morning meeting and planned to get back uptown to the park in time for the races at 11 A.M. But things at work ran late, and I was hyperventilating by the time I jumped in a cab and then ran shoeless across the baseball fields to get to where the boys were racing. As I arrived, I realized I was too late. A well-meaning mother came up and said, "Did you see him? He was great. He won and was so happy." I almost burst into tears.

My son galloped over with his ribbon and said, "Mom, did you see me?" I said, "Yes, honey, you were amazing! I am so proud of you." The rest of the day was a blur for me because of the guilt I felt over missing the only thirty seconds that mattered to Julian, and the lie I had told him. By the time I got back to work I had a name for this scenario: the bad compromise. It means, basically, that by trying to be too many places at once, everyone gets short shrift, most of all me. I had rushed through my morning meeting, I'd missed the race regardless, and I'd told my son a rare lie. It was a losing proposition all around. I was trying to please everyone and ended up pleasing no one.

It was also a moment of reckoning. I vowed never to let this kind of stupidity happen again. Now when I have a conflict like that, when I know I have to take a direct hit, I make the call early, and plan for it. I tell my team at work, "I have to be at Josie's track meet and will make up the time before and after," and sometimes I tell Josie, "I wish I could be at every one of your games, but I can't, so let's figure out which ones mean the most to you and I will block out the time for you and definitely be there." Then I put "Lucy out" on my work schedule so that my top directors can plan around this block of time (I rarely feel guilty since I read for hours late at night to make up for the work time I have to miss, so it all evens out by the end of the day).

I also recognize how lucky I am to have a job that is more flexible than most. Once upon a time I worked at a newspaper where I was a cog in a huge wheel and had to work the hours that my bosses dictated, no matter what was happening in my personal life. I would finish my story for the paper and then have to sit there and watch the copy editor do other work, and when he finally read my story it was only important that I stay so he could ask me a question every now and then. I literally had to watch him eat, take personal calls, and get around to my story whenever he felt like it, so I couldn't leave even though all I was doing was sitting and waiting. The hours ticked by. The next time I had a newspaper job was years later, in the days of cell phones, and I also had a toddler and another baby on the way. I told the copy editor (systems rarely change) that he could call me and I was going home to have dinner with my child. He balked. *If I have to stay, you have to stay,* was his attitude. It felt like all I was doing was putting in "face time." It became another catchphrase for me.

I now don't believe in face time. It's more like "in your face" time to me, since it's hostile and not necessary. Now I run a magazine of mostly women and I tell them: Your work has to be excellent and your personal commitments—kids, doctors' appointments, or whatever takes you away from the office in the day—can't hold up the meetings and work of the monthly magazine we produce. So we juggle our lives around big meetings and deadlines and help one another when someone has a babysitter who doesn't show, or a parent who gets sick, or any other unanticipated event. Beyond that, we all have to live and work and figure it out.

I am immensely proud of the environment I have created at my office since it doesn't involve the bad compromise (unless absolutely necessary) or require face time, and does produce an award-winning product. In my personal life, my kids know I love to work and will always have a job of some kind and they are cool with that. Even if it involves missing some of their games.

I now have a little code with my daughter, which is half-funny, half-serious: I ask her, "Is this going to be a couch moment later?" And she says, "No." And then I ask, "Is this going to make the top ten?" And she says, "Not even top hundred." She also knows that if she really needs me I will drop everything and get home ASAP. She knows this is the case, so she doesn't ask often.

I have always had a "divided" life in terms of work and kids and tell my team, "I always take the call" from my kids, which means sometimes home encroaches on work. But it's a two-way street, and the boundaries aren't perfect, since many nights I have to work at home after dinner. Still, as long as I don't make the bad compromises, it all works out in my emotional office. My pearl here is that you have to be authentic and not worry about what others think (the pinging of the office and the home). For this situation, I also use this pearl: It's not either/or . . . it's both/and. It's okay to have some conflict, as long as you learn from it, or it leads you to make better decisions in the future.

That's Why They Call It Work

Not everyone has the luxury of loving their job, but you can love the things it affords you. The point is to know why you work. Often a paycheck is enough.

The ideal is to get paid for something we like to do or that is rewarding. If you can't combine those two things, though, that's fine. Just be clear that the money supports what you love in your other rooms. Rarely do you get to mix passion, purpose, and paycheck, but when you do, it's magic.

This "magical" state, when you are so absorbed in what you're doing that you feel a natural high, is also known as "flow," a term coined by Mihaly Csikszentmihalyi back in the 1960s to describe anything—an activity or productive mental state—that you can lose yourself in. When you feel flow you are so enrapt in the moment that you lose track of time and focus comes easily. It doesn't feel like work; it is effortless. Some athletes and musicians experience flow—they can be so engrossed in what they are doing that they are almost in a trance. Every one of us is capable of feeling it too.

In our experience, feeling flow at work means that what you are doing can be a source of great happiness, but also stress when the feeling doesn't come and you can't find that "sweet spot." If you are a flow seeker, the stakes get higher, because as you attain that feeling of focus and satisfaction, you add on more challenges to keep engaged. If you're a driven person, your job will likely be both the most rewarding and the most depleting part of your life, depending on whether you're having a good day—feeling flow—or a bad one.

It's not just the extreme personalities who find flow; Catherine has it while sitting in a chair, listening to women talk. "I lose myself in my work. I find it totally engrossing," she says. "It's a privilege to help women feel well, and get paid for it. That's where I experience flow."

Whatever we choose to do with our day, and whatever we call "work," how we feel about it is what matters. For some women, the ultimate luxury is being a stay-at-home mom, and for others that's the ultimate sacrifice. Either way, we all agree that it counts as "work."

The stay-at-home mother may not get a paycheck, but her work duties (cooking, cleaning, chauffeuring, child care, tutoring, etc.), if paid for in the "real world," would be worth about $125,000 a year. The question really isn't whether she is valued—she should be, by her loved ones, whether they express it or not! The more important question: Is *she* happy and feeling purposeful in her day-to-day duties, as well as in her big picture? Catherine and I support any choice a woman makes, as long as she feels it was her choice, and that her day has purpose. That's true for the stay-at-home mother, the lawyer, the toll collector, the shrink, and the magazine editor. But if you are not feeling a sense of self-worth or meaningfulness, then we want you to figure out what is going on and then how to move on and find the purpose you lack.

In this economy you won't always have a choice about what you do or how you spend your day, but you always have a choice in how you *feel* about it.

I MISS MY FAMILY,
BUT I WANT A CAREER

"I came here to follow my dreams, but I miss my family. I know my dad won't live forever and I wonder if I will regret the choices I've made. But then I talk to him about it, and he wants me to stay in New York and live my life and that is what I've chosen to do."

—Kristi, 30; New York, New York

Kristi is a California girl who moved to New York straight out of college to follow her dream of being a magazine writer and editor. It's a tough way to make a living—journalism may look glamorous as it's portrayed in *Ugly Betty* and *The Devil Wears Prada*, but the reality is hard work, long hours, and fierce competition for a dwindling number of jobs with thousands of smart, talented, and driven women. Because of the long hours she has to put in, Kristi can't get home as often as she'd like.

"I missed my sister's engagement party, and when I did come back for her wedding, I got a lot of grief from my friends. I feel like they're judging me. Most of them will marry their boyfriend from high school and never leave the neighborhood, and live the same boring lives their mothers live. I can't do that."

Kristi knows she has made the right choice but feels conflicted when her mother sends her a sweet e-mail describing the family's Sunday ritual of a bike ride along the Pacific at sunset. That makes Kristi want to cry because she feels she is missing out on the mundane things that make their family life so special.

Making her feel even worse about being so far from her family is the fact that her father has been very sick. If he dies while she is in New York she will never forgive herself for missing out on spending more time with him. She can't figure out how to be a successful journalist and a good daughter.

Kristi says, "I'm glad I'm living my dreams and trying to become more independent. I feel like if I stayed home it would be more of the same, and I wanted a change. I have nothing against the choices my friends made but I know I did the right thing by leaving." Her path took her far away from home and her comfort zone, and now she feels alien when she returns. Yet her friends don't understand how she could live so far away, and they're happy staying close.

How do you reconcile following your dream and having to move away from the people and things that you love? How do you find that balance? Is there such a thing?

Catherine's answer: Balance is a beam you try to walk in grade school. The notion of "balancing" sets women up for falling off the beam. You may for an instant hold everything in the balance, but eventually it will come toppling down on one side or another. So rather than feeling like you've failed, you have to pick things up one item at a time, and learn to prioritize.

What gets attention first should tell you something. But that is a rotating list, since one day your child may need you and the next day your boss will. That is the natural flow of your life. So the important thing is to fully engage yourself in this moment before the next comes along. We say: Being present is the new balance. The key to being happy is not trying to do it all, all at once. The goal is to just do—and enjoy—what you're doing right now.

Kristi is coping with a typical twentysomething conflict in a healthy way. She is making the transition between being a girl and being a woman, but her conflict is intensified by living on a separate coast from her family. This separation makes the transition more acute than if she'd done it in her hometown. Catherine explains that Kristi is experiencing separation/individuation as she creates her own life and career, and it's painful but appropriate at this stage of her life. Your twenties are often fraught with the push and pull between the bonds with your family and the drive you feel to create a new independent life and career.

The office and the family room are too close for comfort in Kristi's emotional house, but she doesn't have to see this as an all-or-nothing proposition. In this case, it's not either/or, it's both/and. Which means she can embrace the conflict and try to both tolerate the pain of missing her family *and* enjoy her life in New York. Of course, with new technologies it's easier to try to close that gap, but obviously she can't live in two places at once.

You don't have to live close to your parents to stay connected. Kristi can count herself lucky that she enjoys these emotional ties, and they can continue to thrive from across the country.

Catherine explains: One sign of emotional maturity is to recognize that there is no perfect solution, and that life is full of compromises. You can simultaneously be thrilled that you got a byline in your New York writing job, and also sad that it meant not being with your family that day. That's maturity, and Kristi should celebrate the fact that she is getting outside her comfort zone, feeling good about her accomplishments, and still being close to family members, who, after all, are so proud of her.

SLIPPERS AT THE OFFICE

"Sometimes I get so comfortable at work that I feel like I'm wearing slippers to the office! My best friend works right across the hall from me, and we have so much fun together, but I don't get a lot done. The problem is I want to move ahead, get promoted and have a career. She is able to focus, but for some reason I can't."

—Cynthia, 27; Boston, Massachusetts

Cynthia laughingly describes her job as being in the mind-numbing world of retail accounting. Despite that grim outlook, she has fun in the office, mainly because she gets along so well with her colleague Alice. They are inseparable and spend many hours e-mailing each other about dates, online shopping, and everything but the job they are supposed to be doing. "It's so much fun to go to work, it's like being at home with my best friend, but if I had to be honest about it, I share more with her than

I should. If the boss criticizes something I do, I run over to her and show it to her and ask her to tell me if she thinks it's good. Of course she does, and we then decide the boss is all wrong, and instead of doing my work better, I just feel defensive. I know I should be talking to my supervisor about how to improve, but it's so easy to get Alice to validate my work instead."

Cynthia knows this tactic is standing in the way of her success, and she would really love to be promoted. In fact, Alice did get a raise a year ago, and Cynthia was both thrilled for her and jealous. She realized then that she wasn't being taken seriously, but she was reluctant to change her attitude about her job. And then came the slippers . . .

One day Cynthia and Alice decided to have a sleepover after work to watch their favorite TV show together, so Cynthia brought her pj's and slippers to work. She broke a heel before lunch and had nothing to wear around the office but her slippers. "That's when it dawned on me that I had turned my office into one big cozy sorority with my friend, and as I walked to the vending machine for cookies while wearing my slippers I realized I was acting like a five-year-old in the office and I had to shake that attitude and put back on some heels, before I got fired."

Catherine says that this broken heel was the best thing that ever happened to Cynthia. It helped her realize she'd conflated her office and her family room. She was actually struggling at her job and feeling insecure at work. But instead of focusing on doing the job better and rising through the ranks, she found comfort in oversocializing with her colleagues and creating a dormlike atmosphere at work, reverting to a collegial mind-set and not a professional one. In and of itself, being friends with co-workers isn't bad, unless it interferes with doing your work. And if a pal does get promoted over you, it may adversely affect not only your career but also your friendship.

Cynthia has to learn that she can have relationships at work, but she needs to create boundaries. She and her friends have to understand that if they hope to get ahead, they need to focus on their jobs and behave professionally. It's not that they can't socialize or have fun, but if that's the main thrust, and the work is secondary, you have to believe something isn't working. Perhaps she should even consider a new job where she is engaged and rewarded by the work and not just the workmates.

Cynthia is in the wrong room: She should be in the office, but she's actually in her living room and using work as a big party.

Catherine says Cynthia is "fossilized" or in a state of arrested development, and the way she needs to break this pattern is to grow up at work or leave the place entirely. Her boss isn't holding her back, nor is her colleague; no one is holding her back . . . except herself.

Or put more simply, if you want to get promoted, be taken seriously, and treated like a grown-up, you need to act like one. Cynthia's key process here is that actions speak louder than words, and she is acting like a child. She says she wants a promotion, but she is acting as if she wants to go back to her childhood home or sorority house and be taken care of and have fun. Her pearl: Go or grow. Go along as you have been or grow up and change. It's your choice to make.

I HAVE NO PASSION

"I have a good education but never found the one thing that really turned me on. At school I studied education, but now I just work in schools and don't teach. Going to work feels like going through the motions. I'm not miserable, but I'm bored, and I wish I could do something I feel passionate about. But I haven't found it yet. I wonder, will I ever?"

—Lynn, 42; Phoenix, Arizona

Lynn has been in and out of clerical positions and feels stagnant in her career as a high school administrator. She assists the head of the school, but her days are full of making appointments and answering phones, and she doesn't see a career path out to whatever it is she would find more rewarding. Lynn has been doing this for twelve years, and she still doesn't know what she wants to do with the rest of her life.

She lives with her boyfriend and is happy in that relationship but feels empty at work and isn't sure what her next step should be. "I always thought about starting a business, but I don't have the personality. I am too sensitive and can't take the criticism. I tend to talk myself out of things. I can't initiate anything."

Lynn lacks confidence but not talent. After talking to her for a while it's clear that she is at her happiest when she is baking. Her face lights up just talking about it . . . but she doesn't think she's an amazing baker, or that she could make a living at it. But if she had a purpose—for example, to sell her pies to a local bakery or maybe someday even start her own company—she would be driven to work at it and improve.

Lynn feels lost. She says she might go back to school and learn a new skill but doesn't even know what she would study. Her boyfriend just got a better job in another state, and she is going with him because there is nothing to keep her where she is. She is rudderless. "My parents always told me, Just be happy. Their parents had really pushed them, and they didn't want to put that kind of pressure on me. But I don't know what it takes to be happy."

Catherine says Lynn is stuck in the basement, where her parents still just want her to be happy. Self-esteem is developed in childhood, through pinging from parents, siblings, teachers, and friends. You learn what you are naturally good at and what you have to work at. Some people stick with the things they are naturally good at for the rest of their lives; others find that the most rewarding pursuits are those they had to work hardest at in the beginning.

It's a fine line for parents—you want to compliment your kids but also teach them how to handle criticism and disappointment. It all comes back to authentic pinging. Lynn's parents never gave her harsh (or realistic) feedback, so she never learned to be discerning about her talents, and never dared to fail at anything. She couldn't risk the possibility that someone wouldn't like her work, so she chose to freeze rather than move forward. Lynn's ambivalence—"I guess baking is my passion"—is troubling. She doesn't own up to it, because that, in itself, would be a risk. What if she says, "This is my passion," but no one likes what she bakes?

Yet she won't go down that path because she doesn't want to hear critical feedback, since her parents never gave her any and she never learned how to receive criticism in a productive way. Part of being a grown-up is taking risks and getting feedback and understanding it isn't a personal affront if someone says, "Your apple pie is great but your blueberry pie is a little soggy." Successful people use this kind of criticism to improve. This is a life skill Lynn doesn't have. She doesn't have a career she cares about because she's not willing to put herself out there.

"I enjoy coming up with recipes and figuring out good flavor combinations. That is my passion." So why doesn't she find a job at a bakery and learn how to run a business? On the other hand, if she knows she could never take that path there's nothing wrong with putting a paycheck in the bank and spending all her leisure hours baking. Just because you love to sail doesn't mean you have to be a professional sailor. Be honest with yourself and recognize that your job is a means to an end. Define your purpose (making money or whatever it is) and feel good about it.

By floating through life, following her boyfriend, or just not making a break from her job, she has allowed her life to be determined for her. She's defaulting on her own ability to self-determine. Her inner compass is not pointing anywhere, so she's adrift and allowing the tide to take her where it will.

Her life is being determined despite her own lack of direction. The key process here is that she needs to recognize she is making choices by not making choices. We say, Not to decide is to decide. If she gets up from her chair at work in order to go do something, anything, that she cares about, where does it lead her? To the grocery store to buy ingredients? The farmers' market for the freshest berries? These are clues, and she needs to follow them like bread crumbs to her new life and passion. Her pearl: Take the first step. Then the next. Allow those baby steps to be the start down a new path to a meaningful life.

I HATE CRITICISM!

"I love being right and I hate being told I'm wrong. I can't listen to criticism without feeling my blood boil. When someone says something negative about me they become 'the enemy.' I can dole it out fine, but I hate listening to the critiques that are part of the daily world of the office. I wish I didn't do this, but I do, and now it may be holding me back because I don't collaborate well."

—Lydia, 28; New York, New York

Lydia is a copywriter at a large Manhattan ad agency. She's successful, clever, and charming, and clients generally love what she does. Despite that, it makes her physically ill when she has to walk into a room full of people and let them pick apart her work.

The night before a presentation she wants to throw up. She has headaches and neck pains and is unable to sleep. To soothe her nerves she finds herself eating ice cream around midnight and will sometimes polish off a pint. Finally, at around 1:30 A.M., she drifts off to sleep.

Other than these Sunday night anxiety spells, Lydia loves her life. She has great friends, entertains on weekends, and travels. She is the ultimate go-getter, and right now what she is after is a rocketlike career. Sure, she would love to be in a serious relationship, but she's only twenty-eight, so she figures she has time to work on that. There are still too many other things she wants to do: start her own agency, buy a weekend house, and travel more. The most important thing, though, is her job: She wants to get ahead and make a name for herself so that she can take some of her big clients with her when she goes out on her own.

She knows her inability to take criticism is a problem, since she sees the same kind of behavior in her own father. He always taught her to try to be perfect. And that's a trap—who can be perfect all the time?

. . .

The solution lies in her past. Catherine finds out, after talking with Lydia further, that this all stems from a painful childhood memory (the basement). A screen memory is holding her back. Lydia's underlying problem becomes clear when she tells the story of the "first big critical moment" of her life. When she was seven, she wanted to learn to tap-dance, but her parents forced her to promise she'd try ballet for a semester before she could try tap. Lydia agreed, reluctantly.

That summer she was having trouble controlling her bladder, and she had to go to the bathroom all the time. Often, she would wet her pants. Her parents tried everything, even making her wash out her underwear. Instead of stopping, she got better at hiding the fact that she was wetting her pants, and started washing them out without anyone knowing.

On the first day of ballet school, she was holding the barre and trying to hold in her pee. When the teacher said "Everyone plié!" Lydia kept her legs crossed, knowing if she tried to plié she would pee on the floor. The teacher yelled at her, "Lydia, plee-ayyy!" The class turned to look at her, and as she bowed her legs the pee came streaming out. She ran from the room and refused to ever go back. It was the end of her dance career, and the end of her peeing problem. That accident helped her mother realize that Lydia might have a medical condition. She took her to a doctor, who found that she had a raging bladder infection and needed to be hospitalized immediately. She was put on IV antibiotics to treat the problem.

One day in the hospital, her dad sat at her bedside and apologized for how he had blamed her for her peeing problem. "I should have known it was a medical problem," he told her. "You're still perfect!" When she told him she was worried about missing school, he said, "Don't worry—you're smarter than all the other kids and will have no problem catching up; heck, you're probably smarter than the teachers too!" And they laughed about that. She remembers saying to him, "You know, it's not my fault that I wet my pants," and he said, "I know. It was the infection. You really *are* perfect!" And that was their bond. She remembered thinking she always wanted to be perfect. And from then on, whenever something went wrong, she wanted to scream: It's not *my* fault.

As Lydia tells this story it is clear even to her that this memory is a critical one, in every sense. It's the lens through which everything critical gets filtered. The ballet-class scene and the hospital-bed scene and even the scenes where she wet her pants and washed out her underwear are her screen memories. In her version, the scary ballet lady plays the villain, and her father is the white knight. But she also sees that her dad unwittingly set her up for a lifetime of disappointment, because nobody can be perfect all the time.

The key process to stop "screening" is to start living in the present and decide to, in Catherine's term, "remetabolize" the past. Here's how this works: First figure out if you're allowing a defining moment to affect you today. Next tell yourself those memories are not always accurate. Catherine says they serve a purpose in life—for Lydia they've buoyed her and let her escape her own inner critic—but now they're no longer working for her, and her goal of moving forward in her career is being impaired. By remetabolizing it, you learn to see it from a different perspective: The villainous ballet teacher was actually trying to be helpful; the supportive dad was just blinded to the actual fact that you (an extension of him) are not always perfect. Swap their roles, and you start to get the fact that critical feedback can be helpful. Closing your ears to it can lead to stubbornness.

Lydia's sense that she will not get ahead at work until she learns to take criticism better is correct. As she contemplates opening her own agency, she realizes not many of her colleagues would go with her. They think she is too unbending and is not a good collaborator.

Lately Lydia's been struggling with what's going on at work, and calls her sister for advice. It's during this conversation with her sister, a composer, that a lightbulb goes on. "When someone says my music isn't right for the movie I'm scoring, I take a deep breath and contemplate what they're saying. I wouldn't get any more work if I dismissed it and just said, 'That's because they're stupid.' So even though I wrote it, I try not to take it personally. Just tell yourself it's about your *work*, not about you *personally*."

Lydia begins to understand she can hear criticism without having to hate it or the person saying it. She can even learn from it. She vows to be more of a consensus builder; instead of cutting off dissenters, she solicits the opinions of others and encourages them to tell her the truth. She also practices telling herself, *It's not personal,* and that is a first step toward really absorbing the message and not just rebuffing it, and the messenger. "I try to laugh at myself and say something like, 'Tell me how you really feel!'" she says. "And I'm proud of myself, because my dad never could do that. It's like I finally feel like I am growing, and that's a good thing." We'd add: Sometimes it takes looking backward to move forward.

MAYBE I SHOULDN'T HAVE QUIT!

"My husband and I agreed that when I got pregnant I'd stay home and raise our kids, and we both thought it best for the family, but now I want to do more, contribute to humanity, do something meaningful, like helping to cure AIDS or something else big, to give back. But who am I to complain, I mean, I signed up for this, right?"

—Martha, 37; Richmond, Virginia

Martha has a great life—nice house, loving family—but isn't happy about her lack of career. She spends her entire day with their toddler and has another baby on the way. Still, even with this imminent development, she wants to make a change, find a part-time job, and do more with her day. "Don't get me wrong, I love my son and having kids, but I feel so sidelined and like, I went to grad school for this? I feel brain-dead!"

Her husband, Matt, has a high-powered job as a money manager, and now that the economy is tight and things are tense in his office, he really can't stand hearing her complain, since he feels he walks through fire every day and comes home and wants to be appreciated for the stress he's under. Who wouldn't want her deal? he asks her. Doesn't she know how lucky she is? One day he even says to her: "Wanna switch places? I'll go play golf all day and then you can make the bucks."

Martha has a graduate degree in pharmacology and was working on drug development at a large drug company when she got married. Her dream was to develop the drug that would make AIDS a memory; the reality was that she was in a dead-end department and wasn't getting paid all that much. Together, she and Matt decided that what was best for their family was for her to quit once they got married. Soon after, she also got pregnant, as planned.

"We made this decision together. We thought two careers would be too hard to manage because we wanted kids. We agreed that I would quit my job and come back later to do something that would bring some good into the world. Now he works a hundred and twenty hours a week, and I take care of everything else. He comes home exhausted, and I need a break, but he doesn't help at all around the house. Now that I'm pregnant again, I think: *Wow, sometimes he can be really selfish.* I am totally wiped out, and yet I still have to make dinner, clean up, bathe our three-year-old, and take care of everything else around the house.

"Our last big fight came after I told him he could help out more, and he said, 'There are pregnant women who work at real jobs, and they never complain about their swollen ankles or aching back.' I wanted to throw something at him. Then later that night he wants to have sex. Sex? Forget it, we're barely speaking."

Catherine says Martha is acting out. She's not being direct about what she needs—to go back to work? To have more help? To be appreciated?—and instead is taking out her frustrations and anger on her husband. She may not even know what she needs or realize why she's so angry. Most times when you're acting out it's because you don't know what you're feeling; you just feel the need to change *something*, so you change the dynamic of your relationship by fighting. You act out your feelings instead of talking through them to figure out what is going on.

These two may need to move out of the office and into a space where they can talk, like the kitchen table. (A room note: Many problems couples deal with lead to the bedroom, but sometimes the first stop is to go to a neutral place to sit and talk, like the kitchen table.)

But there's still a lot of denial going on. Ask Martha if she's happy, and she'll say, "Why wouldn't I be? I have a great life, a beautiful son, a second on the way, a nice house, and we're healthy! I shouldn't complain! I know these arguments with my husband are small things and I have the life I said I wanted with the man I wanted. But I also know from not working for the last few years that I need to do something, even if it's just part-time, because I have to contribute, in ways other than picking up smashed peas under the high chair. Maybe I'll volunteer or work at the hospital. But I know there's something more, something that could make me feel like I am contributing to the greater good. I'm still trying to figure out what it is, how I can give back to people who need help out there in the world."

The fact that she is asking herself this question is the crucial step, and too many women never take it. She knows that she wants to make the world a better place, and yet right now she's too busy playing Bob the Builder, and it's making her feel trapped.

Catherine observes that though Martha *says* she's happy and grateful, she sometimes finds herself weeping for no reason. "I just get overwhelmed by the little things like shopping, doing the laundry, and getting my son to his play group on time. I think, *This is my life? I wanted to cure AIDS, and I can't even manage to make my son a healthy supper every night?* And then I'm crying in the shower and hoping my husband won't notice. I mean, I signed up for this. It's exactly what we both planned."

Martha misses her professional life and the sense of purpose she had there. "I could tear my hair out sometimes because when I was young and won a science prize I had dreams of winning the Nobel Prize in chemistry."

One of the reasons Martha is acting out is something Catherine calls the "return of the repressed," which is a Freudian concept for explaining how extreme feelings in the present are actually the result of an unresolved conflict from the past. Catherine's favorite lay expression for this is "hysterical is historical," which means if you find yourself overreacting, weeping uncontrollably, or screaming, the antecedent for the emotion may well be in the past.

The source of Martha's problem is that her parents had a terrible marriage and she vowed never to be like that—a couple of miserable people who never wanted to spend time together. She wanted to make her relationship with Matt her top priority. But neither of them is happy; he would prefer not to be at the office 24/7, and whenever she complains about how hard she has it at home, he says, "I'd trade places with you in a heartbeat."

They both made this bed and now they realize it's broken. They have to change something, but their issues aren't actually originating in the bedroom. She pretends to be sleeping when he comes home from work at 10 P.M. because at this point she's angry that he never gets home for dinner, never makes her a priority, and she isn't going to be "open for business" when he finally rolls in and she's exhausted. It's not initially about sex, but now that they aren't having it, the issues are piling on: It's about everything, sex included, at this point. They need to sit down and rethink the "plan" and make dramatic changes to their situation, perhaps even where and how they live, get a caregiver, make it possible for Martha to return to work, or this one issue—her lack of satisfaction—could cost them the marriage.

Both Matt and Martha desperately want more meaning in their lives and once they start honestly opening up, they'll realize that each brings issues from childhood. He wanted a stay-at-home mom and never had one, and she wanted parents that were loving partners. Now both feel they need to "get it right" for their own kids. But the plan's not working, and they have to reconcile their reality with their expectations.

Catherine suggests leaving the past behind for a moment and talking about what's really making them fight. Matt may find he'd be happier in a less-pay/less-stress job, and he's always wanted to open a wine shop, something he would enjoy doing, and have normal hours. They may actually decide to trade places to be happier, with Matt being the one with the more flexible schedule (he could get home for lunch with the kids if the wine shop was nearby, or drop them off at school on the way into work). She might need to travel to Africa to test antiretroviral meds for HIV trials.

You have to maximize your assets and not play a role, Catherine points out. It's as if they signed up for an *Ozzie and Harriet* view of the world, and neither one of them is enjoying it. These two have to get their view of "family" and the roles of mom and dad out of the basement, and stop trying to create a "fixed" version of their own flawed childhoods and families.

This is why they should first sit at the kitchen table for an honest conversation about what would work in today's world, what they really want for themselves and for their children, and then take the steps to create a new life that reflects who they really are.

They can be happy, but they have to be honest with each other about what they really want, and that means not taking pages from their childhood scrapbooks. They may have to get outside their comfort zone, beyond the traditional roles society once set out for a mother or father, because it isn't working for them.

They also have to be nicer to each other, communicating instead of acting out, since he is staying at work to avoid her, and she is going to bed early to avoid him. The key process in this room is to talk it out, not act it out. Whenever these issues come up, we'd say, be direct. Figure out what you want and express it. The pearl: To have a relationship, you first have to relate.

I MAKE MY OWN MONEY, I CAN DO WHAT I WANT WITH IT

"I should be able to spend what I make! Money is a big issue in our relationship. Even though we both have good salaries and contribute equally to our monthly expenses, I always feel like I have to justify my purchases to my husband. It makes me want to pay in cash or hide the things I buy."
—Anne, 34; Los Angeles, California

Anne is a bright, attractive brunette who is a fifth-year associate at a big corporate law firm in Los Angeles. Her husband, Keith, is also an attorney; he works in entertainment law. They have been together for ten years and still fight about money all the time, even over whether they should share a joint account. He says yes, she says no. She wants to do whatever she wants with her paycheck, and not have to answer to her husband.

Anne grew up in an affluent Northern California family. Her father was a founding partner in a law firm, and her mother was a successful tax attorney. Money was never a big issue for them, but Anne's dad felt his kids should know the value of the dollar and insisted they work every summer to earn their spending money for the academic year. "Dad would always pay for school, but anything beyond that was our responsibility. I realize that I had it good, I mean I don't have any debt right now, and I did learn the value of a dollar. So I resent Keith getting upset when he sees I've bought a nice new suit or pair of shoes."

Keith is from a small town in central California. His father owned a gas station and his mother was a homemaker. They both worked very hard and made many sacrifices to get their two kids into college. Keith took out loans to pay for his schooling and got some merit scholarship money for law school. His philosophy is: Spend nothing, save everything. Hers is: We've got it, why not enjoy it?

Anne's mom always brought her home new clothes, so she sees that as a form of love; shopping is just part of being happy and affirming life and looking forward to events that require you to look pretty and get dressed up. Only after sharing these memories and worries can they see that for Anne spending is a positive thing, an expression of her personality and her desires and her accomplishments. For Keith, spending money is undisciplined, profligate, and even weak. It shows a lack of self-control, like drinking too much. It's not the kind of behavior he wants to see from the future mother of his children. This is serious, and though they love each other, the money fight can drive a wedge between them; they need to sit down and learn to understand each other before it's too late.

Anne and Keith talk a lot about what money means to each of them. While Keith thinks he gives Anne a lot of latitude, he knows she feels she's being watched like a hawk. They have tried to talk about this and they recognize that they come from very different financial backgrounds, but it continues to be a source of tension for them, particularly when Keith recites the Visa bill charges at the end of the each month. "He tells me he's just trying to be helpful, keep us aware of our spending, but he knows it upsets and humiliates me. And to make things worse, he'll have just reviewed our bills and then want to have sex. Is he kidding? I am fuming,

while he can just shut off the bill talk and want to make love. Forget it—
I'd rather go to bed furious and hope tomorrow is a better day."

Not likely, says Catherine, since these two are stuck in the paradigm of
the parent/child relationship, and they are having trouble acting as grown,
married adults. It's as if Anne is reacting against her own father (now
played by Keith), and he is the dad in his family trying to rein in the purse
strings (child now played by Anne). Once again, the unconscious process
is transference. The emotions Anne has for one person (her dad) are played
out and experienced with another (her husband), and the pattern goes right
back to childhood.

She is also experiencing some "return of the repressed" feeling, since
she is saying to Keith "don't tell me what to do," as if it's a response to her
father. But Keith is flummoxed, reacting with a shrug and "I'm not trying
to tell you what to do. No one is. But don't we want to try to build a family
and a bank account together?" Catherine points out that Anne is fighting
Keith as if he's her father, but he's not, and she can choose to break the
pattern and grow up, move forward, and create an adult lifestyle. (As opposed to the kid who blows through her allowance every week.)

First Anne has to recognize she's not in her office but her basement,
full of memories of her father's overbearing behavior, and how money
seemed like power, at least within her family. Having money meant you
got to make the decisions, and not having it meant other people told you
what to do. So once she resets and remetabolizes those feelings, she can
choose to assign a different value to her own paycheck: It's a future plan,
a partnership with her husband, and they both are "investing" in their
family life.

The key process to understanding their relationship to each other is to
think of the Venn diagram, though this time it could represent not just
their relationship, but also their view about how to spend or save. They
can draw a financial Venn diagram, where the shading in the middle is
the money they each contribute to their mutual goals, and the outer areas
are the money they choose to spend or save as they see fit. The middle,
shaded area might need to be bigger, to signify that they share common

financial goals and a common vision, if not a philosophy about money. They need to find areas they can both agree on (saving for a house? a college fund?) and put these in the middle area of the diagram.

You can have different ideas and be close, so long as you work to understand your differences. For anyone pulled apart by money conflicts or different points of view, the key is to remember that sameness is not closeness. You don't have to do things the same way, but you do have to find a workable compromise. Staying close is the goal, not agreeing on everything. Our pearl: It's more important to be close than to win.

I CAN'T SEEM TO ENJOY MY SUCCESS

"I've worked so hard for so long that when I finally made it, it was hard for me to stop and take a breath and actually pat myself on the back. I almost felt like I had to keep moving and better my own best. What was next? I couldn't ever seem to just stop and say, I did it. I just always feel like I should be doing better, achieving more!"

—Karen, 35; Roxbury, Connecticut

Karen is the hardworking co-owner of a small jewelry business. She and her best friend from art school started making jewelry and had some luck showing and selling it to friends and family. They eventually took out a small business loan and rented a storefront on the main street of their little Connecticut town.

"At first, all we wanted was to be able to sell enough inventory to pay our monthly rent. We would literally share a bottle of wine at the end of the month as we sat around the store, doing our bookkeeping, and realize that yes, we could pay the rent this month! Not that we didn't have faith, but it's scary starting your own business."

About six months after they opened their doors, Karen and her partner had done well enough to be able to do a little public relations for themselves. "Our goal was to eventually go national, and my idea was to send our jewelry to the accessories editor at a fashion magazine, so we could see it on a model and hope that the photograph would drive business. We sent it to all the major titles, and what happened next was like a fairy tale. One of our pieces was in a major magazine, being worn by a celebrity. It was a set of delicate gold bangles. One day I got a call from a fact checker at the magazine, who was making sure they had the correct Web site address for us. I panicked. Not only was it good news, but it was also almost too good. I had to quickly make sure our supplier could still provide the bracelets, and that I had time to make up enough pieces before the magazine came out three weeks later."

Karen and her partner worked like maniacs for those three weeks, but when the magazine hit the newsstands, they were ready. Orders started rolling into the Web site, and not only did Karen have to go back to her supplier three times for more bangles, but the other jewelry on the Web site started selling out as well. Karen had to hire a third and then a fourth person, one to man the store and another to answer the phones and work the Web site while she went out to find new designs and create more jewelry. She was suddenly so busy being successful that she never stopped even to have a glass of champagne to celebrate. One day Karen ran into an old friend from school, who said something that struck home: "Wow, you really made it. You must be so happy!"

Once upon a time a statement like that—from this person especially—would have been a major victory. But Karen felt as if someone had just punched her. *Why*, she thought, *don't I feel happy?* She had gotten everything she'd ever wanted, career-wise, and yet she felt that it could all evaporate in an instant if she didn't keep pushing and moving forward, solving tomorrow's problems today.

The joy she'd felt when that fact checker had called was fleeting, like the flash of a camera; but her next thought was panic and then she was racing full tilt to make the most of this opportunity. But she hadn't really made the most of it, just the most profits. "I was so mad at myself because I wasn't able to hold on to the feeling of success. All I could think about was, *What's next?* And *How could we do this bigger and better?* I was so quickly on to the next thing that I didn't take the time to savor that moment, that victory."

Catherine explains that this is an example of idealization/devaluation, which basically means if it happens to you, you think it's not as impressive as if it happened to someone else. In layman's terms, this is the famous Groucho Marx line: "I don't care to belong to any club that will have me as a member." So in other words, just by achieving your goal, it feels less amazing. This is one of the cruelest ironies of a successful life. Karen idealized the hope that her business would get into the magazine, but when it actually happened, she dismissed it because now that it was real, it didn't seem to be as important. In fact it seemed totally unimportant, as if she'd been working for the wrong goal all along.

Some people experience this letdown when they achieve partnership in a law firm and think, yeah, but I missed all my daughter's ballet performances in order to reach this moment where my boss, who I now realize is a narcissistic a-hole, is clapping me on the back. Or it happens earlier, when you get into the Ivy League college of your dreams and realize you would have been much happier at the little liberal arts college that had your favorite subject at the core of its curriculum. Tal Ben-Shahar, the positive-psychology professor at Harvard, once told me that his students will walk up to him after a great class and say, "When do I get to just be happy? I feel like I need to constantly succeed, first to get into Harvard, now in all my courses, and I wonder, when am I allowed to just relax and be happy?" And Tal says to them, "Why not today?" And they look at him like he's crazy. There are expectations of grad school and becoming a Rhodes Scholar and the like, and these driven people don't know how to take their foot off the accelerator; it can become a chronic problem.

The typical type A person is successful in every measurable way but one: They don't value their own success. They lack the ability to appreciate the things they do attain and constantly seek the ones that are just outside their reach.

Usually something or someone in their past is a spark or pilot light to their inner fire. Often it's a critical parent or someone who is devaluing her, and she either can react against the criticism (I'll show you!) or agree with them (I am a fraud). Either way she's reacting, not acting in an authentic way.

Karen's basement is full of memories of working hard to overcompensate for the fact that in grade school she was identified as having mild dyslexia, and she always felt she had to work harder than everyone around her to excel at school. Finally, winning a prize for an essay at graduation was her first "accomplishment" that she had idealized and then devalued. Once she won it she felt it held no real value; it was an award for "most improved," and she didn't feel she deserved all the congratulations that came her way. Only her mother was critical of her, even during that period, saying that she liked Karen's other essays better than the winning one. And Karen felt that her critical mother was the true pinger, not all the positive voices around her.

Karen has to understand why she is seeking further success; is it for herself or to show her mom? For creative purposes or monetary gain? (Or both?) If it's just to stick it to her mom, then it's not going to be enough to sustain her over the long term, and that's why she may feel hollow. It's a Pyrrhic victory, since her mother didn't take any real notice of the magazine that featured her jewelry, dismissing it with nary an acknowledgment. "Oh, that's nice, honey. I don't get that magazine. But my neighbor reads it sometimes!" But no fanfare. Turns out the only person who can validate her is . . . her. She has to understand that her mother may never give her the approval she craves, and Karen can be responsible only for herself, for her own self-worth. If she can do that, she can be happy. She deserves to toast herself and her own success, and not to feel like a fraud.

When something that should bring satisfaction doesn't, you need to figure out your true motivation. What is the passion that brought you here and how can you get it back, reconnect to that thing you love, that started you down this path in the first place? Or was this never the right path for you? We'd say: Act, don't react. In other words, ask yourself, What do I really want? Take the time to figure it out, since the pearl here is to be true to you, and only *you* can decide what that really means. Once you have an inkling, follow it, see where it leads you. Find your authentic self.

I WAS WORKING TOO HARD
AT A JOB I HATED

"I was working a lot of hours in a meaningless job, and I thought that if I'm going to leave my kids every day it has to be for something I care about. So I went ahead and made the leap: I went back to med school. Now I am busier than ever, but I'm happy and glad I did it. Still, I never see my kids. The weird thing is I don't feel guilty about that, being away from the family, the way I did when I worked fewer hours but for a job I hated."

—Abby, 44; Boston, Massachusetts

Abby is a married mother of three (one's ten, and the twins are seven) who began her professional life in an arts-related nonprofit organization in Boston and is now finishing medical school and applying for residency in pediatrics. "I always wanted three kids, believe it or not. I had a peripatetic childhood, and it was very important for me to provide my kids with a stable life and a steady paycheck. I always thought about medical school but worried that the long hours would interfere with that goal. So I built up a career in something else that I liked but never found that fulfilling."

Abby's epiphany came when she put her first child in day care for ten hours a day so that she could do a job she wasn't crazy about. "I was leaving my kids at day care, commuting to work, and had time to think about what I was doing. All of a sudden, it hit me: Why was it better to stay in my current job as a fund-raiser, when I could get just a little more day care and be doing something, like medicine, that I felt passionate about? I knew early on that I was a better mother when all my energies weren't focused on my child."

She moved from the office where she was dissatisfied to the kid's room, where she knew they would be happy as long as she was happy. She got it right, figured out what she really wanted to do in her heart, and then set up her life to fulfill her dreams. Back to the emotional office, where she applied to med school, and four years later she is now being called Dr. Abby by her young patients, and it makes her so happy she wants to cry.

But it was a long journey and one that entailed plenty of sacrifices along the way. "I began by doing volunteer work in a hospital in the evenings. I would wait until my son was asleep, then go off to the ER to get whatever exposure I could to my next career, to prepare for being a doctor— holding children's hands while they got spinal taps, translating for Spanish-speaking patients, transporting patients to the X-ray department. My husband thought I was crazy and would get tired of it. Instead, I loved it and was more convinced than ever that medicine was the path for me." She was using a building block to construct her future emotional office, and it worked for her, because she was willing to do it one little block at a time.

Her parents, who were artists and hated science, thought that her dreams were just that, never a reality. But she realized that her form of creativity was this vision of practicing medicine and helping people, and she had to see it through. "They make art for a living, and I thought: *What do I make? I want to make a difference.* I remember the first time I held my baby and I looked at that perfect little being and thought: *I never want to hold you back. I never want you to hold me back.* This was the realization for me, that to be the best mother I could be I had to do what was right for me. Be the best person I could be. I hope my kids appreciate that someday." It would be years before she saw it to fruition, but eventually she did.

But first Abby wanted more kids, and she didn't think she was quite ready to make the big transition until they got old enough for day care. Until her twins were two years old, she freelanced during the day and went to school in the evenings. When the twins were three, she applied to a top medical school and was accepted. "Money was tight, but the university was generous, and I was able to get a full-tuition scholarship.

"So now I have no money, less time than ever with my family, but I am truly happy and feel zero guilt about my decisions. Should I? I mean, the kids are fine. But does this make me selfish? Because I am doing exactly what I want with my life now."

· · ·

Catherine hears this and says, "Abby is hardly being selfish. She is expressing a healthy form of self-determination, and she is doing it in a purpose-
ful and thoughtful way. If anything, her delaying her own medical career
and then finally choosing to give up her own free time for her passion is
something the rest of us can learn from." Catherine regularly sees patients
who say they wish they had more meaning, more purpose, and a life that
held challenge and reward. The best way to achieve all these things is to
sit down and contemplate what it is your own personal passion leads to,
and when you do that, it can lead you to a career or avocation that is fulfilling and makes you happier, even if you give up things like a big salary
or free time.

Adds Abby: "This was absolutely the right decision for me. My kids
sometimes complain when I'm on call overnight at the hospital, but they
clearly derive much satisfaction from having their mother visit their first
grade class as the health expert." She isn't actually away from her kids any
more than a mother who has to travel occasionally for her job, but somehow the grueling reputation of a medical internship and residency leaves
her open to sniping from mothers who say things like, "I don't know how
you do it." And Abby just says, "Actually I love what I do, I'm willing to
make the sacrifice. And then they mumble something about how their
husbands want them around more, implying either that mine is a wimp or
we have a terrible marriage. I can't let them bother me. We are doing great.
I truly believe that my entire family is better off because of my major life
change."

Confucius said, "If you enjoy what you do, you will never work another
day in your life." It's rare and special when you find something you love,
but you need to seek it out. For some lucky women (I count myself among
them), work feels so rewarding that at times it's like a vacation from the
stresses of family life. Getting to the office, having to do something creative, and helping other women is so much easier than solving a fight over
homework or whose turn it is to walk the dog.

Abby is to be commended—she figured out how to get to the right
room. When she was in the child's room, her desire to be a stable parent

led her to work at a boring job. But she found a way to leave that room for her passion, a career in medicine.

Catherine says such realizations about an enormous life change don't happen overnight. There were clues along the way for Abby, who wanted to go to medical school as a young girl but didn't because her parents, both artists, dismissed it. But when she finally had a moment to step back she was able to follow her inner compass.

You need some space and time to think in order to reconnect to your authentic self, find your own passion, and arrive at your purpose. Here's the good news for the rest of us: If you give yourself a little time and space, and reconnect to what you really love, you can find meaning in your emotional office. Like Abby, you may not be able to get everything done all at once, but you can do it, over time, if you really want. You are never too old to begin.

The final thought in the office is: Whatever you're doing, understand your purpose. If it's to make money, bring home that paycheck, fine. If it's to run your household and raise your kids, great. And if it's to reach that elusive upper echelon in your field (partner, professor, judge, chair, or chief), then that is something to shoot for, but know why you're doing it, and be authentic to you. Not every day will be bliss. And that's a good thing, because knowing your purpose will help you put up with the down days, the menial tasks, the politics of working your way up the ladder (or if you're not on the right track for you, these bad days will help you discover that). Purpose is key, and if you can identify yours, then every day will feel more meaningful, even when there are boring meetings to sit through or long flights to endure, or laundry that needs folding.

Understanding the "why" of the work matters, and remembering what made you *want* to do it in the first place, even if it's only for the paycheck. Remember that you can seek purpose elsewhere and find meaning in other parts of your life.

10

The Bathroom

You're So Vain . . .
and That's Not All Bad

Welcome to the bathroom, the center of all your emotions relating to health, weight, vanity, aging, and body image. The scale, mirror, bathtub, and medicine cabinet can keep many women occupied for hours, and whether you're feeling fat or slim, young or old, pretty or plain, healthy or not-so-much, the bathroom is where you start your day, and it's the last stop before bed. So you're confronted by your image in the mirror—and in your mind—at least twice a day. At the end of the day, as you brush your teeth and wash your face before bed, you think: *How did I do today?* Meaning: How healthy was I and how much did I veer off course in my goal to eat right, get regular exercise, and take care of my body? Often the answer isn't pretty. A mental recount of brownies eaten and laps not swum can make a trip to the mirror or the scale an unpleasant stop. Okay, that's me. But from what I have learned editing *Self*, where we poll women and interact with them on e-mail, blogs, and Twitter, that's millions of other women as well.

Body image is a complicated emotional area, since it involves the bathroom (where the scale sits), the kitchen (where the food you eat contributes to both your weight and your health), the bedroom (where feeling attractive is one component of your sexual self), the family room (Did your mother age beautifully? How does your father's health affect your own attitude about doctors and check-ups?), and the living room (where you compare yourself to other women—your close friends and your faux "friends," such as Jen and Angelina, and all the other professionally beautiful women who come into our lives through TV, magazines, movies, and ads).

And whether you think Beyoncé or Gisele has the perfect shape, you are likely not a doppelgänger for either, which leads to two important questions you need to ask yourself: What is my standard for "healthy and happy"? And, What is the right weight and shape and level of "just right" for me?

When I got to *Self* I realized women generally were unhappy body-image-wise. So I commissioned a poll and we found that to be overwhelmingly true: Only 18 percent of women, fewer than one in five, said they're "just right," weight-wise, while 5 percent said they were too thin and the rest placed themselves in the "I'm too fat!" category. They called themselves either "chunky" (46 percent), "overweight" (22 percent), or "obese" (9 percent), so a whopping 82 percent of women were unhappy with their bodies. It was clear to me that women needed guidance, both in getting healthy and thinking healthy.

Along with giving them the tools to eat right, exercise regularly, and be healthier physically, we needed to arm them with new thought processes to feel better inside about the outside. Instead of punishing themselves for dietary infractions, they needed to think positively about their bodies and do the right thing, to treat their bodies well by treating them right. The message is: Love your body and cherish it and it will love you back and become the body you want. (Hate your body and go to war with it and you are in for a lifetime of hang-ups, health issues, and unnecessary weight swings.) For most women, especially in their twenties and thirties, before gaining the perspective of having friends or loved ones with health issues, it's easy to allow the number on the scale to dictate whether it's a good day or a bad one. That attitude then follows them from room to room, distracting from the events that could be more enjoyable. It's as if instead of "hello," these unhappy-with-their-weight women greet everyone they meet with the thought bubble *Do I look fat?* I am living proof that this attitude can and must be shaken off, and that once it is, your body gets better, and so does your life. Removing the obsession with the last ten or fifteen or twenty pounds frees up space on the mental and emotional hard drive. The most important thing to think about in the bathroom isn't your scale, or even your mirror, but the value you place on your health.

Easier said than done. But I would also defend vanity, at least in moderation. Caring about your looks can be a healthy motivator for many women—it pushes us not to let ourselves go, but to stay healthy for as long as possible. It can even be a lifesaver. But only if it leads to positive behavior.

Feeling fat? I go for a run or curtail the late-night sweet treat. Not wanting to get wrinkles? I slather on the SPF and spray on the self-tanner. I know vanity pushes me to want to bike and not to eat a pint of ice cream before bed, but I never realized that vanity is recognized in the medical community as an important aspect of recovery from life-threatening disease until I met a very special and courageous woman who had battled cancer and was winning. Here is her story:

Jennifer Linn was diagnosed in her thirties with a rare form of cancer, called sarcoma, which is hard to diagnose and harder to treat. She had just had surgery to remove the tumor in her abdomen and was about to face chemo. The doctor asked her what she needed most, and she said: "I need to exercise. You can make me bald, but you can't make me bald and fat. Then I won't recognize myself and I will feel as sick as I am. I really need a stationary bike in my room." So she got a spinning bike next to her bed, and started to bike, even if only a few minutes a day, while recovering. She got stronger and later would start a charity called Cycle for Survival to raise money to research cures for cancers. One day she had a heart-to-heart with her doctor. "Do you think it's bad that I am vain when I have cancer?" And he said to her, "No . . . Vanity is a healthy thing. The patients I worry about are the ones who've given up on how they look. When they no longer care what they look like, I know I should worry."

Jen's story shows that a little vanity is one way of being healthy and self-preserving, so long as it's not an obsession.

The pearl that reminds me to appreciate my well-being, even when I'm scrutinizing my hips and dimply rear end in the mirror, is a single word. It's *squander*. As in, don't squander your health, or do anything self-destructive that could imperil your future, with quick fixes. I won't take supplements or even (unless I'm truly suffering) a painkiller. I don't believe in fad diets or starvation (I rarely skip a meal), and the idea of doing anything to lose weight other than eating right and exercising is anathema to me. The idea of doing something that could harm my health, in the hopes of improving my appearance, is just crazy to me now.

I wasn't always this wise.

"You have great health," a doctor friend told me one night when I reached for what was to be one of my last-ever cigarettes. "Why would you smoke? Why would you squander your good health?" I was in my late twenties, sitting at a bar, trying not to eat or drink (or gain weight!), so I smoked back then, because I was young and dumb. His words hit me like a bus. That word, *squander*, just clicked for me. I don't waste milk, or leftovers, or money. Why would I squander something as precious as my health?

It took several tries, but finally I quit smoking. The word *squander* has since helped me reframe my thinking about my body, my health, and all the God-given gifts I have received. Now the range of emotions in my bathroom is less about self-criticism, and more about self-care, and gratitude for the healthy body I can try to be good to.

I REFUSE TO EVEN GET ON THE SCALE!

"Some women have bad hair days; I have bad weight days, ones that are miserable from the start because I wake up feeling heavy and guilty about the food I ate the night before, and I don't even want to get on the scale because I know I won't like the number it will tell me."

—Jenny, 44; Portland, Maine

Jenny has grappled with body image issues for many years, even though she has always been fit and healthy and never truly overweight, though every now and then she says, "I feel a little flabby, especially around the middle." She never felt so fat that she had to diet, since she considered eating a form of self-love and she enjoyed her treats. She thought this was a good attitude, mainly because she was active. "After I'd go running, I'd think, *I deserve my chocolate cake for dessert!*" But the pounds crept up on her over the years. "Sitting at a desk all day, I didn't burn enough calories to justify what I was eating. I got heavier and more unhappy about my growing waistline."

Then she had a health scare—at the age of forty-two she felt her heart racing and thumping in her chest, and thought she was having a heart attack. Her doctor explained that the racing heart had nothing to do with an impending heart attack, but did indicate that she was under too much stress. She also told Jenny that she had high cholesterol, and unless she changed her diet she'd have to go on a medication to lower it.

"I gave up ice cream and cheese and cut way down on meat, ate more fish, and guess what? I lost ten pounds in about six weeks, and now I think totally differently about food. It's about being healthy, and my cholesterol dropped from 275 to 205, and it's still going down, so now I know that what I eat really matters." Jenny now wants to eat well for the *right* reasons, not because she feels fat, but because she values her healthy body.

The problem was that Jenny liked herself enough to indulge in the post-run chocolate cake, which was sabotaging her health. The unconscious process at work here is a form of "undoing, where she does a good thing (running), and undoes it with another (eating cake)." Not only was she undoing all her hard work, but she was also threatening her good health long term. Once she realized that, she could learn to stop eating like a teenager and think of herself as an adult who had to take care of herself.

Most people don't understand that in a few quick minutes of noshing you can eat more calories than you could burn in two hours of working out at the gym. For Jenny, the fact remains that her body image is making her unhappy, but it may not be because of the extra pounds she's carrying—though those are her focus—but because of the self-destructive patterns she's engaged in. She's sabotaging herself by undoing her own hard work. After trying to be disciplined and healthy, something or someone upsets her and she rebels against her own better instincts, acting out, in Catherine's words, by emotionally eating and soothing herself with food.

For many women, it's easier to think of food as an either/or situation. You *either* diet or you enjoy food, but actually one can do both, by shifting the paradigm to see that healthy food can be delicious, and that "treating" yourself means treating yourself right.

Instead of automatically reaching for a brownie or other reward for being good at the gym or surviving a tense day at work, Jenny realized that she simply had to take a moment to think about what was stressing her out. Once she realized she could take a breath and either start to constructively solve the problem or think about a "next step" to take, it no longer became a matter of eating her way through the stress, but a decision to push it away, and the unhealthy food with it.

It took a scare for her to begin to enjoy eating better for her heart health, but she finally made the decision to choose the healthiest foods, consistently, and soon she loved how it made her feel and look.

This is another case of "go or grow," meaning go along with the status quo and be unhealthy and emotionally tied to food, or grow and evolve and become a healthier eater by understanding what was driving you to the cupboard. The pearl for Jenny became: Treating yourself means treating yourself right.

I DON'T FEEL OLD.
WHY DO I HAVE TO LOOK OLD?

"I feel so vain saying this, but aging is a big issue for me. I used to think I was attractive, and now I see my wrinkles and gray hair and sagging skin and think: *Is it all over for me?* I never thought I'd consider plastic surgery, but now I think maybe it's a good idea."

—Marissa, 50; Harrison, New York

Marissa is a social, active, and fit housewife who was loving her life until she looked at her friends recently over lunch and realized: "Wow, none of us is young anymore, and that makes me upset, because our parents are aging and our kids are now out of the house and this should be the happiest time of our lives. But instead, I'm thinking, *I don't want to grow old!* I feel young, and I still can work out and sail and do all the things I've loved all my life. But for how much longer? I look at my hands and think they look like my mother's hands and I want to cry."

You could say Marissa is spending too much time in her bathroom, and that is bad, but in fact Marissa is right to want to stay healthy, and for her it's as much about vitality as it is about vanity, and the two can intersect in a healthy way.

Marissa's active life brings her pleasure, and appearing older than her friends distresses her. She wants to stay looking young without being overly fixated on youth and the exterior image she presents to the world. For some women, having plastic surgery can be a way of matching the outside with the inside, but it can also become an unhealthy obsession if done for the wrong reasons. Erasing every wrinkle isn't necessarily going to make you feel better, so you have to understand why you're getting "something done" and what your goal is—and if it's only to appear younger, and you think that will make you happier, think again.

Catherine says healthy narcissism is a way of being self-aware or self-preserving, and Marissa is doing that. Unhealthy narcissism is an *over-involvement* with the self, either positively or negatively, which is what some women get caught up in when they start aging and don't like what they see in the mirror. It may take a decision to change how you think about yourself in the world, but it's possible to turn off the light and leave the bathroom behind and stop thinking about the image in the mirror as the one the world sees. You have the power to create another image of yourself, an image of you being involved in other areas of your life—whether it's community service or work or family or a hobby you're passionate about.

In doing this, you're filling yourself out into 3-D, instead of seeing the two-dimensional image in the mirror as the "you" the world sees. Want to experience yourself differently in the world? You can do it any number of ways. What's important is to try to make *this* the self-image you are investing in, since the one in the mirror will not always match the way you feel.

You can't completely control the outer self because aging is inevitable, but you *can* control the inner self. You have the opportunity here to bring meaning to your life from the inside out. The mirror is not the real you. What you do, outside the bathroom, and how you contribute to the world around you, is.

Marissa is well on her way to accepting this notion of actions making her happier, and of listening to her inner authentic voice. She says that when she is feeling good about herself it's because she has done something positive for others, or challenging for herself, like volunteering or rock-climbing or taking an extension course. She likes to tell herself, "Happiness is a choice. I choose happy!" And it's this upbeat personality that makes her so attractive and her laugh lines beautiful.

So we say: It's important to spend enough time in the bathroom to take good care of yourself, but stop obsessing about your reflection. Get out of the bathroom and back to your life. And remember that a smile is gorgeous at every age. And that smile is best when it comes from within.

Marissa's pearl works for her, and it is simply: Happiness is a choice. "I choose happy!"

LIFE WOULD BE PERFECT IF I LOST WEIGHT, SO WHY DON'T I DO IT?

"I feel fat and unattractive and even when I'm on vacation I look in the mirror and think, Here I am in paradise—I should be having great sex with my husband, who totally loves me. But then my life would be too perfect and it's like I always need to have something wrong, but I don't understand why."
—Casey, 39; San Diego, California

Casey had zero sex drive because of her body image issues. The scale and bathroom were making her unhappy, but she took it out on her marriage, in the bedroom.

She wasn't having sex even while reveling on the island paradise of Maui. "I had no sex drive, I wasn't feeling any desire at all. So when we got back, I went to my doctor and said, 'This just can't be right!' She tested me, and guess what? I had nothing wrong except that I was mildly anemic. The doctor told me women feel this way all the time—that I should take vitamins—but more important, I had to take better care of myself. She used a word I'll never forget: She told me, 'You *deserve* to take better care of yourself.'

"That was *so* interesting because I never thought I deserved anything. I had too much, and had been given so much. And now it's like it was doctor's orders: I *deserve* it. I decided to make my health a priority. My doctor's 'prescription' made it okay somehow—I now felt that I deserved to sleep more and eat well and exercise and get back in shape."

Deserve is a tricky word for women, because it implies that we have to get permission in order to be happy, to be successful, to have it all. The church, our families, and our upbringings teach us not to stand out; it is drummed into us to be modest, supportive, helpful.

Most men consider winning to be the goal, particularly in competitive endeavors like sports and work. Women prefer collaborating to competing. If you sense you are "ahead of the pack," you may hold yourself back in one way or another. Casey did that by being heavy, which was a comfortable place to exist.

She had to resolve her feelings about "having it all" and "that's too much." Where did they come from? The answer wasn't in the bathroom; it was in her other rooms, including the family room (her mother and siblings), the living room (where friends would be envious), and the basement (she was brought up with a good dose of Catholic guilt). Her feeling of not *deserving* success follows her from room to room. "People are starving in Africa, and I am so lucky and fortunate and it doesn't feel right to me to be so blessed."

When Casey thinks back, she remembers the nuns at her Catholic school always telling her not to be "piggy" at the lunch table, that God would punish her. "I remember thinking I was going to burn in hell because I used to take a second roll and put it in my pocket and sneak-eat it in the girls' bathroom after lunch. And when I was successful in school I felt guilty, like I didn't deserve it because I was a pig." The idea that she "deserved" something, coming from a doctor, was enough to turn this screen memory on its head and give her the clarity to realize she was thinking about "deserve" in a negative way. "I do so much for others, I finally realized I do deserve to take care of myself."

Catherine says, "This is an important issue for many women who feel that when too much is going right, something bad is bound to happen. The fear of being envied can make a woman feel uncomfortable." They would rather eat the birthday cake at the office party—the cake they don't even really want—than be called out by co-workers for trying to "better" themselves and pass on the cake. If Casey were true to herself, she would say, "No thanks, I'm on a diet," and even though her co-workers might say, "You look fine!," the helpful ones would not pressure her to eat. We would say to Casey, Be true to yourself and don't let the pings of those who want you to stay the same bring you down.

Casey thought being fat made her more likable and less threatening. Avoiding potential criticism, jealousy, and even animosity from her peers was something that, until now, she cared about more than her own healthy body.

But this came at a personal cost.

Casey was sabotaging herself by overeating, which meant that she didn't have to deal with the issue of sex, since she didn't feel attractive. Food became her turn-on. "I could eat till the cows come home," she says. "It was filling a purpose, and I didn't know what that was until my doctor said I deserved to put myself first. That's when I started to turn things around."

For Casey, her pearl came from her doctor: "I deserve it," and suddenly she realized she was entitled to her success, a healthy body, a good sex life, and everything else she wanted. She changed her approach to food, and for the first time in her life started planning her meals, her snacks, and her shopping list. She added workouts to her schedule, and they became a part of her new "job"—taking care of herself. It wasn't something to feel guilty about—it was just another item on her to-do list, stripped of all the emotional baggage that she'd brought to it for years. She's lost thirty-five pounds in a year and is keeping it off. She exercises and eats right and her sex life is back and her energy level is high. Her body image is soaring, but she continues to work at it daily.

Now, instead of saying "I don't deserve to be happy," she says, "We all deserve to be happy, and when I make myself happy I can better help all those around me." Being overweight or feeling down about herself took up so much of her energy that she was unable to get outside herself. "I now know that the best thing is to be good to myself and *then* go out and give back. Trying to be less than who I can be was not giving back—it was giving up."

So the pearl here is: You deserve to be happy, healthy, *and* fit. You deserve it all.

I NEVER THOUGHT I'D HAVE LIPO
. . . BUT I DID IT

"I tried everything—I ran, ate right, and went to the gym several times a week, but nothing I did got rid of my saddle-bags. After twenty years of hating myself in a bathing suit, I wanted to make a definitive change, so I had liposuction. I'm glad I did. It's one of the best things I've ever done for myself."
—Connie, 45; Denver, Colorado

For years, Connie resented her older sister Noelle because she had had liposuction and looked amazing. "It became an issue between us, and I gave her a lot of grief about cheating while I spent hours at the gym doing it the right way."

This tension came to a head when Connie had her first child and didn't dress the baby in the outfit Noelle had given her for the christening. After Noelle made an innocent inquiry—"What happened to the gown I gave you for the baby?"—Connie lost it, screaming things like, "You don't have the right to tell me what to do!" and decided to have it out with her sister right in front of the guests. There was nothing particularly offensive about Noelle's inquiry, but Connie felt bad about herself—she was still carrying extra weight four months postpartum and, as always, was jealous of her sister's slender body—and decided that Noelle was being Little Miss Perfect again. "Everything comes so easily for you . . . why do you think you deserve to have it all? A great job, beautiful kids, a nice husband, and a perfect body, even if you did have to pay for it! Forget it, you can have that outfit back!"

Even as those harsh words flew out of her mouth, Connie knew she was overreacting. Catherine calls what she was doing "displacing" her own body issues onto her sister. This wasn't about Noelle and her perfect body; it was about Connie's own saddlebags and self-image, which she couldn't get rid of, no matter how hard she tried.

Catherine says that Connie was exhibiting what Freud called "the return of the repressed," or, in more user-friendly terms, "hysterical is historical" behavior, in which a minor event becomes major, since it brings up some unpleasant baggage from the past. The emotional outburst is informed by years of accumulated pent-up feelings, and they finally come rushing out in an inappropriate way. In this case, Connie's hysterical reaction to Noelle was not a result of how she felt about her sister's body, but of how she felt about her own. She had displaced her anger and pain and turned it on her sister.

For Connie, the bathroom was connected to the family room, as well as to the bedroom. (She wasn't feeling sexually attracted to her husband. The thought bubble was: *I'm gross, so how could you possibly find me attractive?* She started treating him badly as well.) Clearly she needed to change her body image and perhaps even her body.

She got a trainer and started working out five days a week and watching her diet. The baby weight finally came off, but even after a year, the shape of her upper legs hadn't changed. Connie finally had to admit that the saddlebags were never going away. Naturally, that is. She refused to tell her sister or her mother that she was going to get liposuction because she was so embarrassed about how contemptuously she'd acted toward Noelle over her decision to do it. After the swelling went down postsurgery, however, and Connie saw how great she looked, she couldn't wait to put on a bathing suit and show off her new backside to her mother and her sister.

When the annual family beach vacation rolled around, Connie looked stunning in her suit, and Noelle was thrilled for her. And Connie had an epiphany: "I didn't hate my sister for being perfect. I hated myself for being flawed. The fact that she was so happy for me made me realize there was no malice on her side. I was bitter, and it was all about me."

That "all about me" attitude can emerge in the bathroom when you have too intimate a relationship with your mirror. Your actions toward others are based more on how you feel about yourself, and it becomes hard to be empathetic or feel connected to those around you, except as far as how you feel about yourself in relationship to them.

Connie was acting out her negative emotions toward her sister. If she had been able to explain that she was feeling bad about her body, her sister would have been sympathetic.

For Connie, the pearl is to be honest with yourself, then to express yourself and be direct. Others (husbands, sisters, friends) may be more supportive than you can imagine, and that may lead to a closer bond between you. And close ties are an important factor in lifelong happiness. So by being honest with yourself and others, you can live a happier, healthier life.

TOO FAT TO GET MARRIED

"Sometimes I feel like I'm too fat to ever get married. It's like my weight is standing between me and a man. I know how ridiculous this sounds, but I can't help it. The first thing I think when I'm meeting a guy is, *Does he think I'm fat?*"

—Lori, 42; Los Angeles, California

Lori is a self-described "big girl," with long black hair and bright blue eyes, who works in commercial real estate. She says, "Being a size fourteen or sixteen has always plagued me. I feel best as a size ten or twelve, but that's not easy for me. For most men, my size is an impediment, even if they don't actually say so. My thin girlfriends—even those who aren't as nice or as attractive as me—always had dates, serious boyfriends, and are now mostly married with kids. The only thing I can figure out is that my weight turns people off."

Even so, Lori finds dating a much more pleasant experience these days because of the Internet. "It's just easier to get a date. Before the Internet I would go a whole year and maybe be fixed up once or twice. Now, if I want to go on a date, I can go on a date." And she doesn't go out with just anyone. She pores over profiles and has very high standards. "The men have to be really smart, interesting, and motivated. I really don't want to waste my time if they aren't my type."

Because she believes her size turns some men off, Lori posts several pictures of herself on her dating profiles that hide little. "I want them to know what I really look like. No surprises. It's too painful to worry if they are going to flip out about my size when they meet me. Let them know ahead of time! And if they don't like it, don't go out with me."

Food has always been a major topic of discussion in Lori's Italian family. "I wouldn't say my mother force-fed us, but she did, kind of." Lori smirks when she talks about the family meals. "Eating was almost a form of recreation in my family. My sister got lucky—she found a man who loves to eat too, but he's always been thin, and her weight (she's built like me) doesn't seem to bother him. I couldn't be with someone who wasn't an eater.

"All our lives, my sister and I have watched what we eat, and bonded over our endless diets and exercise routines. Then we get frustrated and pig out. We grew up with this rule: If you blow your diet, you can eat anything you want that day until midnight, but then the next day you try to be healthy again. I know that's not perfect, but it has been my food psychology over the years."

Work is the only thing that distracts Lori from her food obsession, so she's in the office early and late, which leaves her even less time or opportunity for meeting new guys. "Nowadays I work all the time and have lost touch with friends. I start to think: Food is my friend."

·   ·   ·

Catherine says Lori's issues may not be as much about the bathroom as they are about the connections she craves, which she wrongly associates with food. She really wants to connect with people, but the only people she's connecting with are her family. She even says it: "Food is my friend." She needs to get into the living room and be more social. She and her sister are close, and if she's not at the office, she is in the family room, where she grew up (and ate and enjoyed big dinners), and neither place is allowing her to be independent and a sexual being. She knows she's smart and nice and should be able to find a guy, like her sister did, regardless of her weight. But she can't.

Lori's life is very comfortable, so she is resistant to change. Food and family has become a substitute for being with friends, finding a man, and starting her *own* family. She isn't really in the bathroom (where she beats herself up), or the kitchen (where she is "treating" herself, and food is her friend). She is stuck in the family room, using food and family as a security blanket to keep herself swaddled in the safe space where she doesn't have to go out and take a risk or eventually grow up.

Why does she allow her size to be her defining feature? She has to shed the safety net—the overdependence on family and food—and get out there and risk being herself. She's begun to do so by online dating. She may or may not choose to lose the weight to be her true self, but either way it's not about food and weight. Saying, "I'm too fat to get married" is just an excuse for staying in the bosom of her family.

Lori can't live in the past, or in the family room, thinking about all those wonderful family dinners. She needs to launch herself out of the cocoon. After all, food isn't going to abandon her, and neither is her family. The pearl for Lori is that she needs to take risks and not be afraid of what she will find out there. It might even be a husband.

I HAVE TO EXERCISE!
I AM GETTING FLABBY.

"I had so much fun in high school playing lacrosse. I wasn't great at it, but I loved being part of a team. After college I kind of lost the ability to just have fun doing something active. Exercise became a chore, there was no joy related to it. But now I want to get to the gym three times a week and connect back to what was fun. Instead I'm always sitting, and I feel like I'm melting at my desk."

—Pamela, 32; New York, New York

Sitting at a desk working as a tax attorney for the past eight years had taken a toll on Pamela's body. She was never fat, but one day she realized her hips were spreading and that her "muffin top" was getting harder to lose. Exercise became a necessary evil, so she dragged herself to the gym and started seeing some impressive changes in her body and her energy level.

"I thought about how to make getting in shape more fun and I discovered that trying to push myself to do something a little better than last time worked. So I go for a jog on the treadmill and I think, *Let's see if I can go a little faster today.* I turn the speed up just a little further or go a little farther. Or I try to lift one slightly heavier weight than the last time. It's suddenly like a game. I look at another machine and think, *I haven't tried that one before; let me see if I can do* that."

In just three months her body got more toned and her clothes fit better. She used to notice herself getting down over little things at work, and now she is able to ignore minor assaults in her emotional office, such as when her boss asks her to work late and she has to cancel dinner with friends. "I actually enjoy being at the gym, and I can tell my mood is improved on the days when I work out. For the rest of the day I just feel better, like I can handle anything because I did this cool thing for my body. So everything else seems less upsetting."

. . .

Catherine says that Pamela is unconsciously creating what is known as a "parallel process," through which one good event spills over into others and starts to ignite a chain reaction of emotion. So the positive area for her now is the bathroom, since she was able to lose weight and get in shape and that is now creating a ripple effect. Her new confidence is having positive benefits in her office, and she is better able to withstand the stresses of work.

This is how making one room clean can help you tidy up the rest of the house. You feel better and get more done, and that means you have more time for relationships and perhaps even a new romance—all from just starting to work out regularly before the workday begins.

"Someone once told me I always looked sad at work, and I realized this was a problem at my job," Pamela says now. "Work was what I called a 'happy-sucker,' and I knew I had to make an attitude adjustment. Now I don't let myself get too down about what happens at work anymore since I refuse to connect work to my mood."

Pamela has a new personal motto, or catchphrase: "'Up the happy!' is my little code for cheering myself up, and now I do as much as I can to 'up the happy' in my life. This starts with going to the gym and working out, because I realized part of what I loved about lacrosse was actually running around and feeling winded and exhausted afterward."

So Pamela's key process is to work out, "up the happy," and then take that attitude to the office. A recent review of data shows that people with better cardiovascular health (through exercise) have fewer depressive symptoms than the general population. So research backs up what Pamela felt intuitively: Working out made her feel better, look better, and even perform better at work.

Getting regular exercise may be one of the best things a woman can do for herself, since it benefits her wherever she goes. Study after study shows if you're physically active and fit, your mood will improve, and if your mood is up, you'll not only have more energy and be more productive, but your success will spill over into every area of your life. The bathroom therefore connects back to the living room (Pamela found a new social scene at the gym), the office (she's a rising star at her company), and the bedroom (she's feeling sexier and more open to dating possibilities). For Pamela, the pearl is "up the happy," meaning, get up, get going—to the gym, to the park for a jog, or to the pilates studio for a class—and you'll be happier too.

I WANT TO LIVE. BEFORE IT'S TOO LATE.

"Our bodies are not infallible. Things start to go wrong as we age, and it has started me thinking differently about the next half of my life. I started to think, *Oh my gosh, I've been here all this time and now I better try to do some of the things I want to do, before it's too late.*"

—Liz, 55; Brookville, Long Island, New York

Liz, a freelance fund-raiser for nonprofits, had a major health scare a few years ago when her husband had a tumor, which turned out to be benign. She believes that even the transient fear of losing him was a wake-up call, which, she says, changed the dynamic for both of them "in terms of how we related to friends, family, jobs, everything. How we view the world basically shifted." They thought they might not have much time together, and they wanted to spend it in a meaningful way.

"Suddenly we decided to act on ideas and fantasies and everything around us because there was something hanging over our heads. I think it was very positive for us, not that everything wasn't going well anyway, but it did change the dynamic within our family."

How she related to others was part of the equation, but the biggest shift was how she chose to fill her days. Liz decided she no longer had time for things she found trivial, like gossip and needy friends who sucked her energy. "I realized that most people bug me and I am happiest with my family, my very best friends, and my sculpting."

She has friends she plays bridge or tennis with, but she finds she is opting out of more foursomes these days. "I am *so* not interested in the chatter. I don't care what so-and-so said to her, and what she said back . . . blah blah, blah. If you tell me gossip I will probably forget it anyhow. I don't have time for it. Something that really annoys me is when a friend complains, 'You never answer your phone!' Doesn't it occur to them that maybe I don't want to talk on the phone at this moment?

"I have a new passion, which is sculpting. I go to a studio where there are other artists and the people are so happy to be there, and we all feel so lucky to be able to do what we love. Everyone is so supportive of each other's work that I feel like it's a new family, a cocoon of sorts, where it's safe to be creative."

Catherine points out that often it is a health scare, even someone else's, that is finally what it takes to feel totally alive. You suddenly realize that you have been wasting your time with things that don't matter to you. You can feel dazed or in a rut until something jolts you and makes you realize that your life is passing you by. You suddenly "wake up." Rather than being a bystander in your life (and letting the gossips and petty annoyances take over your time), you need to take action and be the scriptwriter of your own plot and next chapter.

Here the key process is to take the wheel. You may need to tell your friends they won't be seeing you as much, since you are spending time on something other than, say, bridge, and that you are working toward a new goal, such as your first art show. If they are truly your friends they will support you and these new interests, even though they miss you.

Liz's husband's health scare led her to new places and interests and people. Her world shifted, like after an earthquake, and the landscape now looks different. Liz says her new motto is "Don't waste time—in any part of my life." That's her pearl, and it's making her happy every day.

WHEN I HATE MYSELF
I TAKE IT OUT ON OTHERS

"Some days you're not feeling good about who you are and you're judging everything about yourself. 'Oh my God, I have a wrinkle here!' or 'I gained two pounds this weekend! I look ugly! I feel ugly!' And then it spills over and I'm not even nice to my husband. We all do it, but I think it's important to try and keep it under control. And it's not always easy."

—Julia, 48; Seattle, Washington

Julia has three kids, ages twelve to sixteen, and lives in a beautiful house in a Seattle suburb where most of the women stay at home and raise their children. She knows that caring about her looks is superficial, but she can't help but feel uneasy when she doesn't look her best. Plus she feels she has so little to show for herself these days, other than being a great mom. "After my kids go to school I go straight to the gym every day because, whether I'm at my target weight or a little over, the physical activity clears the cobwebs out of my head."

Julia may need to examine how she is spending her time and why. She is so busy getting her children to school, to dance classes, to soccer practice, and to all the other extracurriculars that she feels like an air traffic controller, keeping everyone on the right path.

She requires that the family gather for dinner every night and "spend an hour, at least, catching up and reconnecting. I insist on it, because otherwise we never get to see each other together. The kids need that family time, and I do too."

But it doesn't always happen, because some soccer matches can last till six and then dinner gets delayed and the youngest one has to eat, so she eats alone, and then the homework starts and Julia's plans for family time are forgotten. "It stresses me out and then I just want to cry because I can't control how our days are getting away from us."

Julia also gets anxious when she compares herself to the other moms.

"I feel like all the other mothers are so competitive, and if they say their child is doing something like taking music lessons, then I have to sign my kids up for that too." That means she is so overbooked that she never has time to pursue her own interests. Not that she has that many—"Honestly, I feel that I am boring, because the only things I really feel passionate about are working out and being a great mother." Julia is stressed-out, exhausted, and her gym time isn't making up for all the other ways she's not taking care of herself. She feels depleted, emotionally and spiritually. When she feels down about her looks she has nothing to fall back on to boost her self-esteem.

"I love the way I feel after I exercise. My stress level goes down, and I think I handle the crap that's thrown my way a lot better. I know if I haven't exercised in a day or two then I can feel the way I process things slow down, and it's not the same." Julia is doing the right thing for herself by exercising, but it can't be the only thing she does for herself. It's as if every other room is full of the needs of others, and her bathroom (aka taking care of her body) is her only sanctuary from the chaos.

Catherine would tell her that her exercise is great, but the rest of her life is out of control—though she's trying so hard to control things. She is so overbooked with kid duties that she hasn't set aside enough time for herself. She has to leave the bathroom and get to the kid's room and say to them, "We are doing too much. Which activities do you want to keep and which do you want to give up?"

Julia should use the same "I need my gym time" mentality to fill in the blanks on: *I need my ___ time.* That could be solo time, to read and reflect and write, or do whatever she loves. It could be a hobby or a passion. She needs to value her inner self as well as her outer self. She is not taking the time to nurture her intellect, her spiritual side, and her emotional life.

The key process here is for Julia to recognize she is giving too much of herself and her time to others. Too much of a good thing is a bad thing, and in this case she isn't able to take care of herself emotionally. So she needs to learn to say no, or to ask for help from carpooling moms, her spouse, even her kids, who can help manage some of their own chores (and do their homework without prompting). Knowing your limits is the answer here, and asking for what you need to be healthy. We'd remind her to "put her own oxygen mask on first," and then help others. She needs to "value" her own time and herself. We all do.

How to think in the bathroom? Take care of yourself, inside and out, but don't let the mirror or the scale become an obsession. Vanity is fine, to a point, since being healthy is connected to looking and feeling your best. But beyond that it can be a major time suck, using all your energy (Have to lose weight! Want to look younger!), and you can waste years, decades, being too preoccupied with these repetitive self-criticisms. Your beauty truly resonates from within, when you're comfortable in your own skin. To have that happen, spend less time scrutinizing yourself and more time liking yourself and connecting to your passions. The mirror can be a useful reflection, but don't let it become your reality. Remember, it's just a cheap piece of glass.

11

The Bedroom

Love, Sex, and Unmade Beds

Welcome to the bedroom, where the bed is the largest and—for the purposes of this discussion—the only piece of furniture. Other than sleep, which we put in the category of "taking care of yourself" (a bathroom issue), there are only two things that happen in that bed that interest us here: one is the kind of sex you're having, and the other is the kind you're not having but are fantasizing about.

Different Kinds of Sex, Partners, and Self-Images

We all know there are different kinds of love and intimacy, but has it ever occurred to you that there are also different kinds of sex? No, we don't mean positions and orifices. We are talking about the emotional commitment you make to "the deed": some nights you want "rock star sex"—when there's electricity coming from every part of your body; other nights there's just "good sex"—the kind that satisfies but won't go down in the history books; and then there's plain old "I love you" sex—you may not be in the mood, but he is, so you take one for the team because you want him to be happy.

There's also "vacation sex"—it's fun to anticipate, fun to plan, and fun to have. It's "vacation sex" because it's easier to slow down and take the time to really enjoy it on a leisurely day off, or away from home, whether in a mountain cabin or a tropical beach hotel.

There are also different types of sex you have with different types of partners, and what you crave may depend on what you're getting, or what you're *not* getting. You want a "caveman" when you need to be swept off your feet and be "taken," because he is aroused by you beyond any ability to hold himself back. Caveman sex, or "Take me!" sex, is visceral and often characterized by a secondary turn-on: You're aroused because he's aroused, by you! (It's a form of sexual pinging.)

Then there's the Prince Charming fantasy of a man who woos you and respects you and carries you off into the sunset, proclaiming, "You are my princess, and I will cherish and respect you and take care of you in my castle." That fantasy is most appealing when you want to be "taken care of" rather than being "taken." Women who have a Caveman may find themselves fantasizing about a Prince Charming; those who have a Prince may wish he were more of a Caveman sometimes. In either case, when it comes to being swept off your feet, you just want him to take charge.

If you're lucky you have a guy who's a bit of both, but then the challenge is figuring out how to tell him which man you want to take you into the bedroom: the one who's going to grab you by the hair (figuratively speaking) and throw you down, or the one who is going to caress you gently and touch you lightly and lovingly? Guess what? This is your job. Sorry to tell you, but first you need to know what you want and then you need to let him know also. How to do that can be tricky, since many women will say, "Why do I have to tell him? Why doesn't he just know by now?" But neither the Prince nor the Caveman is a mind reader. One of the keys to a successful relationship is communication, and that brings us to door number three.

There is a third scenario, in which you come to the relationship as a strong, independent being, neither needing nor seeking validation or security. You *choose* to share your full life with an equal partner. You are not looking for someone to "complete you," in the famous words of Jerry Maguire, because you don't need completing.

As if.

We recognize it's almost impossible to achieve, but it is doable, with a big caveat: It takes a lot of work to get to the point where you can honestly walk into a marriage or relationship fully and wholly your own person. But if you're looking or waiting for someone else to complete you—even in marriage—you could spend your entire life feeling unfulfilled and lonely or dissatisfied, even when the rest of the world thinks, *She has it all.*

First you have to learn to know, like, and respect yourself (maybe not every second but most of the time) before you can do it with another person. Going back to the Venn diagram, each of you is a full circle, and you overlap as you love and enhance each other—but even when you are "happily" married, you're still an individual.

In Catherine's wedding ceremony, she insisted on a quote from Rainer Maria Rilke, which essentially says that we are individuals who love each other even as we retain our separate sense of ourselves:

> Once the realization is accepted that even between the closest human beings infinite distances continue, a wonderful living side by side can grow, if they succeed in loving the distance between them, which makes it possible for each to see the other whole against the sky.

In the last episode of *Sex and the City* there is a line regularly referenced by women in Catherine's practice, which says: "The most exciting, challenging, and significant relationship of all is the one you have with yourself. And if you can find someone to love the you *you* love, well, that's just fabulous."

That show might as well have been called *Love and the City*, or *Loving Yourself and Trying to Find a Man You Can Really Talk To and the City*. The best case scenario is to like your spouse as well as love him.

The bedroom is about sex, but the first question for most women is, are you and your partner even communicating at all? Before you can think about connecting physically and emotionally, you have to connect in other areas, share other stuff, even the little things. You may share kids, a house, a bank account, a family, a dog, and even a bed, but if you aren't also sharing the details of your daily life, then sex is going to be less satisfying and less interesting, and ultimately it will fall to the bottom of your to-do list.

Want Some Intimacy Tonight? Go Walk the Dog!

Part of the problem is the expectation gap: What's realistic when you're married may not be vacation sex every time, or even rock star sex on a regular basis. In fact, you may not be having sex at all. The point isn't to wake the neighbors, but to connect with each other. This is a marriage we're talking about, not a booty call.

That is where "I love you" sex comes in: Sometimes he wants to do it and you don't, or you want it and he doesn't, and there are nights when you'll say, "No thanks," but then there are other nights when you rally and get yourself into the mood because you're doing it for the other person and for the relationship. And though you may want to do it at the end of a lovely dinner, after hours of talking and catching up, there are times when the schedule (work, kids, trips, etc.) doesn't allow that to happen, and you have to decide whether it's okay to "connect tomorrow" and do the deed tonight.

Or not.

We are *not* saying you should do it against your will—certainly this is an important point. But do it if and when you choose because you love the other person, and because you realize that he does things for you because he loves you; think about all those times he's been nice, gone somewhere and done something for you, when he may not have felt like it. He hates musicals, for instance, but he went to one with you, or he hates shopping but went to the mall to keep you company. He can't stand your aunt, but gamely sat through her long, dull birthday dinner. You do things for each other because you love each other.

The healthiest thing for a relationship isn't rip-your-clothes-off sex but bonding and connecting on a regular basis. You have to make time for this kind of intimacy. One recent study showed that couples who walk the dog together or devote a small amount of time at the end of the day to connecting (fifteen minutes can be enough) stay together longer and are happier than those who don't.

That mundane "catch-up" period sounds insignificant or trivial, but it's the glue that keeps couples together. If something big happens at work, your spouse won't understand the significance of it unless he's heard the backstory leading up to it. You have to connect on the small details of your day in order to keep the relationship close. Even if you're exhausted, connecting is essential. Sometimes you may choose to have sex when you don't feel like it and simply because it's "I love you" sex, it can be helpful in your relationship. Of course sometimes you just say *I love you* and roll over and go to sleep. Promise him a little vacation sex some other time.

Venn You Really Love Someone . . .

The bedroom is about intimacy, where two individuals come together but don't completely merge. Picture the Venn diagram of your emotional life. You are a whole circle (touch your forefinger and thumb tips together in a circle), your significant other is another circle (do the same thing with your other hand), and now bring them together so they overlap in the middle, showing the space that represents your relationship. Link them if you like, but keep the circles intact.

Ideally, the middle and the outside slices are about equal. The overlap is large enough for a rich relationship, but the outer area is large enough so that you can each have a life as an individual. That independence strengthens the emotional bond you share. (Not currently in a relationship? The diagram is still instructive and can help you find the right person, since you need a partner who overlaps but doesn't eclipse you.)

Catherine says, "To marry is not to completely merge." Taking his name is one thing, but giving him the essence of what makes you *you* is completely different and not advisable. We are all for a complete commitment to marriage, but we also are committed to helping women keep a full sense of themselves.

As we evolve, our relationships have to as well. Your Venn diagram is not static. The circles move toward each other some years (you're newly married or raising babies together) and away again after a big shift (a new job, or the kids leave home), and suddenly you're thinking about your future and free time and what you want to do with your next chapter. Your focus may shift toward work or volunteering or being more creative or even spending more hours in the yoga studio or on the tennis court. Whatever it is that brings pleasure and passion shifts the circle, either toward or away from your partner's circle. The same is true for him, if he finds himself playing golf all the time, or wanting to spend hours fishing or choosing any activity that takes him away from the relationship.

You can survive these shifts through communication and caring and mutual love and respect. One half of the couple may become obsessed with gardening, the other wants to travel. You have a choice: to share your passion or not; but your real choice is whether to stay sufficiently overlapped. The overlap needs to be mutually satisfying in order for the relationship to survive.

Everyone should be changing and evolving on her or his own, and there are times when the tectonic plates shift and the earthquake can shake you to the core. If you are committed to the partnership, to the interlocking circles, you need to get back to the point where you are willing to help make the middle area larger and stronger again.

The overlap is where the intimacy happens, and sex is the physical expression of that connection.

So let's get to the bedroom, where so much of the drama of the shifting circles plays out in the form of intimacy, sex, loving expression, or, conversely, infidelity, alienation, and boredom. If you pay attention to the Venn, you can head off the unhappiness and get back to relating the way you want to. Let's hear how it's going between the sheets.

I CAN PUT UP WITH ANYTHING, EVEN SEX WHEN I DON'T WANT IT

"He basically warned me before we got married that everyone in his family of doctors has affairs. It's like they all have some kind of macho notion that because they save lives they are above the normal rules of marriage. So my way of coping is to dampen his urge to cheat—we do it every morning when he

wakes up. I think of it as an insurance policy against him going and jumping on some nurse."

                                   —Elise, 38; New York, New York

Elise swears she's happy in her marriage, but her way of "staying
happy" is to keep her husband satisfied and distracted, which means having sex when she doesn't want it . . . or even know she's having it, since
she's usually still asleep when he rises before dawn for his early shift at
the hospital and rolls over onto her. She doesn't have to "participate" in
this predawn sex, just has to be there and be willing. That's enough for
him, so it's enough for her too. Elise says she got the idea from a friend—
when they shared worries about their husbands—who gives *her* husband
a blow job every morning to keep him from straying. Elise thinks "that
would be too much work," and so she has arrived at her own compromise.

She is convinced her husband will have an affair if she doesn't submit to
this morning ritual. He's told her his dad fooled around on his mom (even
though they stayed married for fifty years) because it's impossible for the
men in his family to stay interested in one woman for a lifetime. "The men
in his family have this kind of Superman ego that allows them to play god,
or at least not feel judged by God, because they save lives for a living. So my
way of coping is to let him do it with me every morning. I am fine with it,
because it's my way of claiming him as mine, every day. Don't get me wrong,
I like sex, but once or twice a week would be enough for me. He could do it
every minute, every day, and my libido isn't like that, but I think, *Just go
with the flow.* I don't want to hurt his feelings or let him think he has to get
it somewhere else. It's a little bit of a burden, but I can handle it."

Catherine says Elise and her husband, Peter, aren't actually in the bedroom, since the "family lore" is that the men inevitably will cheat (unless
they get a lot of sex). He brought this baggage to the marriage, but Elise
brought some baggage of her own. Her father cheated on her mother and
it devastated the family, since a nasty divorce followed and her family
never recovered, financially or emotionally.

This morning routine they have may be sex, according to Catherine, but it's still coercive; Peter is an emotional bully, since he has implied that if she doesn't give him what he wants, he will seek it elsewhere. Elise is complicit in this imbalance of power because she goes along with it. Instead of acknowledging that she is a victim, she tells herself she is in charge of the situation by *choosing* to participate. She's not complaining, since she has fooled herself into believing that she is using her own "power" to control his actions. However, in her most private thoughts, she fantasizes about the "Prince Charming" in her past, the college boyfriend she almost married, and how differently he would have treated her.

She's trying to control her life, keep the house clean, keep the husband "tucked in" and not straying, trying to keep everything under her thumb. But Catherine says in fact Elise is "identifying with the aggressor." Here, she is choosing to emotionally divorce herself from the loving aspects of sex. It's not an authentic connection if she just does it as a prophylactic act to stave off his cheating. What is going to keep her husband faithful and her marriage intact is a true connection.

She loves her life, her regular tennis game at the club and all that, but she fears she would lose it all if she got divorced. She thinks, *How bad is this, really? It's not like he hits me. It's just sex every morning.*

We don't need Catherine to tell us the balance of power is totally wrong in Elise's marriage. She needs to acknowledge what she's really feeling and tell him, "This isn't working for me and we have to talk and make some changes. Hopefully, we can find a way to compromise." But first she has to understand what is going on. Why does she fantasize about the sweet college boyfriend, and why did she marry a Caveman, whom she lets "take" her whenever he feels like it? She loves her lifestyle but perhaps not her life.

This is another way to think of A + B = C, since she is actually trying to control him instead of working on herself. Elise needs to be honest with her husband, tell him what is and isn't working for her, and start to connect for real. You can't control anyone else's behavior in the long run, or stop a spouse from cheating just by having sex when he wants it. You *can* work on yourself and figure out what works for you in a marriage. Stop worrying about him and live the life you want, from morning to night, with or without the prophylactic sex. The pearl: Whatever bed you make, remember, now you have to lie in it!

I'M TOO TIRED TO HAVE SEX

"I feel so guilty. There is just too much going on in my life, in our lives, really, and it takes a toll. Something has to go, and it's usually intimate time with my husband that gets left out. I just am too busy and tired to have sex. And he is the one who suffers."

—Jean, 38; Little Rock, Arkansas

Jean is the mother of two young boys, helps out with the luncheon after church services every Sunday, and visits both her in-laws in their assisted living facility at least once a week. Her to-do list is long—she has unfinished work on her laptop, she forgot to put gas in her car, and her mother is going to be annoyed that she never called back from earlier today. When she does have a spare hour on a weekend, she'd rather sleep than have sex.

Her husband, on the other hand, can flip a switch and be in the mood no matter how tired he is after a long day at the office. In fact, even when he's sleeping and she quietly slips into bed next to him, he wakes up and wants to do it. "We are so different," she says. "I need to get in the mood, and he just needs to be breathing to be in the mood."

And even when she can muster the desire and the energy, there's another problem: the kids. They roam the house and could walk in at any moment, and this makes her feel inhibited. "I love him, I just don't feel like making love to him."

Catherine says "being too tired for sex" is "one of the biggest epidemics facing women today." These women show up at their doctor's office, wondering if there is some medical problem that will explain their lack of libido . . . and is there a pill that can fix it?

A top doctor with a thriving ob-gyn practice in Manhattan says, "They are exhausted, worried they are having a thyroid problem or are low in testosterone, and feel really bad that they don't want to have sex with their husbands. They would love to find a physical reason why they are feeling this way, but rarely do we find something specific." That ob-gyn tries to help with the physical symptoms, and Catherine treats the emotional fallout. "Women feel guilty," she says. "Women think they should be lusting after their husbands. When they don't, they first think there is something wrong with them or their marriage, but in fact they may just be wiped out, stressed-out, and pulled in too many directions."

Patients regularly ask Catherine, What's a normal amount of sex? The question is simple, but the answer is not. There is no right amount. This can be reassuring or not, depending on whether you're looking for guidance or for permission to want it more . . . or less. The right amount of sex is whatever *you* want to have, and what works for the two of you.

"The popular idea that married couples are having sex twice a week on average is probably wrong," Catherine says. "It's probably closer to once a week. Women often compare their lives to sex scenes in TV shows, movies, and novels, and I have to tell them that those are works of fiction. That can be validating for a woman, because it's hard not to think something's wrong with you when every female protagonist on the big screen is frequently enjoying the perfect sexual experience."

Catherine tells women to feel free to say yes, no, or "if *you* really want to, but don't expect fireworks from me tonight." "If you or your partner is interested in having sex more often," she says, "then create a language that works for you, to express your needs and not fight over it. This is where the rock star sex versus 'I love you' sex paradigm becomes useful. One woman told me how liberating it was when she finally accepted the fact that she didn't have to have rock star sex every time. She said, 'I would feel bad if I wasn't that into it or didn't have an orgasm. I know women who feel so bad about this that they fake orgasms.'"

There's no need to fake anything. You may not actually be "tired" but upset with your husband for not helping around the house, or not doing the bills. Be honest, with yourself and with him. Get to the kitchen table and talk about what's going on. If you really just need sleep, then sleep, and ask him for a rain check until you're rested. You can also have "I love you" sex if you just want to show him a little appreciation. Think about the kind of sex you want and tell him. He may not be jumping you because every night you push his hand away, but what you really want is for him to "take you" and have a passionate encounter.

You may even want to develop signals for when you really mean "not to-night" and when you don't. Want to feel like a "rock star" one night? Blast the tunes and start dancing around the living room. Whatever code or language you and your partner use, sometimes it's okay to tell your significant other: This is "I love you" sex or "I'm doing it for you" sex.

And make sure he knows there will be times when you will initiate sex . . . and will sometimes want to be the rock star. In other words, it may be healthier for the relationship if you sometimes say, "Tonight, I just need to get some sleep." Our pearl for Jean, and any woman who wants to say no sometimes: There are two of you in this relationship and you need to communicate. Have a language that you share to signal yes, no, maybe, or throw me down! Whatever your turn-on, or -off switch, you both need to know how to operate it.

I COULD TELL BY HIS TEXT MESSAGES THAT HE WAS HAVING AN AFFAIR

"I found out my husband is having an affair, and now we are getting a divorce, even though I could probably forgive him and move on. He says it's over. He's ready to pack it in. We have two boys, a house, a mortgage, and my mom depends on us for income. How are we going to afford this?"

—Sarah, 41; Greenwich, Connecticut

Sarah thinks she is the "victim" of infidelity. Victim is in quotes here, since, when she's not fuming, she knows she somehow participated in the dynamic that led to the demise of their marriage. Beyond the initial emotional shock, she is also wondering, "How are we going to pay our bills, now that we are going to have to pay for two homes and two of everything else? I work so hard, but he's always made more money than me, and now I won't ever be able to retire, much less take nice vacations or afford things for my kids that I think they deserve. Our lives are literally in financial ruins, and it's all because the asshole had to sleep with his secretary. What did I do to deserve this?"

Sarah works in marketing, and though she never made it to management level she has a good, secure job and is proud of being a diligent worker and a great mother who makes sure all the homework is done and the school lunches are packed. In other words, everyone's needs are met except her own. She thinks her husband stopped being aroused by her because she was always too tired to have sex, and she's always had body image issues as well. He wants to go on a kid-free cruise, or to Vegas, but that doesn't interest her. She would rather be with the kids, even if it means a vacation at some family theme park. Sarah and her husband never spend a night alone together, which means they rarely have rock star or vacation sex.

They live in a bedroom community, and he works late, sometimes missing dinner, but she knows he has an enormous amount of work, often on deadline. She never thought they were unhappy until she was looking through the bills and saw one for a midtown hotel across from his firm's office, and she just knew he was having an affair. She wanted to throw up.

She then went through the cell phone bills, the e-mail trail, his text messages, and the history on his computer, and she found everything she needed to confront him. "He wasn't even trying to hide it. He'd gotten so casual about it that I don't think he bothered to cover his tracks anymore. It's like he wanted me to find out."

That night she had the bills all lined up on the kitchen table like a prosecutor's evidence, and the minute he walked in the door she said, "I know everything. How could you? Don't you love me, the boys, or our life?" And he dropped into a chair, his coat still on, clutching his briefcase. He said, "Do you want me to move out?" No denial and no apology.

He's too good a lawyer to even try to plead not guilty—he went straight to the bargaining table. "What do you want me to do?"

This upset her even more, because she wanted him to fight for her and say he was sorry. But instead he was ready to walk. That is when she burst into tears. Now she had no bargaining chips, because she couldn't even use his remorse to get him back. He was already gone. It seemed to her that he didn't care.

He said he'd earned his freedom. He worked all the time to support everyone around him, and who supports him? Not his wife. She doesn't show the least bit of interest in him, or in sex, so he thought he was doing her a favor by getting it elsewhere and leaving her alone. At least that is what he had convinced himself of before that confrontation at the kitchen table.

Sarah knew, deep down, that she had been neglecting her marriage for years. She never listened when he suggested they spend time alone or make a regular Saturday night date. And what sex they did have was uninspired—for her, it was just going through the motions, like taking a shower.

Catherine points out that though Sarah can take some of the blame herself for neglecting the marriage, she isn't responsible for her husband's affair. He chose to cheat instead of talk. Sarah had unconsciously checked out, and so he did the same, physically and emotionally. The question is, Did they ever truly connect and talk and share intimacies? They were coexisting for years, and in the Venn diagram of their marriage their circles barely touched. The kids were their only real connection.

Can they pull their circles together? It's not so clear. They have to decide whether to try to put the marriage back together or let it go. This is going to take work, and they both have to want to engage in the process. To Sarah's surprise, her husband decides he doesn't want to lose the life they have together, even if it's not perfect, and they start talking.

Each of them has issues. One of the biggest problems: Sarah needs to build up her self-respect before she can be a whole person, or full circle, in the Venn diagram. A healthy marriage has two whole circles overlapping, not two halves of a circle making a whole. Sarah, like many women, doubts she can be independent outside the identity of marriage.

Though she works, her emotional identity is wrapped up in her family life, and being a mother comes first for her. She can't imagine a life outside of her marriage and has no desire to start over. She took for granted she would always be married, without ever paying attention to the state of her relationship with her husband. She realizes that she now has to focus on herself as well as rebuild her life, including interests outside of parenting.

Catherine would tell Sarah to ask herself why she couldn't see the signs that things were falling apart. There were clues along the way, but she "chose" to ignore them to maintain the semblance of normalcy. What did she need from her marriage? Just for it to continue? He was asking for time alone with her and never got it. What did she want? She didn't have the self-esteem to ask or even know what she needed. Once she can answer that for herself, she can have a successful relationship. But it may be too late to have it with her husband. Still, she won't be able to have a successful relationship later if she doesn't figure out what went wrong in this one. Only then can she be fully present, her own complete circle, in any marriage. Here is the sometimes painful truth: It takes two people to create a marriage and two people to allow it to wither and die. You have to question how you participated in your own life outcome. Only then can you determine your next move and ultimately be the master of your own destiny.

I THINK I'M IN LOVE
WITH FACEBOOK MAN

"I would never cheat, but I spend all my time on Facebook talking to this old pal I used to work with. He is such a fun person, and though we're both married we like the spark that seems to exist between us. I call him Facebook Man, and he makes me like who I am better than anyone else, even my best friend or my husband."

—Fiona, 43; New Orleans, Louisiana

Fiona's twins keep her busy every minute she isn't working as an administrative assistant in a large law firm. She never would even look at one of the lawyers. It's not that she wants to have an affair, but when she is online she is the person she can't be at work or at home. She loves her family, loves her life and her twin girls (now approaching two), but this secret flirtation is her way of escaping it all. She feels she deserves it, since the rest of the time—covered in baby spit-up and taking little ones to the playground or the doctor—her life is not her own. She doesn't recognize herself—the tall, lean, confident, and powerful working woman is now wearing sweats and hating how she looks most of the time.

Enter the world of the Internet, where your social life can be whatever you want it to be. Facebook Man is a new phenomenon—you once had to go to your high school reunion to reconnect with that guy who sometimes pops up in your fantasies. The answer to "I wonder whatever happened to so-'n'-so?" is now just a few clicks away. People from your past are now at your fingertips 24/7. You are free to imagine this person, in all his potential perfection, as your long-lost soul mate. He laughs at your quips and flatters your ego. On Facebook, you get to edit your storyline and present to the world the side of your personality you like best.

Meanwhile, at home, all hell can be breaking loose. But on Facebook you are the persona you present to the world, in albums and funny comments and "shared" content on your wall. You can give a quickie thumbs-up, and it's like you're reminding them: "I'm here . . ." And then wait and see if anyone nibbles on the baited hook.

"I have connected to this person online who I knew in college, and he really digs me, but I don't think it would necessarily work out. I just love to check my in-box and see what he's written, and usually it's so flattering and funny that I blush. It makes me feel like we're dating or something, when in fact I am married and not even interested in looking at another guy in real life. Still, it makes we wonder what I'm capable of. I mean, I love my husband and he loves me, but this person makes me feel much younger, more alive, sexier. But then I think, *If my hubby loves me even when I look a wreck, isn't that the real thing?* I should be happy that he appreciates me, even when I think I look horrible. My kids still want to snuggle, and when I later look in the mirror I think: *They see me as a beauty, and I see a mother who's let herself go.*

"Facebook Man doesn't know that, though. He just knows that I'm a busy working mother who has a good head of hair and can type out a funny turn of phrase. And that's exactly what I want him to know. Nothing else. What part of me needs this? It cuts into time with my husband, because he thinks I'm working and he just goes to bed without me. If I didn't need my 'Facebook Man fix' we'd probably have more fun together, watch a movie, even have sex."

Fiona is in the wrong room. She is not in the office (where her computer is located) or the bedroom (where she thinks she should go to spend more time with her husband). She is in the bathroom, where the image of herself in her real life isn't what she wants it to be. And on Facebook she can imagine that best version of herself that she wishes she could recreate, even though her life is booked up with the twins and a job and all the other to-dos on her list that keep her from getting to the gym and eating healthfully. Meanwhile, her online "lover" is reflecting that perfect image of herself back, and she loves this view of herself, so she thinks she loves him.

Facebook can function like a grown-up version of Harry Potter's magical mirror where you see only your heart's deepest, "most desperate" desires. It's called the "Mirror of Erised"—*Desire* spelled backward—and for Fiona that reflection would be a cleaned-up version of herself, as a pulled together and attractive woman, not one with thirty-five extra pounds and nothing in her old wardrobe fitting. She wants to see herself the way she was before the babies: slender and sexy and appealing to everyone, herself included.

Many women find themselves flirting for all the wrong reasons. They flirt not because they are so unhappy at home, but because they constantly need positive affirmation. In fact the husband may say, "Honey, you're beautiful, and I'm still attracted to you," but because the woman isn't happy with herself she devalues his opinion and thinks: *He's an idiot. Because I hate myself, now I hate anyone who loves this version of myself.*

Fiona needs to get back to that place where she likes herself, even if it doesn't mean acquiring the perfect pretwin flat-abs figure. Instead she has to define the new version of herself and who she wants to be now.

Catherine points out that Fiona is split. On Facebook, she's that gorgeous, flirtatious girl of her fantasies, and at home she's the frumpy mom in sweats. Splitting is a defense mechanism; it can happen when you need an escape hatch, like when you've had a big life change or are under undue stress. You create this fantasy version of life, where it's all good over here, in one area, and all bad in another. But both are exaggerated, two extremes of the spectrum. Fiona has to integrate these polar opposite sides of her personality, which means finding a comfortable middle ground where she can like her life.

Fiona doesn't have to give up the fun side or the mom side of her identity. She can be the awesome do-it-all woman of her Facebook profile, the fun-loving wife her husband married, and the upbeat energetic mom who directs all that energy to her kids. The point is to be her best self within the context of her family, not finding a fix outside of it in order to be happy.

So Fiona has to stop splitting and start integrating. She needs to get to the bathroom and take care of herself: start to exercise and eat right, get a new haircut, and look her best so that she can be the person she wants to be for real, not just a Facebook fantasy. The pearl: Integrate, don't separate. Meaning: You can be a complex woman. The key is to appreciate the whole person with all the many different facets of your life.

I HAVE A WORK HUSBAND.
IS THAT BAD?

"I spend all my time at work confiding in a male colleague, Matt. It's like he's become my work husband, and I look forward to being with him. It's not like I'd ever sleep with him—he's happily married and so am I—but I tell him more than I tell my husband. I feel like I'm cheating. But I love to talk to him, and I don't want to give it up. And I don't feel like I should have to."

—Amanda, 36; Boulder, Colorado

Amanda loves her husband, Dave, but doesn't feel passionate about him these days. In fact, a mother of three—ages three, five, and eight—working part-time as a radiology technician and shuttling the kids around 24/7, she's angry that he doesn't seem interested in the details of her life. She remembers feeling passionate about Dave, a paramedic, when they first dated. "I can still think about our first kiss and get that butterfly feeling in my stomach!" She has numerous stories about how much fun they had back then, and how adventurous they were, skiing the backcountry, camping out in the desert, and having sex all the time. "But that was before we had kids and had to get serious about building our family and careers. We just don't have that much time together anymore . . . the kids have been our joint focus, and all the rest of our energy gets poured into our jobs. We both like to excel at work and have gotten lots of compliments on how hardworking we are. It's very important to us both."

Amanda still believes Dave is the guy for her. He's smart, honest, loyal, loving, a wonderful husband and father . . . plus he's good-looking. She isn't planning on having an affair, but isn't shutting that door completely. "I mean, there isn't anyone I have in mind, but on occasion I feel that little zing when I'm talking to a handsome man who is really interested in what I'm saying and intently listening to me. It's a turn-on!"

Amanda is conflicted about her work husband. "I really don't think we have crossed the line, but he is so attentive and always remembers to ask about my mom's health as well as complimenting me on a nice outfit or new haircut. I really like the attention. Dave has been pretty busy with work and coaching soccer for the kids, and he doesn't seem that tuned in to what's going on in my life." Amanda was okay with that arrangement until another mother at a soccer game showed an interest in Dave, listening to his stories and laughing at his silly jokes. Amanda was intensely jealous and suddenly realized what was happening to her marriage: She was losing the connection to her spouse, and he was picking up friendly signals elsewhere. It was a wake-up call.

Amanda is realizing one of the universals of marriage: The early child-rearing years can be some of the toughest on many couples. They lose touch with each other as the kids become their focus, and they prioritize everything else first and each other last. They are failing to connect on a regular basis, and intimacy often gets overridden by the daily grind. It's easy to channel all that emotional attention to your kids at home and your colleagues at work—the people you're around the most. You have to make an effort to spend quality time with your spouse. Sometimes it has to wait until the last hour of the night, after the kids go to sleep and before you collapse into bed, exhausted. It may even need to be scheduled. Maybe you have a natural rhythm of connecting, but otherwise you have to put it on the to-do list . . . preferably near the top of that list.

Though Amanda isn't cheating physically, she has crossed an emotional line, and she knows it. "I love him as a friend, and that would be so uncomplicated if he were a woman, but because he's a man I feel guilty, so I don't tell my husband about it. I know he'd be pissed."

Catherine says Amanda is disconnecting, and getting her emotional needs met elsewhere. She has transferred her feelings from Dave onto Matt. Part of what's making her do this is that Dave isn't showing much empathy for her hectic life, or her mom's health problems. She's acting out by overinvesting emotionally with Matt and has started to withhold her thoughts and feelings from Dave.

Amanda saw at that soccer match that this isn't a harmless game. "I thought, *Oh my god, he's adorable and if I'm not nice to him, some other woman will be and I could lose him.* I made my way over to where he was and started chatting warmly and complimenting him on raising such an athletic daughter. He clearly liked that, and I realized how rarely I ever say anything nice to him anymore. In fact, I don't give him much of anything anymore, and I have to start doing more for him."

Amanda needs to understand that this all started because she was angry at her husband for not reading her mind, which is not something he (or, last we checked, any man) can do. She shut him out and then he started paying less attention to her, and that became a vicious cycle. The two of them need to talk and share their grievances. She has to acknowledge that she is participating in the deterioration of their marriage. It's easy to focus on your spouse's shortcomings, but far more helpful to look at yourself and assess what's going on inside.

Amanda was acting out rather than expressing how she felt. She needs to start letting Dave know what she is feeling and going through, and listening to him as well. She needs to start confiding in her real husband and stop putting so much attention into her relationship at work. If she wants to salvage her marriage, she has to start emotionally investing her time and effort at home. The pearl: No man is a mind reader. Tell him what you need.

HE'S RIGHT FOR ME IN EVERY WAY EXCEPT IN BED!

"I've tried everything to get my boyfriend to do what I want in bed, and it's not working. It's like he's reading from an instruction manual. There's only so much I want to tell him; I wish he could figure out the rest on his own. I can't spell it out for him. But I still love him and maybe that's enough!"

—Charlotte, 35; Long Beach, California

Charlotte says she loves her boyfriend, but making love is often less than inspiring. She wants to marry him, but after three years, their sex life is still banal. From the get-go, he just never had the moves. He used to make her heart flutter by walking in the room, but that wore off, and then she got even more critical of the fact that their sex life never had fireworks. "Basic is the way I'd describe it. Nothing bad, but nothing amazing either. I mean, I've had one-night stands that were more memorable than any of our nights together. And I get frustrated, because I really love him, but I'm not turned on by him most of the time."

Charlotte broached the subject gently with Shep one time, and he said, "I think our sex is pretty great," and beamed at her, implying that he was just happy being with her in bed.

"For him, it feels good no matter what," she says. "Shep doesn't ask how it feels for me, since he assumes it's fine. He doesn't know what to do for me. I've tried to tell him, but it seems to me there is only so much you can communicate verbally on that front." Now he's trying even harder to make her happy and she doesn't want to hurt his feelings.

To her great dismay Charlotte had a one-night stand after a late night out drinking with friends recently, and it was amazing. "On some level, I wanted to find out if the boring sex was my fault. I had to know: Had I lost it? But also, I just wanted to have hot, steamy sex, and I knew this would be my chance. Shep was out of town and he'll never know. But I feel bad, even though we're not married. I can't tell him, but I also think it's partly his fault because I am so *not* satisfied. It's almost like being hungry: If there's no food in the fridge, you have to go out for dinner. It's just a physical need. We all have them."

Now Charlotte is wondering whether she should get married to Shep—if she is cheating now, what's it going to be like in ten years? Will she have what it takes to stick with him and make it work? She is at a crisis point in her relationship and needs to answer this question pronto.

She's rationalizing, says Catherine. On the one hand, she's right: We all have needs. On the other, she is in a committed relationship and telling herself that she can break the rules. She has to decide whether she wants to be Shep's partner. If she chooses to stay and work at their relationship, then she has to sit down with Shep in a neutral space (kitchen table, here we come!) and talk about what is going on with her, emotionally and sexually. Tell him what she is feeling and believes she needs to be satisfied. One of the problems is that she's not communicating well enough—and that may be because she doesn't know what she wants clearly enough herself. So Catherine says Charlotte is acting out by cheating rather than expressing her dissatisfaction to Shep.

Charlotte *thinks* she told Shep how she feels, but he didn't get it. She's trying not to hurt his feelings by disparaging him in bed, but she's hurting him behind his back in a way that's far more damaging and could ruin any future marriage in the long run.

According to Charlotte, Shep is too much of a pushover and so loving that she's too much in control of the relationship. She wishes he were more Caveman than Prince Charming. Many women have tamed their spouse to the point where he can't do *anything* right, even "take her" in the way she imagines a one-night stand would. Catherine says they are both responsible for this dynamic, since now he's trying so hard to please her that he can't be himself in bed. Charlotte's now walking all over him while complaining that he has become a doormat. They have to step back and take a break, or take turns being in charge in their life, and in their bed.

For starters, Charlotte has to come clean with herself and figure out what inner conflict is blocking her from knowing what she really wants. She likes to blame Shep, but is this more about her lack of satisfaction with herself? She needs to look inward and remind herself of her lifelong struggle with self-esteem. Shep isn't there to make her whole. Only she can do that.

Feeling worthy, pretty, smart, sexy, or whatever it is you want to feel cannot be supplied by another person, at least not for long. You have to generate those feelings from within in order to have them be sustained for more than a fleeting moment. A partner can enhance good feelings, but can't provide them for you. If he's the only one providing validation for you, eventually you stop believing it because you can't internalize the positive self-worth. So you continually seek it from others, and are never truly satisfied with the partner who tells you how great you are.

Charlotte wonders whether she should tell Shep about her one-night stand. Catherine says women who cheat often want to know if they have to confess. But usually it's for the wrong reasons. Women want to relieve their guilt, but Catherine asks if the admission is going to be useful and important in rebuilding the relationship. If it's just "truth dumping," then you're making a big mess messier. Many times, the hurt caused by telling is the injury that lingers. It can also derail you, since he gets focused on that other person and misses the bigger picture, the real issues that were bringing you down.

Charlotte *can* tell Shep what she needs in bed and in their relationship, and redefine what she considers "great sex," since sometimes it can be more about expressing love and making an emotional connection than how many fireworks she's seeing. Charlotte and Shep can work on making things better in bed, but she can also appreciate him for his many good qualities: Maybe there will never be fireworks in bed, but there are lots of other highlights. Is it enough? Only you can decide if the good outweighs the bad. Make a decision and enjoy your life.

SELF-RELIANT TO A FAULT

"I won't allow myself to get hurt, so I have certain rules, like when we can have sex and how long before I'll think about marriage. I have to be in charge of the relationship in every way. If someone loves me enough, he'll understand."
—Kimberly, 29; Arlington, Virginia

Kimberly is dating seriously but not eager to get married. She is so guarded that she won't let herself need anyone, and it may end up costing her this relationship, because he wants to get married.

Kimberly was raised in a chaotic household by an abusive stepfather who regularly told her she would amount to nothing. She felt neglected at best and abused at worst. "I won't allow myself to care that much about anyone, so that I can't get hurt. I refuse to put up with anything but perfect behavior in my relationships, like if my boyfriend says *anything* mean, I'm outta there. I am the only one I can depend on. I know that makes it hard for me to be in a relationship.

"Look, my honey is great, but he's trying to move closer to me, and it makes me pull back and I feel suffocated. It may be unfair, but I feel like he's trying to take control of my life. My way to deal with this has been to set rules about how many times a week I spend the night at his place, and even taking every third weekend totally off. If a guy can't respect that then I'm like, See ya! I've always liked it this way, but now I wonder, Am I holding myself back? He can't understand why I am so rigid. Yet I wonder if I let down my guard, will I still keep enough of me intact? I don't want to lose everything I've built for myself: my independence, my life, my career, my own personal happiness."

As a teenager Kimberly considered running away but knew she couldn't support herself. She considered suicide but couldn't stand causing her mother that much pain. So instead she put up with her stepfather's verbal abuse for years, even giving it back to him at times. She finally left home at eighteen and put herself through community college by working two jobs. "Leaving my mom was hard; I cried every tear I could as a teenager. I felt completely alone and depleted. It was as if I could not go any lower, and it was up to me to build my life from there. I always think of myself as my own hero, and I never let myself rely on anyone else."

Kimberly is so self-protective that it's as if she's wearing emotional armor, which makes Catherine ask: Is she really as fragile as she thinks she is? Would her sense of safety be so easily lost if she took off all those defenses and shared herself more fully? What does she think will happen?

Kimberly has reason to be proud of her own accomplishments. But she still has a huge streak of insecurity. "I finally accepted myself this way, but now that I've been with this man for two and a half years and know he really loves me, I realize it's causing a new problem: If I can't change, I might end up alone for the rest of my life."

She wants independence and has built walls around herself, yet deep down she hopes someone will scale them and take care of her. It's a terrible conflict, and she is still in the basement of her childhood memories, working through issues and unhappy memories of her mother (a doormat) and her stepfather (a bully). Meanwhile, neither she nor her boyfriend can understand why she feels distressed when he tells her, "I would fly to the moon for you." To Kimberly it feels like he's trying to hold her back.

Catherine points out the unconscious process of "transference" at work here. Kimberly has made all her love interests into the wicked stepfather, and she spends all her energy guarding against pending injury or hurt. Whether you get caught in this pattern or another one, it can become a "repetition compulsion," because you end up doing the same thing over and over, and this can keep you from evolving in your life. Only when you realize you're stuck in a pattern can you change it. Even then, it can take years. You literally have to relearn how to act. If you're lucky, you realize there's a good reason to change; Kimberly now knows she could stand to lose the best relationship she's ever had, with a wonderful guy who gives her exactly what she needs—security, safety, love, and respect.

"I realize I have to learn to open up. I am teaching myself this in baby steps, and I'm finally learning to talk about my feelings and trust other people. I figure if I can do it with them I can learn to do it with my boyfriend too." It would be easy to blame her lack of ability to get intimate on her tough family dynamics, but she has to step up and work this out for herself.

Kimberly is in the wrong room and needs to resolve her basement issues so that she can be happy in her relationship and in the rest of her house. Otherwise she will end up finding a guy who is aloof and disconnected, and not really safe and secure at all. Her current boyfriend seems like a man who could be a great partner. But she has to let her guard down a little to create a new level of connection—within the relationship. It's about giving up some of her independence in order to gain intimacy and trust. Her pearl: You have to give a little to get a lot.

I HAD AN AFFAIR AT THE OFFICE. I DON'T FEEL GUILTY; I'M SAD IT'S OVER.

"When I got married I really felt great about it. We had a great connection in every way—spiritually, emotionally, physically—and shared the same values and hopes for raising a family together and of course staying together forever. And so far it's gone pretty much as scripted. Nice house, great family, solid jobs, the usual fights but nothing extraordinary. More love than aggravation. But fast-forward ten, fifteen years and you get to the point where you need to feel sexy again, and you find that that happens more outside the house than within it."

—Jackie, 42; Brookline, Massachusetts

By everyone else's standards, Jackie is a together, happily married working mom living the dream. And yet she found herself having crushes on men and enjoying a lusty fantasy life. She never acted on those fantasies, until . . .

"I lost weight, I got in shape, and my husband never even noticed," Jackie says. "Other women *and* men were telling me how great I looked, but I never heard this from my husband." Jackie was feeling so much better about herself that she switched careers and got a more exciting job.

She met a guy in her new job, and they worked closely together day and night. He was younger, available, and admired her very much. "I already had myself a smart, solid, good-looking man and yet I was completely lusting after this guy." She started sending flirty text messages and then began communicating with him constantly. She kept pushing the limits because it was so exciting and dangerous. Then she started lying to her husband and saying she was going out for drinks with friends. And she wasn't. She was meeting *him*.

"Who could resist?" Jackie says. "He made me feel sexual and funny and confident and smart." Their affair lasted just two weeks. He called it off, saying, "I am not going to be the home wrecker. I want to get married and have kids."

Jackie was devastated. She wanted to be adored. And she wanted to keep having what she calls "crazy-good sex." She skulked home and realized her husband never even noticed that "drinks with a friend" went way too late, or that her time texting had increased immensely. She was crying out for him to catch her cheating, want her back, and woo her romantically, but instead he was indifferent.

This marriage is in trouble but not necessarily over.

Catherine says that Jackie acted out her feelings of not being noticed and appreciated and of wanting to be validated for her new figure and job. Her key process could have been to talk it out and be direct with her husband and tell him how she was feeling and what she needed and wasn't getting. But what she is lacking—self-esteem—isn't something another person can provide.

She may tell her husband, "I don't feel loved and adored and noticed." But he may feel that he is giving her everything she wants and needs—the big house, the fancy car. Regardless, she doesn't feel like her emotional needs are met. And she is starving for his attention and affection. Back in her marriage now, with no other man in her life, she's depressed, isolated, and angry.

Jackie is hoping that someone else (her own kids or an adoring man or an exciting new job) can make her feel whole. But they can't. It's as if she is part of a person and wants someone else to complete her and give her meaning and fulfillment. She has some soul-searching to do, since in her marriage, she allowed herself to be half a person, half a circle, hoping another would "fill" in the rest of the drawing. But she never developed herself fully, became her own person, defined her own ideas and desires. When the kids were able to take care of themselves, and her job was on autopilot, she woke up to see that her marriage was dead. Having a hot, younger man adore and ravage her was fun, but it won't sustain her. Now she needs to learn how to better define herself, be "whole," and draw in the rest of the line herself. Her pearl: Only you can make yourself whole. No one completes you but you.

I HAVE THE SINGLE BLUES!

"I'm still single and I'm forty-two. I don't even think I could have a baby if I wanted one. I feel mad at myself for spending years in relationships that were going nowhere. One guy, who I dated for seven years, was so clearly not going to commit, but I totally loved being with him. And most recently, I ended a six-year relationship with a married man. Why do I pick such unavailable men?"

—Andrea, 42; New York, New York

Andrea is singing a sad song. "I know that one reason I stay with the wrong men is that I hate being alone. Like on a Friday night I look for pals to see a movie with and everyone is either paired off or has kids by now. My group of friends has gotten younger and younger as my usual peer group has moved to the 'burbs. It's fun to hang out with younger people, but they all want to go to bars and get drunk and I think, *What am I doing here?* I feel the blues come on and think I'd have been better off at home. But at home I feel lonely. And when I do choose to stay home, I feel like such a loser and like I should get out there and meet people. It's like I'm never in the right place . . . since I always feel like I should do something else.

"So I'm stuck. I host dinner parties, but whenever I ask pals if they know any single men, they don't. Which is why I think I stayed in those two long relationships as long as I did. It was like, What did I have to break up for? There weren't a lot of other options. But now I think I blew it. I may never have a family, and I love kids. So I get depressed. Then I think: *If I were a guy I wouldn't want to date me either.*"

Andrea has lost her ability to focus on the other things in her life— her great job, her love of reading, her desire to write a screenplay, and even her physical health, since she's staying out and spending time with people she doesn't care about, rather than following her inner compass and being the person she wants to be.

If she wants the next chapter of her life to be different, she has to do some reevaluating. She thinks that she always chooses the wrong guy, but why? And was "he" wrong? Guy One, it turned out, had no money, so she discounted him as a potential spouse. But instead of looking to what she later would jokingly call "my poet" to be both a romantic poet and a meal ticket, she could have made her own money and decided that he would have been a great stay-at-home dad, since his teaching and writing life would have allowed her to have a built-in caregiver.

"It's like I do something that drives guys away. Maybe I'm too needy or available, because after a while they don't want to marry me!" Andrea is like so many women who seem independent, but once they're in a relationship they lose their identity and it becomes all about the guy. Men experience her as desperate, and this pushes them away. What is sad is that Andrea is a woman of substance. She is smart and has many talents and lots of creative energy, but once she is comfortably ensconced in a relationship, she "forgets" herself.

Catherine says Andrea is regressing, reliving her childhood emotional patterns. When she finds herself in a relationship that is comfortable and consistent, she relates it to when she was a young girl and her father always treated her like daddy's little princess. He took care of her and made her feel special and doted on her, so now a male admirer finds himself thrust into the role of "daddy" when he wasn't prepared to be that for her. She never did find a partner who would be both boyfriend and father, and that's where the breakdown happened.

Until Andrea understands that no man will replace her beloved father, who dotes on her still, she will be unable to come to a relationship on adult terms and not as a needy child. Her arrested development is something that can be worked through. The key process here is to understand how her past (basement) is intruding on her present (bedroom) and to decide to make some changes in her inner self-image. Once she does this for herself (like not hanging out with much younger people in bars) and finds a peer group who share her interests in writing and moviemaking, she will start to rebuild her own life from the inside out. Only then can she truly grow up enough to have an adult-style relationship.

When someone is regressing they first have to recognize what they're doing and decide whether they want to do it differently. The pearl: "Go or grow" means go along with the status quo and keep repeating your patterns for the rest of your life, or grow up and find a new future with an appropriate partner.

Here is a great thought to take into the bedroom, straight from one of Catherine's favorite poets, Rilke:

> For one human being to love another; that is perhaps the most difficult of all our tasks, the ultimate, the last test and proof, the work for which all other work is but preparation.

We'd say: Marriage is a choice, and you choose to stay married by sharing your life with (but not giving your entire being over to) this one special person. Sex can be loving, powerful, fun, playful, stress-relieving, hot, or just ho-hum. As with any other form of self-expression, there's a range of styles, and it's up to you how it plays out.

You have the power to control or change how you feel in bed—attractive, desirable, or not so much. It's nice to hear from someone else that you look amazing, but it has an impact only if you believe it yourself, and when you do, it's an affirmation of how you're feeling. (If you don't believe it, no amount of flattery will penetrate your self-critical bubble.) So the attraction that others are radiating in your direction is actually the reflection of how you feel inside.

Others can compliment you and even complement you. But again, the only person who completes you is you.

12

The Kitchen

Can't Stand the Heat?
Must Be in the Kitchen.

I love doing some chores, not others. Changing sheets, no; folding laundry, yes. Cooking, no; baking, yes. Unloading the dishwasher, no; loading it, yes. When I fold laundry I look at the person's item, say, my son's T-shirt with the logo from his favorite surf shop or band, and I feel closer to him. I lovingly turn it right-side out, then smooth and square it off, as if it were new, and stack it like you see at the store. It's my way of showing him I am there for him. Then I get to my T-shirt and it's inside out and I barely want to bother pulling the sleeves back through the right way. It's not that I don't love myself, but I don't need to show it to myself. One woman told me that she folds her kids' clothes and her husband's, but leaves her own stack of clean clothes in the garage out back where the washer/dryer is. One day she realized she had to run naked from the waist down, from her house out through the backyard, to get some pants. In that moment she thought, I quit work to raise my kids and I'm glad I did, but I was great at my job and I'm only so-so at being a domestic goddess. There are things that remind us every day that we aren't perfect. While that's okay, when the neighbors look out their window and see a white-tailed mom dashing for clothes, it drives the point home. We always want to do better, especially if someone else is watching!

For me that means ordering in less and trying to make dinner a couple of nights a week. My kids know that the doorbell rings and it means dinner (like actual Pavlovian pups, trained that the bell brings food). My mother was a great cook, but not me, I just can't get it together on a weeknight to get to the store and find the ingredients and whip up a tasty and healthy dinner at the end of a long day. I wish I could.

Still, my kids are healthy, and now they are teaching themselves to make the basics: scrambled eggs and toast, spaghetti and tomato sauce. And of course they are aces with the phone and a stack of take-out menus. Living in the city makes that an option, thank goodness. But the kitchen in this emotional house isn't only about food: The most important thing happening here is emotional nourishment and the "coming together" of the family several times a day. Plus, this is where the division of labor in the household takes place. All those dishes to unload!

And then there's the iconic kitchen table, where we find ourselves having the "real" conversations of the family. The business of who's doing what at work and at school during the tricky teenage years of peer relationships, bad behavior, meanness, and the like. We tend to really get into it at the kitchen table since it's intimate and informal, and unlike in the family room, we're facing one another. Sometimes we'll hold a "family meeting" to make a big decision, like where to go for a vacation, and we always know that means taking seats around the table: I have mine, my husband has his, and the kids have theirs. We never sit in one another's seats, even when the other person isn't around.

It's as if we are all at our posts, playing our roles. I call it my kitchen cabinet (like the president has) since each of us offers advice and an honest point of view to the others. (I like it when the kids offer up their worldview and a real discussion ensues.) Most of the time it all works out and we sit down to dinner and have a family gathering, conversation, or meeting. But when I get peeved over the little things: snacks left out to rot or the dishes on the table, or the dishwasher full and clean (my least favorite sight), I get crabby and nag at someone to "Puleeeeaaaasssse" help a little more around the house!

When it's going well, the kitchen is usually a place for me to come together with my daughter and bake something: cookies or brownies or a special dessert for a Saturday night dinner party. Baking tells me that this is the best time in the kitchen, since it basically says, "I choose to be here with my daughter, spending time on a chore that doesn't really need to get done but is a nice diversion while we talk and share the details of our lives." Silly conversation leads to emotional connection, and for us it usually takes place over a bowl of unbaked cookie dough. Even at a fast-paced breakfast before school, in just a few found moments, we'll connect in the kitchen, have an abbreviated conversation, and touch base before racing off again. And it's through these casual, often mumbled conversations over coffee and cereal that we "feed" one another emotionally.

The kitchen is where Mom used to rule supreme, but now families are more complicated, and chances are she's working, so in the morning everyone is whirling around, fending for themselves because the school bus is about to roll up and the train is about to leave the station.

The kitchen is not always a tranquil space. It can be full of frantic, fraught exchanges—Did you walk the dog? Who's picking up Suzie from practice? How late are you working?—and in the evening, there's dinner to make, homework to oversee, and laundry to fold, because it's also the family work space.

Even if you live by yourself, the kitchen can be the heart of your house. It's where the pictures on the fridge remind you of loved ones; it's where the stack of bills and that list of important numbers remind you that you have pressing responsibilities. It's the organizational center of your "emotional" house.

For our purposes, the most important piece of furniture in this room is the kitchen table, because that's where the family talks about fundamental issues, such as the division of labor, finances, and respect for one another. This is where you share the minutiae of the day or, if necessary, have it out. Maybe you don't have a kitchen table—you hash things out over the kitchen counter, or somewhere else. In our discussion, the "kitchen table" is just a concept; it's where your family connects and where you learn what matters most to them. And to yourself, in terms of time and how you spend it.

MY HUSBAND DOESN'T DO JACK!

"I feel like I'm all alone. Am I married or not? I might as well be a single mother. I do everything for everyone—my kids, my husband, my dog. When can I ask for help from them? The second shift isn't a myth, even for the mom who stays at home. I think, *where is my relief?* I don't even get one minute off."

—Tracy, 43; Lima, Ohio

"I chose this. I love what I do and I'm lucky I get to stay at home. My mom thought it was her job, and hers alone, to take care of the household. My dad had to get up and go to work and that was that generation. But now it's different and most women work. I used to, but when I had my first son, Jack, I quit. Steve, my husband, never touched a wet diaper or wore the BabyBjörn. To this day, Steve will come home and expect dinner whenever he walks in, even at 9:30. I always have a sarcastic retort and say, 'Oh, you can't warm it up yourself?' But then I do it. I really don't mind. But then he leaves his dish on the table and it kills me. That's what we are trying to teach our kids, 'Put your dishes in the sink,' so when I ask, 'Steve, did you forget something?' he will put it in the sink and say, 'I was about to!' but I swear if I hadn't said anything it would be encrusted on the table the next morning.

"Finances are at the root of our major arguments. Even if it's couched in the kids' sports or school. I never tell him he should make more money, but I would like to. For me, there are no pay raises, bonuses, or reviews of a mother's work. You mostly get people complaining or bitching about how they can't find their (fill in the blank) soccer socks, printout, or phone! No one ever tells you what a good job you're doing.

"If my husband comes in and comments about the messy house I get crazy. I feel like he walks in and is immediately negative. I say to him, 'I don't criticize your work.' But I'm more sensitive, and I take it personally. I want him to be supplying praise. I want to give him a list of what to say: 'You're such a good mom, cook, friend.' 'You look great.' It's like he needs a script."

Meanwhile, Tracy cleans up the dog throw-up in the laundry room and brings the dry clothes to the TV area to see if Steve can help her fold them, and he asks her to move them, since she is now blocking his view. He can't find the car keys, or his sneakers, or the food in the fridge. It's as if she has to do everything for him. He's learned to depend on her. As the firstborn in her family, she is a giver, and as the last born in his family, he's used to being given to, and it's a pattern they have grown up with all their lives. But now it's time for a change, since her older son, Jack, is ten and her younger one, Sam, is seven and she is eager to ask them to help out more. And maybe Steve too.

"My job starts when I wake up and it ends when I'm putting the last load of laundry in before I go to sleep at the end of the day, like eleven, so the thing about being a mom is the hours suck and there's zero pay. It's not like doing brain surgery, but it's constant. Relentless. When I try to explain that I like things nice for the family, Steve says, 'Calm down, everything's fine,' and that drives me crazy because if I didn't do it no one would. Yes, I chose my lot in life, and I'm actually quite happy, so why am I complaining so much? What is my problem?"

Clearly, Catherine points out, there are some issues that need to be resolved. Tracy needs to sit down with Steve, not when he's watching TV, not by piling heaps of laundry on him when he's relaxing, and not yelling at him to find his own damn sneakers! She needs to calmly tell him how she feels, and that she needs a break. And boy does she ever. But it's not going to happen because Steve says, "Yes, honey, you need a break."

The truth is there are lots of rooms involved here: the office, which includes their finances (he bought a motorcycle without telling her and she realized they are not equal partners in the money management side of things), the kid's room (he isn't a 50-50 dad, and never has been), and the basement (they each were reared in traditional homes, and he was the baby so was coddled and waited on by his doting mother). The bedroom is involved, since he could tell her she looks pretty, bring her flowers (especially when he asks for a 9:30 dinner and she is ready to put her feet up), and generally show some appreciation for his beautiful and talented wife. But the number one problem is that she isn't getting any time for herself and she is at her wit's end, in every room of the house.

Catherine says, "She isn't getting any time for herself because she isn't *taking it*. She literally has to be the one who manages this problem as well as she does all the other ones in front of her. She gets the laundry done and the dinner made and the kids off to school and the dog walked. She simply forgot to put herself on her own to-do list. It's the "to do" that never gets done. And it's an epidemic in American households: the overly tired, overwrought, overwhelmed, and "over it" moms who can't understand how, once they've decided to stay home, it takes such a superhuman effort. But they have to be their own champions. It isn't, as Tracy says, rocket science, but it is human science: The brain and body need a break, to replenish and recharge and relax. If she put an hour of "me time" on her schedule and treated it like a doctor's appointment for one of her kids, she would be well on her way to solving this.

The other truth is that if she doesn't, her body will break down, she will get sick or injured or fatigued beyond what is healthy, and she will be forced to take a break because you simply can't sustain an effort at this pace without time off (either forced or otherwise). We feel strongly that all women have to do this in order to take care of themselves. You have to be whole and strong and healthy in order to take care of those around you. It's not selfish, it's self-preservation.

If your family loves you, they will understand. Your job is to explain it to them: This is mom's time-out. You have to make it real to both you and them.

Remember, too much of a good thing is a bad thing. She is not only hurting herself, she's doing a disservice to her family, since they will never learn to be independent if she does everything for them.

It's up to Tracy to ask for the help she needs, to suggest little things the family can do to help her be less harried and worn out. Steve can pick up dinner on the way home some nights, or Tracy can go away for a girls' weekend, and it will be good for everyone. Things won't fall apart. It would force Steve to step up and do more. Even just a day at the pool by herself, says Tracy, with a book and some music, is a fantasy at this point. Whenever she goes to the local pool with her kids, she sees it as a harried, hellish experience. But she can empower them to be more self-sufficient: put on their own sunscreen, carry their own towels, bring their own books, toys, and music, so she doesn't have to be the packer and schlepper and supplier of entertainment.

Tracy needs to create a chores list and sit each person down and discuss it. If they are the dog caretaker that day and the dog pees on the floor, they get to clean that up. If they are the dishwasher that day, they are responsible for loading the dishes and turning on the machine after supper. They can even help fold laundry or sort socks. It can be fun and a time for chatting, depending on how it's presented and carried out. Maybe each task earns a reward. Extra video game time for the kids, or something they have been badgering Mom for. This is a chance to explain that she is not the maid, and her job is as valuable as Dad's.

"When they say to me, 'Well, Dad makes all the money, you don't work,' I get furious and say, 'Listen to me, I have a master's degree and I choose to stay home. To be with you guys. This *is* work,' I'll tell them. 'And it's the kind I *want* to do, to be here for you guys, but you can pitch in, because we're a family and we help each other.' I never realized how underappreciated I would feel. Some days I just want the good mother's award."

Catherine would tell her: Only you can really help yourself in this situation, by feeling good about your choices, appreciating the things you do well, working on things you don't, and enjoying both as much as possible. It's nice to have other people's recognition, but you have to feel it from within and know that you are happy with what you have and do . . . and not just wait around for the recognition of others. First of all, it may not come (and you may get aggravated waiting for their kudos), and second, by the time you do get it you may be so resentful that you don't appreciate it when it does come.

The best reward is being good to yourself and taking care of yourself, and Tracy hasn't figured out how to do that. Now that she's at the breaking point, she has to. "Other people think I have it so easy, what do I have to complain about? You want to say right back to them, 'I was at the pool all day doing everything for my kids and I can't take it anymore!' Then I realize, most people would have loved to be at a pool all day. It sounds great but it was really hard. Now whenever I am ready to snap I tell my kids, 'I'm at my throw-down-the-apron moment.' And they know exactly what I mean and they give me some help or a break or they carry their own bags to the car.

"And then when they are all sweet like that I realize they aren't *in* the way of my having a good day—they *are* the way." That's where, ultimately, Tracy found her pearl. She even created a needlepoint pillow with her favorite saying on it: "They aren't *in* the way, they *are* the way." And it may be hard sometimes, but in the end she knows it's worth it and they do appreciate her. They just don't always say it. She has to remember to appreciate herself and *take care of* herself. She's the only one who truly can do that. So it's up to her to do it—for herself and her family. Value yourself, and other people will value you too.

COOKING IS LIKE SEX FOR ME. IT'S THAT SPECIAL.

"I know I can please people by cooking for them, and I won't cook for just anyone, because it's my thing, my art form, my talent. It's more intimate than sex for me. If I cook for you, it's a really, really big deal. Once I do I feel totally invested in you. It's like food is my personal identity. If I cook for you, you had better love it. And me!"

—Tess, 28; Ann Arbor, Michigan

Tess, a graduate student in history, with a focus on the history of foods of different cultures, knows she uses cooking to get love and approval. But that's how it's always been, how it was at home with her family. While she knows it's a bit odd, she can't really see how it gets in the way of her relationships. That said, she is well known for brief love affairs that never really get anywhere.

Tess is a self-described serial monogamist, and she's in the early stages of a new relationship and doesn't want to screw it up this time. "But I haven't invited him over for dinner yet. Strange as it sounds, I'd probably sleep with a guy before I would cook for him. Anyone can have sex, but only I can make osso buco in my very special way. I can always tell when I'm really falling in love. I get these tender fantasies of shopping for and feeding the guy. There is this distinct switch when my feelings start to deepen."

Catherine points out that the downside of Tess's love affair with food (and men) comes when the recipient of her creations doesn't appreciate her efforts. "They don't have to lick their plates clean," Tess says, "but I count on seeing their satisfaction. I feel kind of rejected or insulted if the person I'm cooking for doesn't like it. I wish I didn't feel that way, but I've always been someone who likes to please others, and I like the singular attention I get for making an amazing meal. It fulfills some need in me. I'm getting their approval, their love."

Even Tess knows that her "food as approval" equation isn't really about food. Substitute food for anything you do that has a performance (and praise) component to it and you will have the same issues. Is it your writing of proposals at work? You beam for days after your colleagues say you write the best proposals in the business. Maybe you play the piano, and the sole reason you love doing it is the feedback when you play for others. It could be arranging flowers, baking scones, or even playing tennis—the attention it brings you is addictive. And when you don't get it you're like a junkie without her fix. This means you are dealing with issues related to vanity, self-esteem, and validation.

Tess is using food as a way of pinging, Catherine points out, since she is eager to get approval and affirmation, which she has lacked since she was a girl. Both her parents were hypercritical academics who made her feel as if she was never good enough. But her cooking always won kudos from friends, boyfriends, and others, and she could even get her parents to oooh and aaah over her special dinners. It was the only time they ever truly praised her from the heart. Now she is seeking that same kind of love in her relationships.

Once Tess realizes that she is playing out the patterns of her youth she can stop performing for others and start enjoying her cooking for what it is—a personal creative act. Still, she has trouble asking others to take care of her the way she likes to take care of them. It's almost impossible to have a meal and let it just be about the food, plain and simple. That's when she should tell herself, "I like to cook, but sometimes other people can cook for me."

Tess needs to find self-love and then serve others because it brings her pleasure, not because she is feeding her own neediness. Let her kitchen be the place food is kept, prepared, and served, not the throne room where she is the queen and her subjects kiss her ring, and her cinnamon buns.

THE SATURDAY SNIT

"Weekends are the time we all look forward to most in my house. Saturday morning, we wake up, and because of my high expectations, the day is already full. I go into such a state about everything we have to accomplish: get to the soccer game, the mall, get a haircut. Plus there are all these things we want to do around the house—yard work, laundry, errands—everything that I put off during the week. And I've also planned family activities back to back—we're meeting this family for brunch, and that family for dinner. So I start nagging everyone over breakfast and ruining the day, right off the bat. They see me coming and run away."

—Sharon, 35; Princeton, New Jersey

Saturday should be Sharon's happiest day, but instead, it's her worst. She wishes she could enjoy a free day with her husband and their three kids. Instead she wakes up tense, with too much to do and not enough hours to get it all done. This perfect storm of expectations versus reality leads to what she calls "the Saturday Snit."

Sharon realizes that she's holding herself and her family to an unrealistic standard. "I have this constant thing hanging over my head that I should be perfect. I have a Martha Stewart fantasy for my home, but I really hate cooking, and I really, really hate cleaning. But I still race around, trying to have the perfect home, still trying to be the perfect host.

"I try to talk myself out of it by saying, 'What's the worst that could happen?' What if one of my friends came over and my house was a mess and I had no food to serve them? Really, would that be so terrible? None of my friends have neat houses or food to offer me, either, and I don't judge them. So I don't know why I feel this way. I feel like I'm constantly keeping chaos at bay.

"I either overschedule to the point where I'm pissed if things don't go exactly according to plan, or I try to be laid-back and give my husband, William, stuff to do. But then I second-guess everything he does, and I make him crazy too. That's a big issue between the two of us.

"William and I are trying to embrace the fact that when you have three little kids, there's always somebody acting up. But when it's actually happening, we feel angry and overwhelmed and frustrated, even though we know it's gonna happen every weekend.

"My husband and I often turn to each other and say, 'I just need a break.' But I've come to realize that *nobody* gets a break. We're both really busy with work. We're both really busy with the kids."

Sharon's weekly weekend crisis finally blew up after her daughter's season-ending softball game. William was in charge of the team party, but Sharon couldn't let go—instead of letting him just order pizzas, she decorated the whole backyard, put flowers on the picnic table, made Rice Krispies treats, and sliced and diced fruits and vegetables for the parents. While she was doing all this, she told William to clean the playroom in their attic. "No one is going up there!" he said, and she screamed at him, "They might, so do it!"

It's an impossible situation, because even if the playroom gets cleaned and the snacks get baked, the guests will walk in to see Sharon and William yelling at each other. If that happens, Sharon's "awkward moment" won't be running out of pizza; it will be a knockdown marital bout that will keep the team moms gossiping for months.

Catherine would ask, "What room are you in, Sharon?" Her mother might have been a Martha Stewart type—but she didn't have a job outside the house. That's a key difference, since Sharon works three days a week in Philly at an art gallery. She remembers that there were always healthy homemade treats in the kitchen when she was growing up, and she wants that for her children too, but at what cost? She clearly can't have every moment be that perfect family scene she fantasizes about and remembers (inaccurately, as it turns out) from her childhood.

Sharon knows she is expecting too much of herself and her family but can't help herself. The next time she sees her mother, she says, "Mom, I don't know how you did it!" Her mother smiles and says, "Honey, 'it' is a figment of your imagination!

"Your upbringing was far from perfect," Mom says. "Your dad and I fought all the time, mostly because I thought he drank too much. I once threw a plate of hors d'oeuvres at him at a cocktail party. You had a happy childhood, but it was far from something out of a magazine. We weren't perfect. No one is!"

That news was life changing for Sharon, who now tries to remember that her mental snapshot from childhood isn't the one her mother sees. Catherine says this is a classic case of screen memories messing you up, since your childhood imagery is never accurate. Sharon is looking through scrapbooks, seeing only the idyllic moments of parties perfectly executed and her mother dressed in Jackie Kennedy–type shift dresses, but what she doesn't realize is that it looked like that only while the picture was being taken. Beforehand the wet dog was rushing about, shaking pool water on all the food, and after that picture was snapped, the men drank too much and burned the steaks. But the fun was real and what matters most isn't a clean playroom but a bonded couple, so Sharon and William should agree that chaos will prevail and go with it. Her standards and expectations have to come down.

Sharon needs to remember that it's not either/or . . . it's both/and. Life is rarely perfect . . . or a disaster. It's a mixed bag—you can have fun at your softball team party, even if the dog snatches a pizza and drags it around the yard, your cupcakes are burnt, your youngest daughter spills ketchup all over her new white shirt, and the playroom has been declared a toxic waste site. The both/and also applies to Sharon's childhood—there were highs (she only has great memories of her dad) and lows (those flying hors d'oeuvres).

So it's back to the kitchen table for Sharon and William. They sit down and talk. She tells him about her (imperfect) childhood memories and her new understanding, and they realize that at least during their softball party fight she didn't throw anything at him! They agree that they can't wait to have a nice, relaxed weekend. Next Saturday.

Here's how to think about weekend life: Chaos can be fun, if you go with the flow. Stop controlling, start connecting.

GET YOUR FILE CABINET
OUT OF MY GARAGE

"I live alone, and I like it that way. I get to eat what I want, sleep when I want, and not do anyone's laundry but my own. My boyfriend recently brought some of his stuff over, and now I'm feeling a little suffocated. Why does everyone assume I want a full-time companion?"

—Lorraine, 59; Phoenix, Arizona

Lorraine is a young fifty-nine and works as the office manager of a doctor's office. She has been single for four years, since her divorce. Her two grown children are married, and both live in nearby cities.

She says these last four years have been the happiest time of her life and readily admits that she stayed too long in her marriage. "Maybe fifteen years too long. But the kids were young, and I felt financially dependent, so I made the best of it. And now that I am living a solo life, I realize that I am happy and not interested in going back to being someone's wife."

Looking back, she says the divorce was rough, but she is happy she got through it. "If I'd known I would feel like this, I would have done it sooner!" But the best news for her was that her kids supported her all the way. "I'm a pleaser and a caretaker and it's most important to me that my children and my then husband were comfortable and cared for. How I was feeling didn't matter so much. When I was in that marriage, I wasn't depressed, but I now know that I wasn't happy either."

At some point during her marriage she finally realized her husband was an alcoholic and she was an enabler. Couples can survive that, of course, but for Lorraine, the biggest problem was the backseat position she took in her life. It wasn't until after her kids finished high school and went off to college that she decided to finally get a divorce. Making a new life as a single, older woman wasn't easy at first, and she felt lonely. But once she "cleaned house" (literally, in this case, hauling all her ex's stuff to the dump), she started feeling better. She got into a nice routine: early-morning yoga, work, and laps in her gym's pool three days a week after work. "It was so odd at first to not have to rush home and make my husband dinner. I've started cooking and eating so differently now that I'm on my own, and I've lost ten pounds!"

About a year ago, Lorraine met a sweet, smart man who, unlike her ex-husband, doesn't drink. "I feel really fortunate to have met such a wonderful guy at this point in my life, but part of me is lamenting my loss of freedom. I mean, he's not asking me to cook him dinner, but last week he needed a place to put his file cabinet—his son lives in their family home and is running his own small business from the house—and it 'magically' appeared in my garage! He didn't exactly ask, and I didn't exactly say no either. I don't want to hurt his feelings, but I *don't* want him living with me. So the dilemma is: What if I put my foot down and I ruin a great thing?"

The situation becomes a crisis for her when her boyfriend invites two of his friends over to Lorraine's house for dinner, and suddenly she feels like she is back in a marriage—cooking a big dinner and cleaning up afterward—which is not what she wants! She knows she has to get up the nerve to say: "That file cabinet has got to go. I love you, but I am not interested in living together. I feel like I just got my life back and you are a great addition to it, but I am not ready to be 'wifey' again."

Catherine explains that Lorraine has finally found some freedom and her own voice, and now fears giving it away bit by bit. Although she doesn't realize it, her unconscious pattern, all her life, has been to be a pleaser, a fixer, a rescuer. She puts everybody else first: her kids, her ex, and now her boyfriend. But she is starting to realize that she has earned this new independence and doesn't want to give it up. At first she feels selfish, but then realizes she is not. Because she failed to have a conversation about that file cabinet beforehand she is now forced to have an even more painful one. She has never liked being confrontational, but she forces herself to bring it up. By bringing that file cabinet over and having friends to her house for dinner, Lorraine's boyfriend infringed on her space and her freedom. She's clearly thriving living alone. Her whole house is now her "tenth room," where she can think, create, breathe. She finally has a space she can call her own.

Now that Lorraine has finally found her own domain, she has to be willing to protect it, even from someone who loves her. "I promised myself after my last marriage that I would never let my own needs be ignored again. It's like I woke up from a long sleep and thought: *Stay alert, it's important to be in charge of your life.* I want my kids to be proud of me and see me as the person I am today, not for the wimp who put up with all that for years with their dad."

Lorraine told her boyfriend he had to pick up his stuff. "If that means you want out, then good-bye," she told him. He was perplexed, but it wasn't a big deal. He got his stuff, but he didn't break up with her.

Lorraine learned it's not either/or, it's both/and, which means she can have her space *and* a boyfriend. He can come for dinner and leave. He can sleep over and not keep his stuff there. She doesn't have to give him a key or a drawer either. And if he pushes back, that's fine. Conflict is part of every healthy relationship. The pearl: Being true to yourself doesn't mean you will lose the other person. But just going along may mean you'll lose yourself.

WE HAD THESE AMAZING PANCAKE MORNINGS WHEN I WAS A KID

"I'm hoping the kitchen will be the spot of many happy memories for my family. I know it sounds corny, but the kitchen was

the happiest place in my house when I was a child. Whatever
problems we had—overdue bills or a bad report card—seemed
to disappear when we'd do a family project in the kitchen."

—Rebecca, 31; Atlanta, Georgia

Rebecca says her dad liked to cook elaborate gourmet meals and
would get all his kids involved in his productions. "He'd have one of us,
usually me, at the sink cleaning vegetables, my middle sister at the cutting
board slicing and dicing, and our youngest brother usually did the mea-
suring and mixing. We were like a well-oiled machine." Rebecca's mom
didn't like to cook, but she did the shopping and the cleanup, so everyone
had a role.

Rebecca has her own family now—a husband and two young children,
three and five. She is happy to report that her kids love to sift the flour
and wash blueberries as their mom makes pancakes on Sunday mornings.
"When we're all in our pajamas and the girls are with me in the kitchen
making breakfast, I get this warm feeling that everything's all right."

Chuck, her husband, is thrilled that Rebecca's a great cook (he can
hardly use the can opener), but he has noticed that she seems happiest
when she's in the kitchen with the girls. He wonders, What happened to
his attentive wife, the one who used to cook for him? Even Rebecca has
noticed this change in their relationship. "I get so much satisfaction being
with my kids that maybe I'm not paying as much attention to my husband
as I should." She understands Chuck's complaint but confesses that she
just doesn't feel as connected to him as she did when they were first married. In fact, she is a little annoyed that Chuck can't "find a role" in the
kitchen and enjoy his family there.

What's going on here? Catherine would point out that Chuck is feeling neglected because Rebecca has shifted her intimacy to the girls. She
identifies with her father and enjoys the closeness with her kids. But
Chuck is left out. Though serious conversation can happen at the kitchen
table, it can't when the table's covered with flour, sugar, eggs, and kids.
Chuck and Rebecca need to come back to the table when it's quiet and
the kids are in bed. They can bring up memories and listen to each other.

She wants to re-create the security and happy hearth her dad provided, and Chuck craves the coddling his mother used to give him with meals and praise and hugs. He also wants to say to her: "Just because you have kids, don't forget your husband."

Rebecca knows she is too kid-centric at times and needs to throw a little heat in his direction. They can make this work, but only if they both agree on what they need from one another and how to get it. Maybe she cooks for just him one night a week, a candlelit dinner after the girls are in bed. Rebecca can agree to give him more attention, but perhaps not on weekend mornings, when her focus shifts to the kids. She loved those family bonding moments from her childhood, and she wishes he could understand her desire to re-create them. But he doesn't cook, or enjoy being in the kitchen, so she can't force bonding when to him it feels more like bondage. Chuck can spend time kicking a soccer ball with the girls. The point is connecting, not necessarily cooking.

Catherine says Rebecca is "screening" and that she has to stop trying to relive scenes from her childhood but instead try to create new traditions. Her key process here is to ask herself, What am I trying to achieve by forcing the pancake mornings? Am I succeeding at creating family togetherness, or am I missing the point? She wants to connect, but she is too busy controlling and trying to create a happy scene. She needs to be aware that her screen memories aren't shared by everyone. In fact they are making it difficult for her husband to feel included. He hates being in the kitchen, so she shouldn't insist that he be there! Anytime you get big resistance from a family member, you have to ask yourself, What am I trying to accomplish? And if it's connecting, you may need to find a new way to do it.

Once Chuck and Rebecca clean up the bedroom (where she isn't attentive enough) and the basement (where childhood memories are driving her behavior) they can reenter the kitchen Sunday morning and maybe even show Chuck how to crack an egg. They can all laugh about the fact that the three-year-old is better at flipping pancakes than Daddy. The pearl here is: Now is it! Enjoy this moment, even if it's cereal and burnt toast. Rebecca may not be having perfect pancake mornings the way she did as a child, but she can create new memories that her kids will torture their own families with later.

WHY DOESN'T HE LISTEN?

"We get together at the end of the day and talk about things, but most of the time, I might as well be talking to myself. Sometimes I want to shake my boyfriend and scream at him: Are you listening? Do you care? I love him, but I may have to leave him. He's just not there for me the way I think he should be. The way I deserve."

—Marianne, 27; Portland, Oregon

Marianne is a second grade schoolteacher at a public school, and she knows that not every single story about seven-year-olds is going to be riveting to her dates. But she feels as if she must sound like the teacher from Charlie Brown, whose voice is translated into: "*Mwa mwaw, mwa mwaw!*" because her boyfriend glazes over, or worse, interrupts her or just thumbs his BlackBerry while she is telling him a story.

"The point is, he should care what happens to me during the day, and he just doesn't seem to. My dad used to listen to us all at the dinner table, and we never were allowed to interrupt each other or we'd be punished. He was an old-school kind of guy, and he expected perfect behavior, even when we were little. So if you wanted to talk, you waited your turn and respected whoever was speaking."

When Marianne started dating Brian, she immediately noticed (and was upset) that when she'd tell him something she thought was important he wouldn't follow up with appropriate questions or comments. One time a waiter interrupted her, and when they'd finished ordering, Brian never asked, "What were you saying?" She was taken aback.

"It's like he'd listen, but not hear. Or it was like he didn't *want* to talk with me about this subject, especially when it was something really deep. He'd be kind of quiet, and then change the subject. It felt awful to me. I felt really unheard. Even though Brian was starting to say he loved me, I knew something was wrong if he couldn't even follow conversations that were important to me. He didn't really *know* me."

When Marianne tried to talk with Brian about this, he was perplexed. He'd always considered himself a good listener. That's when she really knew she had a problem. "I see these kinds of conversations as the essence of a relationship," she says. "Needless to say, I don't see this relationship lasting much longer."

Catherine says Marianne is right; the reason it's called a relationship is because you are supposed to be relating. But there is a big clue in her story, which is that Brian avoids the heavy stuff, because, Catherine would guess, he feels uncomfortable with it, doesn't know how to fix it, and that makes him feel helpless. Yet Marianne's response to his signals (he changes topics, or just zones out) is to talk more and insist on his listening. But it becomes nagging.

She says, "I'm just trying to share the details of my day with you! But you never want to listen to my stories." Brian doesn't seem to get it, but she can't change him by insisting that he listen, and she's only driving him further from her. The result: They aren't able to make meaningful conversation.

Everyone comes to a relationship from a different place, so when Marianne realizes her needs aren't being met (after she is sure she has made herself clear), she has a choice: She can accept Brian, limitations and all, or leave, and find someone who wants to hear what she has to say. In the relationship equation, where $A + B = C$, A (Marianne) decided that B (Brian) is never going to be the man for her. She wants C (caring and conversing). Her pearl: Before you can build a relationship, you first have to relate.

But before Marianne gets into another serious relationship she should test out the idea that she doesn't have to bring up every one of her students' problems over a dinner date. Or her own dramas, for that matter. She has to check herself to make sure she's not the queen of TMI. Marianne also needs to accept that it may not be possible to replicate that orderly dinner table of her youth. By the way, if you haven't figured it out by now, we're in

Marianne's family room and basement, since she's still Daddy's girl and Daddy never interrupted her and always found her stories fascinating!

Hopefully, the next time she's on a date and the waiter interrupts her story to take her order, she'll know she's found an attentive guy when he says: "Now, what were you saying?"

Her pearl is to remember to relate and not just recite.

SOUL MATE OR HELPMATE?

"Am I his wife or his maid? I mean, I love to cook, but it feels like the only reason he's married to me is that I'm the chef, the cleaning lady, the errand runner, and yes, the sex partner too. (I refuse to use the word *slave* there, but I thought it!) When I'm honest about my life, I feel like he married 'the help'—me. What do I do now?"

—Gina, 32; Tampa, Florida

Gina's new husband, Tom, loves to eat, and she loves to cook. Seems like a match made in heaven—and usually it is. "He will call from the office to see what I'm planning for dinner," Gina says, "and while that's sweet, sometimes, it can become annoying, since that's the only reason he calls. It would be nice if he occasionally called to see how my day was going, or what's new. I know he loves me, but sometimes I feel like the hired help."

When Gina complains to Tom about this, he's baffled. He thinks he is paying her a great compliment. "I love you and I love your cooking," he says. "It makes me feel so taken care of, like I'm back in my mom's kitchen." This is hardly sexy to Gina, since she likes her mother-in-law but doesn't want to be made to feel as though Tom's having sex with a younger version of his mother.

Plus, Gina wants to be loved for more than her meals. "I know I'm being extreme when I say this, but Tom is obsessed with food—and his mother! Sometimes I don't feel like cooking, or I want *him* to make dinner, and he seems so disappointed. I hate seeing his pouty face, but I also feel like I'm getting taken advantage of. That's not the dynamic I'm look-ing for with my relationship."

Food is just one place their friction is apparent, since they aren't even talking about all the other chores he expects of her: taking his shirts to the dry cleaners, getting the car to the service station, calling the cable guy, etc. It's a long list, and the only thing on it that sounds even close to loving is, "What's for dinner?"

Catherine would tell Gina that she needs to understand she is promoting this dynamic—his neediness and her servitude—and in order to figure out why she's doing that, Catherine would ask her to take a break from the stove and walk through her emotional house. First stop is the family room, where her in-laws are feeding her husband the idea that a wife should be a perfect helpmate.

Gina comes from a long line of Italian food lovers who all prided themselves in being great cooks, and she remembers her grandmother teaching her to make delicious meals and then hearing all the compli-ments her grandfather would shower on her throughout the meal. It was as if food was a way of pleasing men, so every woman in her family learned to create delicious meals.

These memories are potent, and one of her favorite pictures is a photo-graph of twenty people from four generations of her family sitting around her childhood dinner table. It reminds her that a big meal is the central part of the family. She thinks about how her father always treated her mother sweetly, always complimented her on the amazing food she pre-pared. Tom is now treating her the same way.

Gina needs to sit down at the kitchen table with Tom—but not over a plate of pasta—and hash out her feelings, explaining to him that when he focuses only on food she feels less like his bride and more like his mother.

The key process here is "too much of a good thing is a bad thing"—she can love the tradition of putting a great meal on the table, but she doesn't have to do it every night. Maybe one night he makes dinner, or they go out. But she has to express how she's feeling before she gets fed up and throws the pot of Bolognese sauce at him.

Tom is shocked when she starts the conversation, saying he didn't know she felt so strongly about this. To him, she had always initiated the dinner conversation, practically first thing every morning, as in, "What would you like tonight? I have to know before I go to the store." Then he felt as if he was paying attention to her by calling in the afternoon and checking on how she was doing. It was meant to be loving, not bossy, he explains. Gina's relieved but also a bit nervous about being thought of as less than the perfect wife. She says, "Don't tell your mother. She'll think I'm lazy or not good enough for you." But by realizing that she brought this dynamic to her marriage as surely as she carried her recipe book into their home, she can put the cookbook away for a night and pick up a take-out menu.

Catherine adds that once you have expressed your feelings, you have to stand by your words and convictions. Don't slip back by dint of habit but respect your limits and follow through with your resolutions. It's easy to fall into old patterns, but your frustration will ultimately return, so you have to be willing to be a little uncomfortable until you establish new routines.

Her pearl: You're not your mother. Be authentic, true to you.

THE SIXTY-YEAR-OLD TODDLER

"I've already raised my kids, and now my husband is like another child, completely dependent on me. I want to tell him to fend for himself, and I want to travel, see my grandchildren, start doing new, exciting things. He's just interested in padding around the house in his slippers, and honestly, if I left him alone for more than forty-eight hours he wouldn't know where to get his next meal. I am so sick of it sometimes that I can't breathe."

—Sandy, 60; New Haven, Connecticut

Sandy is a retired high school principal who now teaches English as a second language at a community college. She loves her work and is very busy running an organization she started that mentors schoolchildren around the city. She also always has had full responsibility for her household, since her husband, Glenn, owns a construction company and spends more time on the site than he does at home. When Glenn is home, he spends a lot of time watching TV, reading the newspaper, and asking Sandy where he left his glasses.

He can't make himself dinner, and Sandy can't even send him to the store for salad dressing or a ripe tomato, because she knows he'll get the wrong thing. It's learned helplessness, and Sandy knows she is complicit in it. "Glenn's a great husband, father, and now grandfather, but he doesn't—and never has—done much around the house." This always irritated Sandy, and now Glenn is starting to feel agitated as well, because Sandy's not home as much, since she has become the go-to babysitter for her grandchildren. Now Glenn is getting grumpy.

"It's as if he's in competition with our grandkids, vying for my time and attention. Maybe I've overindulged him as a traditional wife, but we are both in good health and have a lot of years ahead of us, God willing, so we are going to have to make some changes if our marriage is to survive."

Catherine would suggest that although Sandy's main complaint about Glenn is that he is too dependent on her, she has allowed this to happen. Now she wants to change the dynamic, but she first may need to visit some other rooms, since this pattern started when she was a child who loved to be needed. Her primary relationship growing up was with her mother and was fraught with overdependence, since her mother was needy and controlling, and the way Sandy dealt with it was to comply in order to defuse the tension and keep the peace.

But Sandy's also having issues with the fact that at sixty she's feeling young, fit, and healthy, whereas Glenn is becoming stagnant, more set in his ways, and happy to stay home all the time. If it were up to him, he would leave the house only to play golf.

Sandy's urge is to go off to see those two adorable "little people" who are her grandchildren, and she feels she is missing their most important years. "I want them to know me and rely on me." She explains that Glenn is the love of her life and her life partner . . . but she wants an equal partner. A grown-up who can take care of himself. She needs to drag him into the kitchen and have a conversation with him about whether he prefers a stack of take-out menus or a freezer full of entrées. Or he can make a few dinner dates with his pals at the club, because if she is free to go have "fun," so is he.

Catherine says Sandy has to acknowledge that she is enabling Glenn's dependency, since for forty years she has enjoyed being needed by him. The key process here is "too much of a good thing is a bad thing," since she taught him a form of learned helplessness. She colluded with him in perpetuating the idea that he couldn't do anything for himself around the house.

We'd add this pearl: If you want to stop a spouse from acting like a baby, stop babysitting him.

I'M A NEAT FREAK—AND PROUD OF IT!

"I drive my family crazy—I've cleaned and put away the pots and pans before we even sit down to eat dinner. By then, of course, the food is cold. I don't expect that they will keep the house as sparkling as I'd like it—my standards are high—but is it too much to ask that they not leave every room a pigsty?"

—Brenda, 41; St. Louis, Missouri

Brenda is an executive recruiter who never got less than an A– in school. She took time off after her second child was born ten years ago, and she spends an extraordinary amount of time socializing, entertaining, and yes, cleaning house. She doesn't even mind that her friends call her a neat freak. "I don't think that it's anything to be embarrassed about. What's so wrong about liking to have my home looking beautiful? Part of it is that we don't live in a mansion, so small spaces get easily cluttered."

The other part, she admits, is that cleaning gives her a reassuring illusion of control over her world. "I clean before I do anything. I can't sit down and read a book or the paper when there's a mess. So this means some days I get to the end of the day and realize I haven't done anything but chores, and then I get resentful because my husband comes home and doesn't help."

She is trying to relax a bit, but it's not easy. "I've definitely become more relaxed, but I'm one of those 300 percent people, and anything I do becomes my identity. So when I used to work, I was a raging maniac. Now that I'm home, I'm totally controlling about the house." She is also controlling about everyone who lives there, and she's driving her family crazy.

Bill, Brenda's husband, has never cared about neatness. He walks into the house, drops his coat on the back of a chair in the living room and gets newsprint on the sofa's yellow upholstery when he reads the paper. "I have asked him to hang up his coat, and not leave newspapers on the couch. But he cannot seem to remember this. He says that he works hard all day and doesn't want to be 'working' when he gets home. He basically says that he won't help! I'm not asking that he clean the toilet, or even the dishes, but just hang up your damn coat!"

One night, they had a bigger fight than usual about a late fee on a bill, and she made a sarcastic reference to his giant pile of mail on the desk. "He told me that his desk was off-limits, then screamed, 'I don't work for you!' He slept on the couch that night."

Catherine says Brenda is treating her family like the staff she used to employ, and they are ready to quit! She grades everything in her life—how the house looks, how her kids are acting, how her body looks, and how her husband is doing at work.

From Brenda's point of view, her family isn't making the grade. But they don't seem to care, and that bothers her even more. At times her husband will make a mess or let the kids watch TV on a school night, and she thinks this is his way of undermining her parenting and house-running philosophy.

Catherine thinks these two may have some bigger problems that have been swept under the living room rug. They need to sprint to the kitchen table and talk. Brenda needs to understand that she is overinvested in how her house looks because it represents her ego. She needs to "let go" of her grading system and realize that her family members aren't extensions of her. That is where the problem really lies—in the bathroom. Brenda is a narcissist, since she sees everyone in her personal sphere as a reflection of herself. But the truth is she is only in charge of herself.

She is so busy keeping everything tucked in that she isn't enjoying the unmade bed, or the creative mess that is part of raising kids in a busy world. So the question is: Once she gets to the kitchen table with her husband, what's reasonable? Can she ask that they clean up on a Sunday night and at least get organized before the work week begins? Or is it fair to ask that the kids make their beds and keep their rooms relatively neat most of the time? One sock out of place shouldn't mean an F.

Brenda needs to express herself directly and respectfully and "ask" but not demand that things get a little better. It's not "my way or the highway" when you're dealing with a spouse and kids. To express herself and how she's feeling, she doesn't need to act bossy. Not "Clean up your mess!" but "I'd love it if you could put away your things."

Brenda and Bill had that conversation at the kitchen table, which led her to realize that to change the outcome she had to first change herself, as in A + B = C. She can tell herself, *This is pass/fail, not a graded honors course in AP Neatness.*

Overachiever or not, she isn't achieving the desired result of a happy home. "I promised Bill I'd try to relax on the clean-freakiness, and to stop nagging, and he offered to put his clothes away." So now when the messes happen she tries to take a deep breath and tell herself she can always clean it up tomorrow, or later tonight, when everyone's asleep.

MY TO-DO LIST NEVER ENDS

"My to-do list is so long I never get through it. When I get close, I add more to it. In fact, I worry that I am just making work for myself so that I never have to sit quietly and think about the bigger questions, like Am I happy? and What am I doing? It's like, If I'm busy I must be happy. I'm depressed when another day is over and I didn't get everything on my to-do list done."

—Pauline, 36; New Rochelle, New York

"This little piece of paper kicks my ass every day. I never want to go to sleep because I don't have my work done. And I wake up and think, OMG, I have so much to do! I know the day will go well if I can knock off like six out of eight, but sometimes I don't even get half of it done. I even put some things on my list that are already done so I can cross them off. It feels like a cheat, but I like the look of the list that's partly conquered."

When asked what kind of things are on her list, Pauline answers, "Anything and everything that occurs to me that I have to do or want to do. Things like writing this article I have in mind, reading the newspapers, working out, cooking for the shelter, shopping for the house, errands like getting the old lamp I found at the flea market rewired, getting to the library at school to read to the kids for an hour, making my hubby a special dinner, etc., etc., etc."

She sounds invigorated as she reels off her list, her eyes bright with excitement at the idea of achieving it all. "I try to keep it a mix of big things, little things, long-term plans, and short-term things, easy stuff to get done. Then if I don't do something I feel so inadequate."

But while she can expect to get a workout in or that lamp to the electrician's, she may not knock off the 2,500-word article for the newspaper, and she certainly can't cook every night and get to the school to help out, and make time for her workout. The mix of big and little may make her feel important and busy, but it's also part of what's tripping her up, and she has to recognize that she's in a pattern of overstriving and underdelivering.

And one thing is missing from her list: a breather. Without time for reflection, you're a hamster on a wheel, going nowhere. You never evolve.

And just like a hamster that is always in motion, just going around and around for the joy of the motion is an end unto itself. There is something soothing about the movement, even as it occurs to her it's an artificial sense of accomplishment.

Catherine says Pauline is exhibiting the "manic defense." It's a way of constantly moving so you don't have to look at the bigger questions. If you stay in motion, you don't have a chance to sit still and figure out what's actually bothering you. You feel like you're being productive, and you can fool yourself into thinking that you would have felt even better if you'd gotten more done. But the truth is the opposite. Having more time to think—and appreciate the moment—would have made what you *did* accomplish feel more meaningful.

Catherine would advise Pauline to get to a quiet place, a personal space, where she can figure out what she's running away from. Is she happily married? Is her writing career stalling? Pauline isn't actually enjoying the activities she does manage to cross off the to-do list, and Catherine thinks it's because she's trying to do everything but not sensing a greater purpose in any of it. This is what the Tenth Room is for: thinking and deciding what's important to you. Setting your priorities, finding your passions and purpose.

Pauline never gets a moment of quiet, and so she doesn't allow herself to contemplate what she might learn if she did. If she asks herself the bigger questions, she might realize that she has some big changes to make. But scarier than finding the answers is never asking the questions.

The pearl: Take time for yourself. Take a breath.

So here's how to think about the kitchen: You may not love every errand to run, diaper to change, or dishwasher to unload. But if you ask yourself, *Why is this important to me?* it can give meaning to the mundane. The reverse is true when you have to step over the toys and leave home for another activity, knowing they will be there when you return. Sometimes you have to look past the mess to see the bigger picture. If you can't stand the heat, you're probably in the kitchen, and that means warmth trumps cleanliness. Being present and pleasant is the goal, not perfection.

13

The Kid's Room

Where Everything You Do Is Wrong

Walk down the hall from your bedroom and you'll find the second bedroom, also known as the kid's room. The perfect scenario here involves a beautiful room, sunlight streaming in, with a freshly bathed eight-year-old reading quietly on her bed, surrounded by stuffed animals. Nearby, an easel holds the painting she was just working on.

This cherub plays soccer but also does ballet; she enjoys music and math; she is not a "pleaser" but a natural leader among her peers. She has quirks that distinguish her as a creative and stimulating individual. She loves her parents and her little brother, and is polite to everyone she encounters. And she always makes her bed without being told.

Now for the reality: The room is dark because the windows have been covered with *High School Musical* posters, there's a half-eaten bagel under the bed and stinky soccer socks balled up next to her desk. The cherub, sprawled on the floor, is leaning so close to her computer that she appears to be moving the cursor with her nose. She doesn't look up when you enter the room and never seems to do anything you ask, at least not the first time. Or the third. You feel like everything is a struggle with her, but you love her more than life itself and she loves you too, even though it doesn't always feel that way. Especially when she yells, "I hate you!"

The Messiest Room in the House

We all know there is no room more complicated for a mother than the kid's room, where you constantly grade yourself and almost always find yourself lacking in most ways. (*Not spending enough time with the kids?* Check. *Not being patient enough with them?* Check again.) And even when you do manage to get everything in the emotional kid's room clean and tidy, there is always going to be another "mess" arriving within the hour. And that's okay, because if you aren't having issues here, you probably aren't having a real, engaged relationship with your child. Here, a mess is just part of life.

One key question in the child's room is: Whose perspective are you seeing this from—yours or your child's? You may be doing a great job, even when your child is screaming and throwing a temper tantrum. But if the kid is happy and you're miserable, then you have a problem. As a parent, self-doubt or frustration is a daily occurrence. What shouldn't be? Mom's misery.

So in the kid's room you have to figure out what works for you, as well as your child. As Dr. Spock once said: A happy mother is a happy baby. It's not selfish to try to be a contented parent. There are some serious things to feel guilty about, like neglecting or abusing your child, but short of that, most of us are doing the best we can, and Catherine reminds all of us that being a "good-enough mother" is actually better for you and your kids than trying to be a perfect mother. "Good-enough mother" means being attuned to your child, yet leaving them room to grow, according to D. W. Winnicott, who coined the phrase. Being less than perfect may actually turn out better in the end for both of you.

This lesson is hard won even for the mental health professionals. Catherine describes a typical moment when she and her youngest daughter, Phoebe, square off over issues of control. When Phoebe gets tired, it's late, and she's not in the mood for anything but falling into bed, the fights are classic "hands-on-hips" throw-downs, and it's not pretty, and certainly not something you'd expect to find in a shrink's house. But believe it or not, Phoebe, mature seven-year-old that she is, can also be furious, grit her teeth, and say, "Mom, I am so mad at you right now, I could scream. But you know I still love you." Even an evolved second grader can understand that fighting is part of loving each other.

Me? A favorite line is: "The opposite of love isn't hate. The opposite of love is indifference." I tell it to my teenage son all the time. So when I put a curfew on Julian and he doesn't like it and tells me, "The other kids my age don't have curfews," by now it's such a familiar exchange that I just say, "The opposite of love is . . ." and he says, "I know I know, indifference." And then he smiles, and we begin to negotiate. Midnight? he asks. Eleven, I counter, and then, in unison, we say, "Eleven-thirty!" Done!

It's okay to fight; what matters is how you fight. The conflict is part of the love. In fact, you may never stop having conflicts with your kids, and that's a good thing. You will make mistakes, perhaps every mistake in the book. You will lose your temper and you will raise your voice. So will they. But through it all, your job is to keep loving them. And make sure they know that you do.

WHENEVER MY KID MISBEHAVES
I THINK IT REFLECTS BADLY ON ME

"Whenever my daughter is mean to another child I get so worked up. She's a wonderful girl most of the time, but those rare occasions where she says something mean make me crazy and I can't seem to let it go. And I always think it's somehow my fault that she is acting this way."

—Emily, 33; Houston, Texas

At a recent baseball game, Emily's daughter Grace turned to a little girl on her own team and told her she was a bad hitter. Emily wasn't exactly watching the game because she was busy chatting with friends and keeping track of her other two kids. But Mark, her husband, and the coach, who is a friend and also a child psychologist, both talked to Grace and handled it. When Mark told Emily about it later, he finished with, "It's over. We've addressed it."

"He knew I wouldn't be able to let this go," Emily says. "I have a tendency to overreact in these situations, so I did everything in my power to restrain myself. I went up to Grace after the game and I said calmly, 'I heard what happened, can you tell me why you did that?' She told me she was sorry, that it 'just came out of my mouth.' I almost asked her if she had Tourette's syndrome, but I didn't.

"The next time she did something I didn't like, I realized I was still furious at her and yelled, 'Don't think I forgot that nasty thing you said to Kristin!' I wasn't proud of it. I knew that Mark had dealt with that incident, but I have a hard time not getting involved. I think I'm a control freak."

What room is Emily in? And is she in the wrong room? Of course the answer is yes. This isn't a parenting issue, since Emily knew that Grace had been appropriately parented on the spot not only by her father but also by the coach.

Catherine suggests that Emily has to step back and ask herself why she is so enraged. Often when an original upset isn't fully expressed (or worked through), it can come roaring back over something that doesn't merit a strong response. Freud calls this "the return of the repressed," and in the self-help circles, it's the "hysterical is historical" lesson: Whenever there is hysteria—any overreaction—it is likely rooted in the past. Emily's overreactions are based on her recent (and unexpressed) anger with her daughter, as well as an experience from her own childhood.

"Seeing Grace be mean to a friend is a reflection of me. I definitely said those kinds of things when I was a kid, even as early as the first grade. There was one girl in my class, Rachel. I remember her as if it were yesterday. I made fun of her for not being able to read when I could. I even remember her last name, and I recently Googled her to find out what happened to her, and she didn't show up anywhere. She's gone. It's like she's dead. Not even Google can find her."

It's as if Emily thinks she ruined this poor girl's life. Even though Rachel is probably fine and doesn't even remember the incident, Emily is carrying around the ghost of her, so she isn't *gone*. She is present in Emily's household, an intruder from her guilty past.

Catherine says Emily clearly needs to deal with her feelings about Grace's comment and work through them—with her husband or on her own, or in a nice talk over a family dinner about the mean-spirited way some girls can be toward one another in school. In any case, repressing her feelings has clearly backfired. Grace isn't blameless, but now she's angry at Emily, and the two of them aren't speaking. The kid's room is a mess, due to problems elsewhere in the house, such as Emily's basement and the family room, where her husband told her not to say anything.

Emily has to understand that she is not her daughter and vice versa. She is the mother now. The narcissistic tendency is always to think of our children as an extension or replication of ourselves (mini-me's), especially if they look or act as we did as kids. But it's a disservice to them, Catherine points out, because they need a parent who isn't projecting her baggage onto them. Keep your problems to yourself, and make sure their problems are authentically their own (they will have a few, trust us), and the best way to navigate is to ask yourself: Whose problem is this? Is it mine? Is it hers? Am I conflating them? If it's hers, am I acting appropriately? Or is some of my childhood polluting this situation? You need to see yourself honestly and reflect on whether you are being the parent or trying to "right" the wrongs of *your* past. If your screen memories are impairing your ability to parent objectively you need to do some work in the basement and put those memories in the right boxes, once and for all. Remember that looking backward is a good way to walk into a wall. Also, it's not all about you. This time it's about your child and her mistakes.

The pearl: Here in the kid's room, you have to be the parent. You've already been the child.

MY KIDS LOVE MY BABYSITTER MORE THAN THEY LOVE ME!

"My heart aches when my kids call out Jasmine's name in the middle of the night instead of mine. Or even when they say they prefer her macaroni and cheese to mine. It just kills me."
　　　　　　　　　　　　　　—Shawn, 35; Summit, New Jersey

As a mother of two (ages four and six) who works full-time in a bank, Shawn worries that because she isn't around much on weekdays, her kids love her babysitter more than they love her. "When we were interviewing sitters, I thought I'd found the perfect person—Jasmine, who worked with the same family for ten years, but wasn't able to relocate with them when they had to move out of state. I spoke to the mother of that family at length, and she was devastated about losing Jasmine, saying she'd been a blessing to their family!"

Initially, Shawn adored Jasmine as much as her kids did. So did everyone else, from grandparents to teachers to neighbors. "But then I started feeling like Jasmine was the greatest caretaker and I was the absentee mother. Don't get me wrong, I really enjoy my job and we need the money, but I hate feeling this way.

"Jasmine isn't doing anything egregious, but sometimes I think she does enjoy her status with the kids a little too much. After a long weekend, I have heard her say, 'What did your mother do to you? Did she feed you this weekend? You look so skinny.' I know it's meant in jest, but it's like she is twisting the knife. Jasmine knows I like to be the one who gives them treats, and if I find out the kids had cookies during the day I get ridiculously upset. And now even that is backfiring since sometimes when I walk through the door after a long day at work, they run up to me and beg for candy. Then I berate myself and think: *Do they love me at all? Or am I just the candy mom?*"

On the flip side, Shawn knows that Jasmine is sensitive to her feelings, and often protects her from getting hurt. She tells the story of her oldest child's first step: "Jasmine called me at work one day to tell me that Anna was about to start to walk. And when I got home that evening, she had Anna show me her first steps by wobbling toward me when I came through the door. I was touched. Look, I'm not an idiot—I know Anna took her real first steps earlier that day, but Jasmine knows how I get if I miss something big like this. As gross as it sounds, Jasmine saved the first time Anna successfully went to the bathroom on the potty. She knew that Anna would want to show me . . . and it was a great moment."

Shawn is torn because she knows Jasmine is doing a great job, but she can't help feeling threatened; she even knows someone who fired their babysitter when the kids got "too attached." Shawn says, "I'm not going to go that far, but I do want to stop being so preoccupied with how great Jasmine is and how terrible I am."

Catherine points out that Shawn's complex feelings of competition, jealousy, and guilt mixed up with appreciation and gratitude are common. Whether you choose to go to a job, or work because you have to, it can be complicated emotionally when you have to employ someone to be a caretaker in your family. It often raises questions like: *Am I a good enough mother? Why do my kids behave better for her than for me? They nap, eat, and bathe so easily for her, but give me such a hassle when I insist they do these everyday things.*

Catherine reminds us that this is not an either/or situation—the kids can adore the babysitter, *and* love their mother. Shawn has to remember that more than two people (she and her husband) can love and be loved by their kids. Love is not limited, and having a responsible, caring, and adored "third parent" is a godsend. "I know Jasmine enables me to do my job outside the house. And I do really appreciate that she has the kids call me at work to tell me about important things in their days, or even just to say hello to Mommy."

The most important thing for Shawn is to deal with her ambivalence, or any internal conflict she may have about working rather than being there every moment for her kids. If she doesn't, she may displace these feelings onto her babysitter (or others) by getting upset over minor infractions. It's Shawn's responsibility to make peace with her current circumstances (or change what she can), instead of feeling guilt-ridden and then annoyed at her babysitter for simply being great at her job.

Kids pick up on those conflicted signals, whether it's that you don't want to work but have to, or that you don't have to work, but want to. Either way, being honest about your feelings is healthier and paves the way for everyone to be happier. The key is for you to be comfortable with your decisions and know what your conflict is. You may be feeling anxious about the entire situation (the babysitter is a better mother) when in fact it's really just one thing (I make my kids love me with candy) that needs adjusting. Shawn thinks, *If I don't give them candy, they won't love me!* She can stop the candy flow, and they can be irritated about it, but they will get over it.

Even if you're fighting with your kids, tell yourself this is because they know you have to love them no matter what. This is the mother's dilemma: They feel close enough to you to act their worst, and that's both secure for them and torturous for you since you think, *We only have these precious hours together, and we're fighting!*

They key is to not blame your sitter or yourself. Doing it all sometimes means thinking of life as a pass/fail course, not grading yourself with less than A-pluses every day. Catherine would say it comes back to Winnicott's idea of the "good-enough mother" who tries her best and then has to let the rest of it not get to her. Think of all the things you do with your kids and for them, and not the hours you are apart.

A lot of moms worry, *My kids won't know that I'm the real mother!* You can explain to your child that because you love them so, you helped make sure they are happy, and you love them when you're with them and when you're not with them, equally. It's the love, not the hours, that matters. Many women work two jobs, and have to leave the house early in the morning and not get home until late, and their children still feel the motherly bond.

So here is how Shawn needs to think about her problem: Conflict is okay, but don't pass it on to your kids. If you resent the sitter, you may be displacing your frustration about your work/home balance onto your babysitter (or your spouse, your mom, or anyone else who gets to see your kids while you're not able to be with them). Displacement, Catherine explains, can go in any number of directions: Figure out why you're upset and deal with the source of that emotion. Then walk through your front door and be the best mom you can be while you're with them. The pearl: Your kids know you love them even when you're not with them.

I'M THE "HURRY-UP" MOM

"My mom seemed like the perfect mother. She was always around, drove all the carpools, made the cookies, and served up a hot dinner every night. This was great for my brother and me, but we could never really tell if she enjoyed doing all that. We often wondered what went on inside her head and behind her smile. She was so good-natured, and I constantly feel like I am never as patient as she was. I'm afraid my kids will just remember me for yelling at them to 'hurry up!'"

—Kara, 32; Chicago, Illinois

Shortly after her son Jack turned two, Kara, an accomplished businesswoman, realized to her horror that she was running his life like a drill sergeant, except without the whistle. "When I got pregnant, I hired someone to manage the travel agency that I'd started. I wanted to have a baby, and I needed to put my baby first and my company second."

It wasn't until Kara yelled at Jack for dawdling over a dead earthworm on their way to the park that it really hit her. "Why was I mad at Jack for being a curious, adorable, slow-moving two-year-old? We had set out for the park, but Jack didn't care if we were in the park or if we *ever* got there. He was fascinated by some squished critter on the sidewalk. I was the only one who cared that we weren't getting to our destination. It occurred to me that this wasn't the first time I'd been angry with poor Jack because of *my own* frustrations."

Kara's friend Elaine commiserated with her on the phone that night. "Elaine totally got it. She's a writer and confessed that she is constantly tempted to—and sometimes does—bring manuscripts to the park when she takes her daughter there. Here we are, trying to be good moms, and instead we are being distracted, divided-attention moms. That's not what I want from me or for my kid. No thank you."

Kara grew up in a *Leave It to Beaver* home. "Clearly, my mother was devoted to being a great mom. She had all the time in the world for us.

Mom was so unflappable, she never got angry when we spent too long in the backyard or got our Sunday clothes wet right before she put dinner on the table. I sometimes wonder if she had a double life or some other part of herself we never saw, where she expressed her true self, her inner feelings. But it's possible that was it for her. Now I think: *How could that have been all?* She was Miss Sunshine every single day. It was like the lights were on but no one was home."

Kara also knows now that her mother was not satisfied, and her marriage suffered for it. Kara watched her mom's world get smaller after she and her brother went away to college, and now her parents have a very traditional retirement, where they play bridge, golf, go to concerts, and seem to share barely more than a few words over dinner. When she asks her mom about those days, she answers: "That's what we did. That was just what was expected, and I enjoyed it. I had great friends. I was happy."

Kara always vowed to have a full life when she grew up. "I watched my mom be Sally Stepford, and thought, *Uh-uh . . . not me.* I want it all: the financial independence of working, not to mention having the cre part of my brain firing on all cylinders, *plus* I want the kids and the band. It's not like other women haven't figured this out. Why can't I? then something happens and I explode for no reason and think, m you can't be the perfect working woman, the perfect wife, the pe mom, and not sometimes lose my stuffing."

Catherine has a thought for Kara: When you are going to the park w your kid, it's not just about *being* there, it's about the journey. The simple statement "Let's go to the park" involves logistical challenges not unlike planning a trip to Europe. There's the prep work (pack the snacks and lay out the clothes) and then transportation (The double stroller? She wants to bring her tricycle!) and choosing the route (Through the shortcut or along the nicer longer streets?), and all of that can take more time and negotiation than the actual minutes spent at the playground. All of those moments represent valuable transactions between you and your kids.

These seemingly mundane interactions are what parenting is about, not just getting to the park and watching your kid on the swing. The little things before and after are often more important than the destination. Going to a soccer game? The car trip there and back offers many more chances to connect than the hour-long game. Taking a vacation? Chances are you'll remember the airport delays and the plane ride conversations long after the hotel or hike is a faded memory.

In this case, as in almost every other moment in our lives, what matters is the journey, not the destination. The pearl: Slow down long enough to enjoy this moment.

And the next one.

I WISH I COULD TAKE ALL OF MY DAUGHTER'S HURT ONTO ME

"My daughter feels bad because this one friend didn't invite her to a sleepover and all her other friends are going. I want to call up that kid and read her the riot act. I never would do that, and my daughter would kill me if I even mentioned it, but I get so upset on her behalf. If I could, I'd take all the hurt she feels and experience it for her. But I can't!"

—Julie, 40; Rye, New York

Julie is a stay-at-home mom who used to work in advertising. She was phenomenal at it, winning awards and rising to the level of vice president of media planning. Julie is also an amazing mom, pouring herself into her girls, her husband, and her household. "I find it very fulfilling and I have no regrets about changing from working outside the house to working inside it. I wouldn't swap it for anything."

Julie does have one nagging concern as her kids get older and the stakes get higher. "You know that old saying, 'Little kids, little problems. Big kids, big problems'? Well, now that my girls are ten and twelve, and have just boarded the adolescent roller coaster, I am having a hard time. When I see either of my daughters struggling or feeling unhappy and I can't make it better, I seem to be more affected than they are. I get depressed."

Both of her daughters are doing well in school, but Sophie, the oldest, is having some social issues. "I want to call that sleepover kid up, give her a lecture about the importance of being inclusive and thoughtful, and when I'm really out of control, yell at her! Of course, I'd never do that."

Catherine says Julie's instincts are from a loving place, but she's going in the wrong direction. Like most parents, Julie wants the best for her kids. But she can't *be* her kids. She can only help them acquire the tools they need to navigate through life. Sometimes helping a child see that she can survive a big disappointment can be an amazing growth experience.

No surprise: Julie is in the wrong room, since she can't live in her child's room. It's possible that by experiencing the kid's room as her own, she's even adding to her daughter's disappointment about that "missing" party invitation. She needs to be the parent, and that would take her to the family room, where she can become an adult influencer, as opposed to a kid impersonator.

First step for Julie? Get outside herself, because right now she's making it all about herself. She can't go back to eighth grade (that basement scrapbook we all dread) and refight a battle she already lost. But as a mother she can guide Sophie's experience and help make it better.

Julie must think like a wise adult, not a hurt child. She must be an island of calm and security against the storms her daughters will endure at school (and in life). She needs to see this sleepover flap for the minor setback that it is, not a major social obstacle in her daughter's life. She can even explain to her daughter, "Remember how this feels, because next time you think about leaving someone out, it will help you make the right decision."

Julie needs to be empathic, Catherine adds, by listening and letting her daughter express her emotions, not supplying them for her, which is what you do when you are trying to fix a problem because you feel the pain also. She needs to just listen and acknowledge how hard it must be, but then not dwell on it. Perhaps they can make other plans, go see a movie or do something else fun.

If you become too identified with the drama of the preteen social scene, you allow that mentality to extend into your home. The pearl:

Home life should be a haven from the emotional tempests that rage outside, in the hallways of middle school. Be the parent, since your childhood is over. Act your age.

=====

SOMETIMES I JUST WANT
TO DIVORCE MY KIDS

"When my kids refuse to eat the dinner I've just spent forty-five minutes making for them, saying how gross this or that is, I get furious. Then they get annoyed because if I try to help with homework, I don't do math the way their teachers do it. They yell, and I find myself incredibly frustrated. At my lowest moments, I swear the idea of divorcing them has crossed my mind. It's embarrassing, but it's true! Other people's kids are so perfect, so polite, and mine are just horrors. What did I do wrong?"

—Samantha, 40; Chicago, Illinois

Samantha, a tall, blond health-care manager for a large corporation, says that while she loves her children—a boy and a girl, nine and eleven—there are times when dealing with them gets to be too much and she wants to scream. "I would never, ever do anything to hurt my kids. We don't believe in spanking, and my husband and I try our best not to even yell or act punitively. But I'll tell you, when I've had a particularly hard day at work, I just can't deal with my kids harassing me when I get home: *Why can't I get a cell phone? How come he gets to do that and I don't? That's so not fair, Mom! You are ruining my life!*"

Samantha wishes they'd greet her like the dog does when she walks through her front door after work. "The kids don't want to hear that I had a bad day. They haven't seen me in eight hours and they have lots to tell me. Matt, my husband, usually gets home late, so I have to do everything, from cooking to cleaning to checking homework. And it always seems to end up in a fight of some sort. I get so annoyed that I just go walk the dog.

And the worst part is, I see other parents having nice conversations with their kids and laughing, and I think, Why can't my kids be more like that?"

Catherine reassures Samantha that every mother has had these kinds of feelings during tough times. Part of the problem is that she needs to ask for what she wants, like a nice greeting at the door instead of being bombarded with a litany of demands. Instead of letting her bad day spill over into a bad night, she can spend some dinner and homework time with them and then know that after they go to bed she gets her personal time, to put her feet up and watch a favorite show or take a bath or read a book.

She may be in the right room here, the kid's room, but Samantha has always wanted to be a better parent than her dysfunctional mother, who was an alcoholic; sometimes Samantha would find her passed out on the couch, no food in the house. "My mom was never really there for us, and we had to fend for ourselves so much of the time that I promised to always be on it with my kids, but sometimes I forget to leave a little energy for myself. If I were a drinker I'd reach for the wine! I get totally exhausted and then I need a break and it's not like I really want to divorce them but I feel like it's not good for me to be this tired and stressed. Something's gotta give!"

What's gotta give, says Catherine, is her expectations of perfection. She is the full-on mom she wants to be, but she also works and so does her husband, so the kids need to respect that.

The key process here is "too much of a good thing is a bad thing." Samantha needs to set her limits and ask for help. She is trying so hard that now she's running herself ragged.

She's no good to anyone when she is so depleted. Taking care of herself is a bathroom issue, all about her health and well-being, and in this scenario a long hot soak or a relaxing shower will be more helpful to the kids than a hot, cooked meal and a cranky mom glaring at them from across the table.

Maybe they can order the pizza while Samantha takes a twenty-minute replenishing break and then everyone can come to the table happy and refreshed, ready to share the details of their day. Her husband can step up also, if she asks him to. He could switch off nights with her, so she can come home early three nights a week and he can manage the other two.

Raising kids together requires a lot of give-and-take, but she is the only one giving right now.

Samantha hasn't wanted to ask for help, since she has been too busy overcompensating for her own lack of mothering. But it's not working for her. She shouldn't wait to explode to express herself; she needs to sit down calmly over dinner (at the kitchen table) and tell her kids she needs a little more help from them. A good-enough mother allows her kids to grow up and take more responsibility around the house. Trying to be everything for them doesn't help them be their fullest versions of themselves. One way to think about this: The lifeguard not only learns to be the rescuer, but she also teaches people to swim. That's the pearl.

I LOVE MY KIDS, BUT I DON'T WANT MORE OF THEM

"Pete wants another baby, but I feel like with two kids already, the parent-to-child ratio is working for us right now, and to add more to the mix would mean giving less to one of the kids—and to ourselves!"

—Annabelle, 37; Austin, Texas

Annabelle and her husband, Pete, have a seven-year-old son, Jason, and a three-year-old daughter, Jordan. Annabelle is a stay-at-home mom, and Pete owns and runs a small restaurant near the local university. Annabelle and Pete have been married ten years; they went to the same college but had different circles of friends, so they didn't really know each other until a mutual friend introduced them at a party about twelve years ago. They hit it off and got married two years later. They have generally been on the same page regarding how they live, raise their family, spend free time, etc. But one issue they can't agree on is how many kids they will have.

Pete was one of four boys in a boisterous household with lots of friendly competition and roughhousing with his brothers. Annabelle is the oldest of three girls and says the competition in her household wasn't so friendly.

Both of her parents worked full-time, and "getting attention from them was our form of sport. We were always vying for their time, and it was hard to come by. I felt like we could never get enough from them."

Recently, in a conversation over a late dinner, Pete told Annabelle that he'd really like to have a third child. "I couldn't believe how serious he was," says Annabelle. "I thought we'd put that to rest. He knows how I feel about this. Pete and I are already too busy, and we don't make a ton of money from the restaurant. How could we handle this financially?"

Pete has heard Annabelle talk like this for years, but he is convinced that his "the more the merrier" attitude will prevail. "Annabelle doesn't realize how great she is with the kids and how having *more* kids can actually make life easier," he says. "They will have each other to play with and can entertain themselves. And we already have plenty of hand-me-downs for either a boy or a girl. We can handle this. It's all good."

Annabelle is conflicted because she gets so much pleasure from being a mother that the thought of another snuggly little baby is alluring. "But I'm realistic, and I know how it goes with three—it's complicated, and someone doesn't get their needs met. We are already stretched so thin. But I hate disappointing Pete. Just because he remembers it being 'all good' doesn't mean that's how it will be for us. Did he forget that his father made a lot more money than we do? Things are really good for us right now. We are happy. I don't want to rock the boat."

Catherine says that Annabelle and Pete are both screening—thinking about how it was when they were kids. Pete's trying to replicate that joy, and Annabelle's trying to avoid the pitfalls. They need to go to the basement and bring some of Pete's scrapbooks to the kitchen table, where they can really talk, look at his family pictures, let him express his nostalgia for his childhood, the fun and chaos and endless good times. Annabelle should ask if he can put out that much energy today, with the kids he already has and his thriving, busy restaurant. And how will he feel after a third sleep-sucker arrives? And when will he find the time to give Annabelle her time with him? (This is from her basement full of memories, where no one got any time.) Which takes us to the bedroom, where Pete keeps trying to have unprotected sex.

Pete is not living in the here and now or listening to Annabelle, who is also stuck in the basement. He forgets that his mother was exhausted, got impatient, and that his dad traveled all the time for work and stayed away from the chaos at home as much as he could. Annabelle says adding to the household workload will "break my back, and our bank," since she is already exhausted and their finances are stretched to the limit.

Now, back to the kitchen table, where they are talking. Pete's mom didn't work, but he knows Annabelle eventually wants to go back to her teaching job. The choice of whether or not to expand their family has to be made together, and she shouldn't feel railroaded into having a third baby. Meanwhile, she is worried that if she says no he'll resent her later.

They have some talking to do, especially about his little "jump on it" act in bed, which is totally unacceptable to her. She needs to tell him: "You can't just bully me into getting your way."

The first step for Annabelle: Be honest with herself. Her mind is made up, but she won't tell Pete because she doesn't want to upset him. The "We won't have enough money" excuse is just that.

While she can't change him, she can change herself, and that means being direct and truthful, even if it disappoints Pete. What's delaying this conversation is her desire to get back that loving feeling they had before the kids came. She worries that having this potentially difficult discussion will make it harder between them, because he will become "emotionally unavailable," which is how it felt to her growing up with parents who were distant. But she has no choice but to tell him the truth. The pearl: Be honest, even if it hurts.

GOOD COP, BAD COP

"The kids practically smell dissent, and have started to divide
my husband and me, causing us to take sides and be annoyed

with each other. How have Todd and I ended up angry and on different pages? Am I a bad mom because I don't want my kids doing homework in front of the TV? Meanwhile, he's such a pushover that they know they can always get him to say yes. That makes me the bad cop!"

—Adrienne, 47; Denver, Colorado

Adrienne is a freelance musician married to Todd, a computer analyst. They have two kids, ages eleven and fourteen, who have homework after sports practice most days of the week. By the time the kids get home, clean up, have dinner, and settle down to do homework, they have been going nonstop for fourteen hours straight. In order for the kids to keep up with their studies, "screen time" is very limited on weeknights, and TV watching has not been allowed.

Todd and Adrienne have generally been in agreement about the rules, but recently, the kids have gotten into *American Idol*, and they have been lobbying to do their homework in front of the TV "just on Tuesday nights." Since both kids are doing pretty well in most subjects, they feel the strict TV rule should be lifted for this one show (and as a bonus they say, "We can all watch as a family!"). Adrienne is unmoved by the argument, but Todd has been waffling. As a true TV lover (who considers the remote one of his own appendages), Todd really empathizes with the kids, and he has always felt the house rules were a bit strict.

That leaves Adrienne feeling like the bad guy—and she hates it. "It's awful to be the fun-buster parent. I wish my kids had more free time, but they don't. Todd and I, as parents, can't just cave because they want to watch a certain show. If we give in to this, then what'll be next?"

The bigger issue right now is that the kids have started gently teasing Adrienne about being a "Meanie Mom," and Todd isn't doing much to deter them. "The kids can tell that we are divided on this issue, even if Todd seems to be toeing the line. They are getting bolder in their campaign to change the rules."

. . .

What's happening here, Catherine says, is that the kids are doing what's called "splitting" their parents. Splitting is a stressful dynamic in any relationship and can drive a wedge between even two well-intentioned parents. But it can happen only when the parents allow it to.

The first problem is that most couples think they should agree on everything, but that's unrealistic. You will disagree many times; it's how you handle it that matters. Splitting can happen at every level, big and small—such as what to have for dinner, or whether to allow a rude child to have dessert. It becomes a way of life in some families and the source of much tension in the family dynamic.

It often starts when the kids are young, toddlers even—one parent will bring a crying baby into the bed, and that child soon learns who the softie is. Usually one parent takes a stand on one set of rules (eating vegetables or brushing teeth), and the other is stricter about different areas (shaking hands, being respectful of grown-ups, making your bed). There isn't a single parent that hasn't shot their spouse a pleading "Back me up here!" look.

We have to take this issue from kid's room to kitchen table, pronto. Adrienne and Todd have some talking to do. They may even have to stop in the basement first. Perhaps Todd had a strict parent who made life in his house a misery and he vowed to be more understanding with his kids. Or perhaps the opposite—there was no discipline and everyone needed more structure, and Adrienne wants to create it to help her kids, not to torture them.

There may be areas where you can compromise and not feel undermined, especially when it comes to TV watching. With the Internet, you can watch shows anytime, anywhere. But this is still a parental decision, and how you arrive at a satisfying consensus is what matters, not what you end up watching!

Parents need to recognize splitting when it's happening and whether it's initiated by the children (May I have a sleepover tonight?) or by you and your spouse (I told the kids they could have a sleepover tonight). You may want to have a go-to phrase, such as "Family meeting!" or

"Daddy and I need to talk about it first," to discuss the issue privately and then present a united front to the kids. Remember, it's important to choose your battles, and to become good actors. Practice a straight face when you start your "Your father and I have decided . . ." speech. No hints allowed as to who wanted to give in. Your children are searching for clues, and they will try to pry you apart later, even though you're together (at least publicly), having agreed on a decision.

The parents are a unit, even when they disagree, and kids need this solidarity in order to feel secure. Knowing you have more than one person looking out for your best interests is like life insurance. The pearl: Parenting is a collaboration, even if it sometimes feels like a battleground. Remember, you're in it together.

LIFE WOULD BE SO MUCH BETTER IF I LIVED SOMEWHERE ELSE

"I wish I lived in a huge farmhouse full of kids, like five of them. We'd all spend our afternoons running around green fields, painting, making elaborate projects, being creative, and having so much fun together. I would stay home and help them be their best selves. It's a fantasy of course, because I live in a tiny apartment, have two kids, and work all the time. It's just economics. If we had all the money in the world and space, I know we'd be so much happier."

—Heather, 38; Baltimore, Maryland

For Heather, time and space are connected. So are money, work, and the freedom to be creative. "I want to spend more time with my kids," says Heather, "but by the time I get my work done, or my chores, or my workout, or check their schoolwork, we are all wiped out. We just want to sit in front of TV or veg out. We don't have the energy to be that perfect family. It seems that our together time is always in the car or rushing around. It's rare to have downtime that is memory-making. Life is just too hectic."

So this is where Heather's fantasy comes in. She believes that if she lived in a rambling farmhouse on acres of land that things would be different.

"But maybe I'm delusional, because I know the person who is driving the hectic schedule is me. If there is a test anywhere on the horizon, I ride them like a farm animal to study harder and try to excel. I worry that I am pushing them too hard, and yet whenever I see them goofing off, even if it's at their desk, drawing or doodling or writing, I think: *It's great my kids are creative, but they need to get good grades too.* So I drive them, and then I regret it.

"I love my kids and my hubby so much that sometimes I wish we could move to Montana, and be together, away from all the stimuli that takes us away from each other. Or I fantasize about a round-the-world trip, just us four, on a sailboat, to slow down this moment and spend precious hours together before everyone grows up and splinters off into their own directions. And yet I know in my heart I won't yank them out of school, quit my job, and upend our lives."

Catherine says Heather is suffering from what a professor once told her could be called "geographic dissonance," which means that she thinks a change of physical location will change her emotional self. The popular expression "wherever you go, there you are" tells you how unsuccessful a strategy geographic dissonance is.

Heather knows she's driving this fast-paced life, and it comes from her past, growing up with overachieving parents who expected the same from their kids. Now she is repeating the pattern but hoping for an out.

People often feel that a change of scenery will do them good . . . and it may, but not permanently. Heather's Montana fantasy is her way of saying, "I wish I could step off this crazy merry-go-round." But she doesn't. And she has to figure out why. What is it doing for her? Is she worried that her kids won't succeed unless they are in the red-hot center of the thrumming city? Would a slower, more remote life be *too* quiet? Heather's key process is "it's not either/or . . . it's both/and." It's not a question of absolutes: Heather could live a quieter life in Baltimore, or any city, or she could live a busy, driven life on a farm. It's up to her to decide how fast or slow she races through her day. She needs to stop being so anxious about trying to achieve everything, including the quiet, creative life she is unable to attain. She can slow down and give her kids more free time, but it's a decision, not a move to a new state.

Heather has to stop blaming geography for her problems and see that her emotional baggage travels with her everywhere. Some pearls are about time, as in "now is it." This one is about place, and being happy in your current surroundings. The pearl: Here is it.

I FEEL LIKE MY KIDS ARE MISSING OUT

"I grew up with cousins who were like siblings to me, and I feel so sad for my kids that they don't have this. My life wouldn't have been the same without that big extended family and all the traditions and now I feel like my kids are missing out!"

—Molly, 38; San Diego, California

For the last twelve years Molly, a spunky, creative co-owner of a women's clothing store, has lived with her husband, Richard, a VP of business for an Internet company. They are happy, they have three healthy kids, no debt, and they own their modest three-bedroom house with a small but well-groomed backyard big enough for a swing set and a trampoline. They lack for little ("We could always use more money, but who couldn't, right?") and don't spend a lot of time worrying about their financial security. The kids are in the local public school down the street and have lots of friends in the neighborhood. Molly and Richard are pleased with their setup and feel like they have a great little community, mostly from friendships through their kids' school.

Both Molly and Richard grew up in the Midwest, in small towns where their parents were raised and their extended families lived. Molly's grandmother, who moved into the house after her grandfather died, did a lot of the cooking and babysitting and was "such an important, meaningful relationship for me. My parents were busy, and Gramma would always have time to talk or listen or play cards." Molly's cousins lived around the corner, and they would meet up to ride their bikes to school. "I remember it as such an idyllic time. We had fun, freedom, and family everywhere. Life seemed so easy.

"It feels kind of lonely out here in California. My brother lives back in St. Louis, where we grew up, and now that he has kids, he and his wife don't get out here much." Molly's parents are retired and spend about eight weeks throughout the year living in her den.

Molly laments the lack of geographic closeness but realizes she is lucky to have parents healthy and mobile enough to spend chunks of time with her in San Diego. "Not that it's all bliss, but I'll take their messy suitcases and the loss of our den for those eight weeks. It's still not enough. My kids know them pretty well, but it's not like they can participate in their everyday lives. That's what I'd like, but Richard thinks what we have going is just fine."

Molly fears her kids will never know the closeness she enjoyed growing up. "Sure we have great friends, but family is family, you can't replace that. I don't like to burden my friends, so calling them up to take my kids on the spur of the moment, or come over and celebrate a great performance in the school play, isn't that easy."

Catherine suggests that while Molly's good old days (she's screening) may have been great, there is plenty of fun and connection to be had in the amazing life she has now. Get out of the basement, Molly, with the old Christmas decorations and make some new traditions of your own. Richard and the kids love living on the West Coast and are quite happy with their beach vacations. If it's the traditional white Christmas you're missing, plan a ski trip or head back home for the holidays. There is no such thing as the perfect size for an extended family. Yet she wants to prescribe what it looks like in some imaginary holiday scene. We'd warn

Molly that if she keeps carrying the heavy VHS movies around, she'll never enjoy the new HD digital gadgets her kids can operate better than she can!

Her nostalgia is telling her that she could be happier in the here and now. But to achieve that, she has to recognize what is keeping her back and decide to jump into the present. The pearl: Your kids will think *this* is a memorable childhood.

I ALWAYS WANTED KIDS, BUT FIRST I NEED A HUSBAND

"I know I want kids, but I'm not ready to do it alone, be a single mother who got pregnant with a frozen egg and some anonymous sperm donor. It's hard for me to imagine a child without a father, or me without a life companion."

—Laura, 39; Chicago, Illinois

Laura, who is single and a bond trader, says she is "not meant to be alone. Why I'm alone, I can't tell you. I hope I will meet someone, and I'm trying to think positively about that." But Laura is not only concerned about meeting the right guy; she also wants to do it soon, before her biological clock is done ticking. "I'll be forty in eight months, and I have always wanted children. Of course I thought they'd be my own biologically, with my husband (whoever he is), but time is running out."

Laura comes from an intact nuclear family: mother, father, and one younger brother. They are all close and live in the same community, sharing Sunday dinners at the Chinese restaurant they've been enjoying since they were kids. Her brother is married and has two young children, whom Laura adores. Being "the fun aunt" only reinforces how much she wants kids of her own.

She asked her gynecologist what her options were. The doctor mentioned many ways to have a child (with or without a partner), including adoption, assisted reproduction technologies (like IVF, even using a donor egg if her own eggs are no longer viable), or considering oocyte-freezing.

"Oocyte-freezing?" After the initial shock of learning what oocyte (egg) freezing was, Laura began intensively researching this path. "In a million years, I would've never considered this. But when I checked it out and then met with a doctor who does it, I felt like it could really provide me with an option previously unavailable."

The only stumbling block was the cost, up to $15,000, none of it covered by her insurance. When she brought it up at dinner one night, her mother jumped at the chance to help her. "She said it would be her and Dad's pleasure to give it to me for my fortieth. At first I thought that was weird, controlling, and too obviously self-interested, since I know how much they want my brother and me to deliver more grandkids. But then I realized this is what families are for, and they can afford it, so I said, 'Why not?' It made it more 'all in the family,' which I liked."

Laura is aware that egg freezing is not an infallible process, but she feels like it's worth it if there is even a small chance that if and when she meets the right person, she can have a child that will be hers genetically. "I'm single and pretty frugal. If my parents are offering up the money and happy to do so, why not go for it?"

Catherine notes that Laura was trying valiantly to solve her problem but now has to veer off the path she'd always imagined for herself: the white dress, the groom, and the house with the picket fence and three kids. Now she is forced to give up that vision of herself and rethink her future as a possible single mother with a lab-conceived child. The dissonance here is between childhood dreams and adult realities, and women often have to grapple with reworking their view of themselves.

The key process for Laura may be to rewrite the narrative of her life, but to do so in a healthy way she has to first mourn the loss of her earlier dream and move on. The reality may still have a "happy ending" (she could meet a mate), but she is struggling as she lets go of that dream.

When asked what happens if Mr. Right doesn't come along in the next several years, Laura looks pensive and a bit defeated, but she is planning for either contingency, because she doesn't want to miss out on being a mother.

Now Laura is dating again and trying to keep an open mind about her future. She feels less desperate and more confident and calm about her future, now that she has her eggs "on ice." Maybe she'll find the guy and maybe not, but she's doing everything she can to steer her life in the direction she wants to go. Laura has learned she can be both a traditionalist and a modernist, and she's moving ahead. The pearl: Embrace your reality, whatever it is.

I WORRY THAT ONE BAD GRADE WILL LEAD TO A LIFE OF FAILURE FOR MY KID

"I'm at work, and my daughter's teacher called to tell me that Olivia failed her history test. I know she studied and so I am devastated by this news, but I can't react because there is a roomful of people in my office so instead I have to pretend everything is great and get back to the meeting. Meanwhile I want to cry."

—Joan, 45; Darien, Connecticut

Joan cares about grades and performance reviews and has always been such an overachiever that she is devastated when her daughter gets anything less than As. So when a teacher tells her Olivia is struggling in school she wonders, What did I do wrong? She listens in dumbfounded shock as the teacher reports that Olivia is chatting in class, may need a tutor, and may need to be bumped down to what Joan dubs in her unkindest moments the dummy section. Her stomach flip-flops, and she has to rush off the phone to not say anything inappropriate, as there are colleagues in the room. She has to use her best poker face to get back to the meeting and not say out loud: "I'm a failure. My daughter needs me, and this whole working thing has been a big mistake." Instead she turns back to her meeting, appearing calm and focused, and tries to stop her mind from reeling.

"Nothing can upset me as much as bad news about my child. I wouldn't be upset by learning our numbers were down or we had lost a client," Joan says. But this kind of phone call can torpedo a workday every time.

Catherine says Joan is trying to keep her rooms separate, but she's failing to do so, since a bad grade isn't like a bad prognosis from your doctor. It's just one grade. But to Joan it relates to her self-image as a person who had to work for every grade and even now struggles to be thought of as smart in a room full of sharp-witted people. She knows her daughter is intelligent but not a great test taker. Still, the kid's room and the office are connected for Joan, because she also feels if she were home in the afternoons she could help Olivia study for each test.

"Other moms review and help their kids study, but I never get home in time, and then I think, *She should do this on her own.* I did. No one helped me with my homework. Why is it I blame myself? But then I think: *She won't get into a decent college, she won't get a good job, she'll marry an asshole, and her life will be ruined.*"

Often when parents are disappointed in a child, they need to ask themselves why and take a step back to figure out what part of the situation is so emotionally charged for them. Joan is projecting, Catherine points out, and it may be due to the fact that she thought that would have happened to her if she hadn't worked so hard to achieve all that she did in school and in her career. But this isn't about Joan (get out of the bathroom, where you're looking at your own reflection). Joan is having a screen memory of her own report card review sessions, and she realizes that her loving parents were not always so supportive.

Her parents made her feel as if grades were the number one thing they judged her on, and when she brought home anything less than a stellar report card, they sat her down and gave her a "talking to." The reckoning wasn't pleasant, but it never got violent—just serious and to Joan, at least, lacking in love. It was like being interrogated by the secret police: They would point to a grade that wasn't an A and say, What happened here? And here? Can you do better? You must! You are smart, you have to show it! And she vowed she would.

So when Joan was reeling in that meeting, she was thinking about herself, and how she is perceived by others, and what it takes to succeed in the corporate domain.

Catherine says Joan may or may not choose to share these memories with Olivia. But she has to let Olivia be her true self and not feel that her mother will judge her or define her by her grades. Joan needs to allow Olivia to own her failures and her successes. When she gets it right, she will be proud of herself and her grade, and when she gets it wrong, she gets to feel bad about it but not worry that her mother will love her any less.

Catherine adds that Joan has two jobs here: one is to be a better parent by leaving her insecurities and performance anxiety out of Olivia's equation, and the other is to focus on her job and not let a personal call at work derail her day. The most important thing is for Joan to help her daughter find her strengths and shore up her weaknesses.

Of course you want your children to do well and live up to their potential. But keep yourself out of the equation as much as possible. Even saying something as benign as "I am so proud of you" can set up a dynamic that has them trying to please *you*. A more potentially helpful and supportive way to phrase something might be: "Aren't you proud of *yourself*?" or better yet, tell your child who comes home with an improved grade—it doesn't have to be all As—"You should be so proud of yourself!"

Or if you want a stronger statement: "I hope you are really proud of yourself! I know I'm proud of you!" The point is they should be working for their own self-esteem, not for the purpose of pleasing others, not even you. The parent's job is to create an independent and healthy and confident child who moves appropriately through all the stages of development. (In Mahler's model of separation/individuation, the baby learns not only to separate from the mother but that the mother is a loving presence even when she's not around. Both the separation and the loving presence have to work properly in order for the healthy development of the child to be complete. Without separating and feeling the empathic parental presence there can be problems of individualization and self-esteem.) So Joan's job is to allow Olivia to be her own person and make sure she feels loved all the time, no matter if there are good grades, bad grades, or anything in between.

The key process here is to show empathy without being smothering or overly critical. This is pinging again, but it's empathetic, not critical pinging. The goal is simply "Honey, I support you in all your endeavors."

Joan's not in the kid's room when she reacts to the grade, she is in a meeting, and this is exactly where she needs to be, both physically and emotionally. Her job is to do a great job at work, and then come home and be a great parent. But you can't always parent from work and you can't always work from home—at least not effectively. Joan needs to realize that her job is to help Olivia and not be distracted by her own problems. The optimal condition: Stay focused at work, and it will be easier to be focused when you are home. You will both be the better for it.

The final thought for the kid's room: You're going to make mistakes and you're going to get frustrated. Your children are going to yell and scream and stomp their feet, and sometimes you'll feel like doing it also. The only thing that matters is that you never stop loving them, and that you let them know you do, in every scenario. It's not that you will always be pleasant (or even get through an entire day without a fight, it sometimes seems). It's that you love them and support their efforts to grow into the best version of themselves. After you love them and tell them so, get out of the way. They will be fine, and so will you.

14

The Attic

Expectations and Other Emotional Heirlooms

Let's go up to the attic, where you store your heirlooms, or what we think of as your emotional DNA. Your personality (and your happiness) is informed by who you are related to, living and dead. The stories of their lives passed down from one generation to the next keep certain traits alive.

Your job in this space is to both accept and reject this legacy, as you choose, but that job gets complicated, because every new storyteller brings a twist to the tale and a new interpretation of the truth. "Grandma was a nut who lived with twenty-seven cats" or "Great-uncle Bob was a war hero who kept the Germans from sinking his ship"—the stories are often full of embellishments that would make a Hollywood scriptwriter blush. The teller isn't just telling you what you want to know; they are telling you what they *want* you to know.

For instance, my friend Jim tells his daughter about a moment in his childhood he will never forget. His grandmother was dying of cancer and she walked him down into the basement and opened up boxes of precious china she had kept since her wedding day. Instead of telling him how important these plates were to her, she said, "I want you to always remember me and never forget that I cared more about you than any other thing in the world. Things don't matter, people do." And then she threw a plate against a wall and shattered it.

She handed him a plate, and together they broke every one of those plates. "I was only four, but I will never forget my Nana and how unbelievably modern and strong she was," Jim tells his little girl. Later, Jim's wife tells the story with a different spin. "I have her jewelry, and let me tell you, Nana liked beautiful things, but she hated those plates because they reminded her of the bastard she married. Don't believe everything you've heard about that woman. She was a shopaholic."

That other version of Nana doesn't change anything for Jim and his daughter, who both treasure a legacy of a strong and willful woman who wanted to make sure her grandson never forgot her. And he never did.

Think about it: What traits did your family pass to you through its stories, legends, and wild exaggerations? This is an easy question for me to answer: I'm tough like my grandfather, who was a great businessman and drove a hard bargain. He always told me to put my best foot forward, and I remind myself to do that by literally stepping into any important meeting with my right foot. (Did I mention there is also a slight strain of OCD in my family?) But I'm also a connector, who likes to chat it up with people just like my dad—aka, the Mayor—who sends hundreds of Christmas cards to everyone he's ever met, or worked with, or for all I know, shared a long flight with! I like to be creative and intuitively smart like Mom, the artist, or sporty and strong and outdoorsy like all the women in my family. And of course I tell my kids all about these "strengths" that they have inherited, as surely as the heart disease that runs through the family tree.

The attic is also a place of high expectations. When you ascend into that arid, magical space, it often smells of wood and is hot and a little awe-inspiring, since there could be ghosts up there, and certainly there are ghosts in your imagination, the ones who want to influence your actions today. You bring these spirits back downstairs into the rest of your house, since you don't want to disappoint all the people you love who aren't even there: your ancestors. For some people, the expectation that they will be a success—or a disappointment—is a huge source of stress. These expectations range from who you marry to where you live and how you educate your kids. Not all the ancestors who are influencing your decisions are dead, but some of the most powerful voices are those from beyond. Let's first hear about one woman's money woes, since they come straight out of her attic.

I'M TERRIBLE WITH MONEY AND
NOW I'VE LOST MY SAVINGS

"I felt so stupid. My family worked their whole life for me and I felt like I'd blown it. Plus I couldn't help but feel as if I had wasted not just their money, but also all the time they spent earning it. I couldn't forgive myself."

—Barbara, 34; Newton, Massachusetts

Barbara spends plenty of time in her attic, since both of her parents are dead and she has to grapple with some big issues alone, wondering what they'd think of the new boyfriend, the apartment, the job, and her handling of her finances.

She just got through a tumultuous year—her savings were wiped out when a risky investment went bust. She lost her inheritance, everything she owned, and she is worried that she has let her parents down. "It wasn't my fault," she says, "since I was going on the recommendation of a friend, someone who knows money!" Only now does she realize that she should have taken responsibility for researching the investment. Only after it was gone did people tell her: "Everyone knows that those were high-risk derivatives, and besides, since when do you put all your eggs in one basket?"

She was feeling guilty about this until she was able to get her money back after a powerful lawyer threatened to bring a highly embarrassing and expensive lawsuit. Barbara fully recovered her principal, so there was a happy ending, but she endured many months of worry and hand-wringing and feeling guilty.

"I felt as if my dad was looking down on me with his arms crossed because he was upset, and shaking his head, like he did the time I scraped his car on a tree coming into our driveway. He just stood there on the porch and shook his head at me, like, What a dingbat . . . I know he's proud of me, but that was the image that kept coming into my head . . . Daddy, upset and disappointed.

"Now that I got the money back the image has shifted to one of him smiling, laughing, and hugging me. He has his arms around me in my dreams, and I am cracking up and saying to him: 'Whew, that was a close one! You taught me to be persistent but not piss anyone off, and look—I got the money back!' So I know he's proud of me!"

Before all this happened, Barbara had been very nonchalant about her bills. Worse than nonchalant, she was actually unwilling to put them on her desk or even look at them. When the mail arrived, she would drop the bills into a big basket by her front door and let them sit there for weeks without opening them. "I thought, *Out of sight, out of mind.*" She didn't want to even look at her bank balance.

"I thought, *These are unpleasant things, and I just want to come home from work and have a nice evening, listen to music, relax, and cook and watch TV.*" She eventually puts all her bills in an envelope and takes them to her office, where she feels more in control and the bills seem less threatening, and more payable, since it's where she gets paid. Her home has to be free of all financial stress.

Catherine wants to tell Barbara to get to her emotional office, take control, and not let bills and bank statements scare her. Even if she isn't making the day-to-day investment decisions, she is deciding whom to give that responsibility to, and judging character is as important as picking a stock. Her financial future depends on her taking full responsibility for her fiduciary decisions, including whom she allows into the vault.

Barbara transferred her parental feelings onto her broker, who could not be trusted, as it turned out. Even if he'd been trustworthy, a totally hands-off approach isn't warranted, since no broker could be expected to watch out for her the way Barbara's father had all those years.

Transference happens in all relationships, when you meet someone and ascribe to them a trait you recognize in another person, usually someone you care about or are familiar with (a father, brother, etc.). In this case Barbara fell victim to her own desire to trust, and see her father, in this broker. It wasn't to be. She has to understand that she was a participant in this drama, since she enacted a pattern from her past, allowing herself to play the role of daughter and putting her broker in the paternal role. It was a fantasy scenario and it all came crushing down when the markets teetered and fell.

The pearl here is that you are in charge of your life. That means you need to be comfortable managing your own financial future. This case reminds us that we are all responsible for ourselves, financially and otherwise. You can choose to trust others, but ultimately only you are in charge. Be comfortable being the boss . . . of you.

MY ANCESTRY IS NOT MY DESTINY

"If you grow up in a Vietnamese household, even if it's two in the afternoon and you go out for an errand, your mother says, 'Hurry up and get home. It's going to be dark soon.' My parents were so overprotective that I often want to throw off my heritage completely. But I am proud of my family and its traditions, and now I have to make them my own."

—Maria, 31; Irvine, California

Maria's parents came to California from Vietnam separately, met in a Vietnamese church in their new state, and got married. They clung to their national heritage and passed it on to their children. They also ran a very strict home. "My mother was paranoid as her baseline," Maria says. "This was coming from a woman who'd been through a war and lost lots of family and friends."

Maria's parents put enormous pressure on their children to succeed—to be perfect students and get into a great college. Maria met that goal when she got accepted to UCLA, which she jokingly calls University of Caucasians Lost among Asians. "I wanted to major in nursing, but UCLA didn't let freshmen do that and my mom begged me to go there anyway and go pre-med, so that's what I did."

When she started at UCLA, she rebelled against the expectations of her parents and dated all the wrong men and did drugs, joining the "rave" scene, doing Ecstasy, and crowd surfing into the wee hours. She ended up on academic probation.

"I finally calmed down and got my act together when I realized I wasn't hurting anyone but myself. It's as if I finally realized no one cared how self-destructive I was being but me. After one particularly bad night I knew I had to stop. I realized I was literally killing myself. That's when I thought: My *ancestry isn't my destiny, but neither is the opposite true. My destiny is not running away from my ancestry.* I had to find a healthy medium. I had to start to grow up and own my future."

Catherine says Maria was reacting by acting out in all the worst ways: drinking, drugs, and blowing her academic future. It took a series of extreme and scary nights for her to begin to realize she was stuck in a teenage stage of rebellion. Serendipitously, around the same time she discovered a new potential direction to funnel her energies into, one that would take her away from her family.

"I saw an ad in the school paper that I could join an accelerated nursing program at Columbia, and I signed on." Her parents tried to stop her from moving three thousand miles away, but once she qualified for the program (by raising her grades) they were happy that her life seemed to have a renewed purpose. She left for New York City and finally gained some hard-won independence the right way, not by being self-destructive but by getting on the career path *she* wanted to take.

"A lot of the kids I grew up with hid what was really going on in their lives from their parents, who either didn't want to know or were in denial, since all they cared about were their kids doing well in school and getting ahead. As long as you got good grades you could do anything else. To my parents, good grades equaled happiness."

Maria had to define happiness for herself, and that meant talking to her mother about how unhappy her mother's marriage was and how they only stayed together for the sake of the kids. Maria's father had an injury that prevented him from working, so her mom brought home the paycheck and her father got more and more miserable and more and more difficult to live with. "Roles changed, she became the breadwinner after he got injured," Maria says, "and now we also know more English than he does, so there's very little he can contribute other than to be a jerk and act like the boss of everyone when in fact he has lost all his power in the family. Dad gets depressed and mean, and my brother and I bond together against him.

"One day my father asked for my brother's report card and Johnny said, 'I showed it to you, you just don't remember. Maybe you're going crazy.' And my father flipped, lit a cigarette, held it over his arm, and said, 'When you lie to me, you hurt me emotionally like this. I'm going to show you how much you hurt me.' And then he burned himself. I'll never forget it."

The emotional damage is still spreading through the family. Maria refuses to date a Vietnamese man. "I know my parents want me to marry and give them grandchildren. Of course they only want Vietnamese grand-children. Last Thanksgiving my father turned to me and said, 'Okay, it's time now. You have to bring home someone and get married.' He never wanted me to date or have a boyfriend and now decided I have to get married. I turned to my brother and laughed.

"My mother will be honest with me about how unlikely it is that I'll find a Vietnamese man who is decent and smart and not going to be a chauvinist. All she wants for me is a good man who is smart and capable of providing for my family. But even that is enormous pressure, because it's like she already has a résumé in mind for this future husband, and I haven't found him yet."

Maria has to find a way to please herself and her parents. She was in the attic, but she should have been in the bedroom—her own, not the one from her childhood.

Catherine sees this kind of thing all the time—women who are still trying to please their parents, grandparents, and a whole family tree of relatives through their dating choices, even by marrying the wrong guy to make their family happy.

Is Maria happy? She says yes. "I love my life in New York, I love my job. And I'm excited and optimistic about meeting someone new. Someone really cool."

So she has most of her house together, the office and the living room and all the rest of it. But her bedroom is big, and its walls touch the attic, and the family room. Maria's process, it turns out, is that she is still pinging off parents and grandparents, and everyone's expectations for her. She can please her parents and herself, so long as she is authentic in her own life. The pearl: If *you're* happy, your parents should be happy too.

I FAILED TO SAVE FOR MY FUTURE

"Growing up, money was never discussed, and I thought it was not going to be an issue in my life. Now it's so sad because money makes me crazy. I grew up with plenty and thought it would always be there. I never wanted to think about it, since our family always acted like it was beneath us and other people have to worry about money but we are just creative and philanthropic. Then I realized the old saying 'Clogs to clogs in three generations' was really about me."

—Ellen, 55; Philadelphia, Pennsylvania

Ellen is a social worker and a writer. She never had to worry about having enough money when she was young, but she never felt comfortable spending much. It just never seemed important to her, perhaps because her mother was such a big spender. "I was so unhappy every time she brought me home a new dress, for every special occasion. My mother insisted that we get fitted at this old-fashioned kind of department store, with the same old ladies falling over themselves to help us find the perfect dress for communion, or graduation, or even just a party. It seemed ridiculous and wasteful to me, even as a kid."

Ellen's values were always different from those of her parents, who couldn't understand why she always wanted to take a stray dog home, or volunteer to serve food to the homeless as soon as she was old enough. "They thought I'd grow out of my need to 'save the world,' as they used to say, but I didn't. They were only concerned with material goods, appearances, and social stature. I couldn't stand it. But now that I've done it my way and bucked the family system, I am feeling conflicted because I still need money to live and never have enough of it. I just don't understand this."

She is now a social worker in a community center and does feel good about her life's work. She is involved with a wonderful guy, Hank, who also works at the community center as an engineer. He came from modest means and makes enough money to live comfortably. "I admire Hank so much. He seems happy with what he has and what he's doing. His hobby, making model airplanes, is his love. I'm doing what I love, and I'm not happy, I'm stressed about money all the time!"

Ellen's family home when she was a child was decorated like Versailles, all gilded furniture and ornate moldings, and she hated the look. All she ever wanted was simple furniture from IKEA and modern white walls, like the clean lines of a loft in some artsy neighborhood. She tossed off all the wealth and privilege to pursue her dream of saving the world, but when she got back from her travels in Asia and Africa, the family money was decimated—her father had made bad investments at the end of his life—and now she wonders: How could that have happened?

Catherine explains that Ellen is a product of a family that never thought they would have to worry about money, so they never discussed it. They had so much that they thought it was tacky to talk about it. But in the end they did their children a disservice, since it's important to be educated in the topics of saving and earning, spending and giving. Ellen's family worried only about giving it away and taught her that philanthropy was a responsibility, but by not discussing the other aspects of personal finance they left her without a critical life skill.

She thought nothing of settling for a low-paying job and told herself she'd never have to worry about savings; there would be *something* left over when her parents died. It couldn't *all* be gone. But Ellen turned out to be naive. The money was all gone, and she had no more in the bank than a few weeks' expenses. She would have to work for the rest of her life in order to keep food on the table and a roof over her head.

Ellen needs to take responsibility for her own situation and actions.

This is her deciding "not" to deal with money, and it meant not dealing with her life. She has been reacting to her mother and not wanting money to define *her* in her own life, says Catherine. Now, of course, that is just what is happening. The lack of money is now her biggest stress and is front and center in her emotional house.

For Ellen to resolve these money issues, she first needs to get to the right room: her family room. The truth is, Ellen is still reacting against her mother, long after it's warranted. Her mom isn't buying her dresses, and Ellen needs to stop thinking about the past and start thinking about her future. That will require her to take action and pay attention. Even if it is to the bills, the debt, and the fact that she now needs to earn money.

Her future awaits her, back in the office, where she can start to take control over her financial outlook and reconsider her job or lifestyle choices. It's late, but never too late to take charge of your life. The pearl: Stop reacting and start acting. It's never too late.

EVERYONE TOLD ME I HAD TO GO TO A GREAT COLLEGE

"I was always the smart one in the family, and my grandparents always put all this pressure on me to be the brainiac, go to Harvard, make them proud. My brother was the jock, my sister the beauty. Or so my parents always said. So when I got into Harvard, the assumption was that I'd go, like I didn't have a choice. You should have heard them; they were like broken records trying to convince me. It's like it was more for them than for me."

—Sheila, 25; Cincinnati, Ohio

Sheila and her brother and sister were assigned roles in their family, and though she was always the smart one, she was also attractive and a decent athlete. Her beautiful sister was only a B student, and her brother was both cute and smart, so they pretty much all stuck to the roles "assigned" to them for years.

The three siblings were pretty good-natured about their roles, teasing one another about them. But when Sheila got accepted into Harvard for college, the family pressure to go there felt overwhelming. "It's like I didn't have a choice," she says. "They assumed I'd choose Harvard. I mean, who turns down Harvard? But I knew it wasn't the best fit for me. And I was getting more scholarship money from one of the other excellent schools I got into—which would make it much easier for me in the long run, because I wouldn't get out of school weighted down by a huge debt. But you should have heard them; they were like broken records trying to convince me to go to Harvard. It's like it was more for them than for me."

Ultimately, Sheila turned down Harvard and is pleased that she had the guts to stand up to her parents. "I have to admit, it also feels good to say I turned down Harvard. Sometimes I second-guess myself and wonder if I did it just to prove a point—to my family and everyone else. I think I made the right choice, but it's hard to have your whole family pushing you in a different direction. They all seem to be handling it okay, but it's as if the family roles have been forever challenged or changed. It's weird. I'm still the same Sheila, but somehow they seem disappointed in me."

Catherine says Sheila's grandparents and parents are benevolent narcissists, since they always wanted to go to Harvard themselves, or at least say their offspring did. It was as if Sheila had to validate their intelligence, live out their dreams, and make good on the fact that they'd all worked so hard to "arrive." But this wasn't her idea of the only worthy destination, and they couldn't understand why not.

"I wanted to be my own person, so the more they pushed the more I resisted. Maybe if they had never said anything I would have chosen that school, but by the time I got in I was determined to go anywhere else and let everyone know I wasn't a puppet they could manipulate. I almost decided to forget college completely, go off to India, and just say, Take this acceptance letter and shove it!"

Sheila even told her parents she was thinking of taking a whole year off and getting a job, and they nearly had a stroke. It gave her immense pleasure to tease them. Catherine says Sheila was acting out, not expressing her true feelings of wanting to be an individual, without the entire parade of ancestors following her through the pearly gates of Harvard. Family pressure can alter the very things it is trying to preserve. Sheila eventually chose Brown, which was her way of staying true to herself and also getting the education she wanted. "They will never forgive me, but I don't care," she says. "Now my grandmother introduces me as the granddaughter who's too good for Harvard. It makes us both smile, but she will never forget or forgive. But we love each other for being so fiercely independent. I know I'm more like her than anyone else."

Whether you are stubborn and strong, or caring and loving, or a combination, the kind of legacy that matters is the emotional traits passed down through generations. That's better than a string of pearls.

I DON'T STAND A CHANCE.
WHY MARRY?

"Everyone in my family ends up either getting divorced or committing suicide, and this goes back for at least four generations, as far as anyone can document, and now I don't want to get married, because it's like a curse and I think my boyfriend and I would be better off just living together. But now he wants to tie the knot, and I think: *What if this is the biggest mistake of my life?* I feel like I am tempting fate."
—Nora, 29; Ann Arbor, Michigan

Nora, who is a sales associate at a small ad agency, has been dating Jed, a graduate student in comparative literature, for eighteen months. Because of his many years in school—not earning much money, living (happily) on a shoestring—and her years in the work force—socking away savings as a single woman—they are on slightly different pages in terms of how ready they are for marriage. Nora never thought it possible that she might be able to be in a stable relationship. Until she met Jed.

"But now I have fallen for a guy who is a hopeless romantic, recites poetry in three languages, and has written the most beautiful marriage proposal letter to me," she says. And Nora is nervous. At first she thought it was about the lack of security. He will never be a big earner, and she will likely have to support them. And then she realized her big hesitation is darker and more deep rooted. She thought about her family, her past, and realized, "My parents got divorced, my grandparents had a rocky marriage, and my grandfather committed suicide. And his mother did too. What if it's not in our gene pool, this thing called commitment and happiness? What if I am destined to hate being with one person for the rest of my life?" Nora knows she can be hard to live with—she has her moods and her nasty side. That's all the more reason it's a miracle Jed loves her, she says. "I don't really deserve him. Whether or not we ever have any security, I know he'd stay with me forever. That's who he is, what is in his DNA—a stable and loving marriage for his parents, and they hail from a long line of couples that stayed together for, like, sixty years and then died together. It's kind of sweet, but I also wonder: How does that happen? What kind of person never looks around and asks: Is this it? But then I immediately think, *What's wrong with me?* I am so lucky he wants to be with me, and yet I can't commit."

Catherine says Nora's stuck in the attic, rummaging through the steamer trunks for clues as to why the people in her family can't stay in relationships. One way to get unstuck is to realize hanging around in the attic is more detrimental than moving forward. Catherine reminds us that mental illness runs in Nora's family, although she should understand that this is by no means a certain destiny for her. Still, if Nora feels this issue is "blocking" her, she may want to talk to a mental health professional to better understand what is and isn't genetically programmed. "Marriage doesn't cause suicide," Catherine explains. "Clinical depression and other mental illnesses do, or at least contribute to the problem." Still, some things are more genetic than others, as it turns out. "There is extensive evidence that some mental illnesses run in families," Catherine adds. "But that is no reason for Nora to let her family history determine her future. She may be right to be wary of her emotional DNA, but she can't ruin her life over it." If Nora loves Jed and wants to make the commitment to marriage, she has to take a leap. I would add that the answer to the question "What if this is the biggest mistake of my life?" could be posed as: "What if *not* doing it is the biggest mistake of your life?" As we like to say: Not to decide *is* to decide. In fact, this is an "heirloom" from Catherine's own grandmother. Think about your own family sayings—the ones that work for you are precious and worth passing on to the next generation.

In the attic you can play around, delve into your grandmother's trunk, try on her wedding dress, or leaf through her album. But at the end of the day those heirlooms are just dusty old things. They aren't you, and while you may be proud of your heritage, it's time to go out and make your own history, whatever that may be. Your own legacy is ahead of you, not up there in the attic. Get back to the rest of the house and live the life you choose to live. You'll be happier, and everyone who came before and after you will be proud.

15

The Tenth Room

"Even My BlackBerry Gets to Recharge"

Virginia Woolf had it right when she wrote that all women need a room of their own. For the twenty-first-century woman, that can be an actual, physical space or a mental place she has established with some healthy boundaries.

I'd add that we all need time away from our lives, to think, to relax, to just be with our own thoughts and reboot. Whenever I am stressed it's because I haven't given myself any time lately, which is the one thing we all deserve to give ourselves. I was grabbing a quick lunch recently—as usual, late for an appointment—and I asked the gentleman ahead of me if he was in line for the cash register or waiting for something from the server. He nicely offered that I go ahead of him and I said, "Thank you so much, since I'm keeping someone waiting." His response: "There is an expression where I come from, 'There is more time than life.'" I thought about this and then had to ask him what he meant. (Even taking the time to have this conversation told me I was giving myself the gift of relaxing a little, not charging ahead.) "It means," he patiently explained, "that before we're born, there is time, and after we die there is time, and we are only here for our life, but time goes on and on." Time is bigger than all of us and we just rush ahead and don't realize that it's as precious as space, as air, as any other essential commodity. It's a reminder that the things you can't see or own or control are those that we should value most but that we take for granted. But we shouldn't. Time is the one gift you can give yourself every day to be happier.

I JUST NEED A LITTLE TIME
AND SPACE TO MYSELF

"I am so busy that when I finally get a few minutes to myself in the bathroom and I look down and see my husband's shaving stubble in the sink and little bits of shaving foam on the counter and all his junk left around, I want to strangle him and tell him to move his stuff to the guests' bathroom. I can't stand having to clean the sink before I even get to wash my face."

—Janet, 38, New York, New York

Janet, an entertainment executive and mother of a ten-year-old boy and eight-year-old girl, is always busy—she has a crazy work schedule, monitors all the homework on the weeknights, coaches soccer on the weekends, and barely has time for her own workout. Her idea of a luxury is a bubble bath every now and then, usually late on a Friday night, at the end of yet another hectic week. Most mornings she wakes up early and is on the treadmill in her home office by six (she can watch videotapes for work during her sweat session), and an hour later everyone is racing to get ready for school or work.

Sometimes Janet hardly has time to get ready for work in the morning, and even that fifteen minutes alone in the bathroom is often ruined because the sink's a mess, with globs of shaving cream in the basin, and so she gives her husband a hard time about it, and they have what they call "the first stupid fight" of the day. "It makes my blood boil when he says I get mad at the littlest things, but I feel like I should be able to walk into a clean bathroom, and I have asked him to clean up after himself many times. It's no big deal to him, but to me it is huge. It makes me feel like he doesn't respect me."

Despite this friction, Janet adores her husband. Stewart is a great father to their kids, helps make breakfast for them, and is always trying to be cheerful. But when Janet storms out of the bathroom and says, "Your shaving stuff is everywhere and the sink looks like something out of a frat house!" he acts hurt. "All I want is for the sink area to be dry and neat, a place that doesn't feel gross and wet. Call me anal, but that pisses me off. That and a bunch of other unimportant things that I get on him about . . . and then feel guilty about afterward. Like not folding the hand towels after using one. Or putting the newspaper back together after he reads it so that I don't have to search around for sections. That's stupid stuff, I know, but it sets my teeth on edge."

Janet's best friend, Melissa, has a similar complaint. Her battleground isn't the bathroom (or the morning newspaper); it's her bed. Sleep is very important to her, so she gets aggravated when her kids jump on her while she's still dozing in the early morning or when her hubby yanks the blanket off her as he rolls over. She also hates how much her husband intrudes on her bedtime. "He is jealous of my time, even when I sleep," she says. "He wants me to entertain him 24/7. I am the opposite of that—I want to be alone when I'm in bed. I love my husband, but when he says he has to work or take a trip I am so happy because I can do my own thing in bed."

Janet found the space she needed by moving her cosmetics bag to the guest bathroom, even though she has to keep everything neatly tucked away when guests come over. Melissa thought about getting twin beds and pushing them together so she would have her own "pod"—no blankets pulled off her at night, but she would be close enough to snuggle when she and her hubby felt the urge. "The other day I moved some magazines and the book I was reading off my nightstand and into the guest room," she says. "I even thought about sleeping there, but I didn't because I knew it would hurt my husband's feelings. But I know lots of women who would love something like that. It's the ultimate taboo—separate beds, separate rooms."

For Melissa, it's a bedroom of her own; for Janet, it's a sink of her own.

As Melissa and Janet were walking home one day after dropping their kids off at school, Melissa said, "I plugged in my BlackBerry the other day, and as I did that I thought, *Wow, even my BlackBerry gets to recharge!*"

The fact that her PDA will sit there undisturbed for the entire night made her jealous . . . and showed her that she doesn't have enough time to herself. Pearl: Don't forget to unplug yourself sometimes.

Sometimes I Just Want to Run Screaming from the House

Erin is a working mother who just moved to a nice New Jersey suburb and is feeling isolated. She's far from her brother and sister (who live in Massachusetts, three hours away), and they've always been close. Her kids are three and five, and they always have playdates and birthday parties on the weekends, so it's no longer possible to pick up and go on a Saturday to see her family. Erin and her husband, a banker, moved to the burbs to get a bigger house, a safe community, and a real backyard for their kids. But she gave up the proximity to college friends and work colleagues. Her husband works late all the time, leaving her alone to make dinner and take care of the kids most evenings. Since Erin works part-time at a home-design firm she isn't bonding with the stay-at-home moms in her neighborhood. "We have dinner parties, but our friends from the city think it's this big deal to come across the river. I find myself spending hours on the phone or Facebook just to connect with friends. When I go to the train station and see the PARK AND RIDE sign I think, *Omigod! I've been parked.* I mean, we have this beautiful house and this great life, but sometimes I feel so trapped that I just want to run screaming from the house!"

Everyone Needs to Get Away— and Can, Without Even Leaving

What are these women feeling, and are they in the right room? Melissa wants to be left alone, Janet needs her space, and Erin is feeling trapped, but it's not about the actual rooms for any of them. It's about the "Tenth Room," a place away from the other nine. They—and all of us—sometimes want to "have it their way," to paraphrase a favorite old TV commercial. Often this is hard to do, especially given our busy routines. Many of us who are mothers can count on one hand the number of times we've been alone in our own home. The toddler can walk (yeah!), but now she can follow you into the bathroom, so for the next few years, you can't even pee in private.

Is it asking for too much? To have a little space?

Catherine hears this all the time. "A friend said to me yesterday that she was upset at her husband for being sick because it meant he was going to be home all week. She was pissed. She felt bad for him, but her primary feeling was annoyance because she wasn't going to have any alone time in her house. Is she a bad person? Of course not, but she felt guilty. The real issue here is that you can't just have alone-time when your husband goes to work. That makes it feel like you're stealing those moments. And stealing anything makes you feel guilty. The paradigm is wrong. You need to *create* those moments. You have to have your own identity and your own life. And for that, you need your personal space." This brings up a favorite old expression of mine: "I married you for life, not for lunch!"

And we do love and need those we cherish most, and value our time together, but we also need to cherish ourselves and take the time to replenish our own energies when we feel depleted—emotionally, physically, or spiritually. That is what the Tenth Room is all about.

Can't Fit into a Mouse Hole?
You Just Haven't Found the Right One

The first person in my home to use the expression "mouse hole" was my daughter, Josie, when she was three. My husband and I had just put a big colorful plastic slide in Josie's room, and she liked to crawl under the platform and into a little square space where she would drag a book, a puzzle, a coloring pad, and some crayons. She'd spend hours happily playing in this little space, and when I would check in on her, she'd poke her little curly-haired head through the round hole, and I would say, "What are you doing?" Josie would answer: "I'm in my mouse house." When I asked if I could come in, Josie said, "Mamma, *you* can't fit through the hole. It's a mouse hole, and only I can get through it."

That told me Josie needed this space, this mouse hole, to be hers, and hers alone. It was her retreat. Even a three-year-old knows that every woman needs a sanctuary.

Not all of us are fortunate enough to have an extra room in our houses. For many of us, the mouse hole is metaphysical—it's that bubble bath or your garden, anywhere you feel free to think and close the doors on your other nine emotional rooms so that you can be alone with your thoughts. For some women it's a walk, for others it's listening to music in their favorite chair. Even something as mundane as doing the dishes can provide an escape from the swirl of activity around us. In fact studies show that repeat-motion activities—knitting, jogging, ironing—can be soothing, since while doing them it's easy to lose yourself in your thoughts and let your mind wander.

Some people go to Starbucks to sip a Venti skim latte and read the paper in peace. You can carve out your private space, even if it's in a public park. One woman Catherine knows relaxes as she walks the aisles of her grocery store. "It's a mindless but very cleansing expedition," she says. "I'm by myself, and I get a lot of pleasure out of it."

As much as we love our children, we also need our own "adult" time, just as they need their "kid" time. It's something kids do naturally—the first thing they do upon arriving at a playground is to go running off gleefully, like birds taking flight—but we need to remind ourselves that we need this same time away, free of guilt and inner conflict. I remember one particularly beautiful vacation day with my daughter, who was then six. We were holding hands and walking to the pool across a beautiful garden, and I said to her, "Wouldn't it be great if I didn't work and we could spend every day together just like this?" She said, "Mom, honestly, we'd get sick of each other." I laughed and realized she was right.

You have to be realistic about how much time you can give yourself: If you have a baby, the smallest escape—a long, luxurious shower—may be enough; if you have teenagers, you can give yourself more alone-time, since they're ignoring you anyway . . . until they run out of money or get hungry!

Everyone has an escape hatch, and the key is to find yours and then take it. As often as is healthy for you, find your mouse hole, before being at home feels like being in jail. Then all you can think of is: Bust out! Or more likely you'll act out by being irritable. Take control of the situation before it has control of you. It's not selfish; it's self-preservation. By taking care of yourself, you will be better equipped to help yourself and everyone else around you.

Not having that time, that space, is a source of tension that leads us to being crabby with our family, and having a bad day. We don't want to be bitchy to the ones we love the most; we just want them to leave us alone sometimes. You need to take care of yourself by making sure you get alone-time every day. Don't wait till your husband leaves the house and the kids go off to school and then say, "Hooray, I'm finally alone!"

Conversely, when your mate has his time away, whether it's his regular pickup game or a few hours tinkering in the garage, it's critical to respect that time as well. When my husband goes out with the dog and I need him and call his cell and it rings in the other room where it's sitting on his desk, I get annoyed until I remind myself that he needs his forty-five minutes away too.

The Tenth Room is all about regeneration, about recharging the batteries of your being. Remember Melissa being jealous of her BlackBerry because it gets recharged every night?

"I need to recharge because everyone is trying to suck the life out of me," says Melissa. Catherine would tell her that they can suck the life out of you only if you let them. Often she will ask a patient who is having these issues, "How do you think this happens?" And she'll say, "They do *this* to me and they do *that* to me . . ." and Catherine will say, "Do you think you participate in the dynamic in any way?" And of course the patient typically will smile and admit, "Well, I must, right?"

The key is to be aware of your role in this exhausting routine. It may sound like yet one more "to do" on your list—Take time for self; check!— but it's liberating and healthy and essential.

The neat irony here is that to truly clean up your emotional house you have to sometimes "leave it" and come back later. Spend time in your Tenth Room and you'll return to the other nine refreshed and with a healthier perspective. This will allow you to see that no one is *trying* to suck you dry—your kids and your husband, your friends, all of whom love you—it's *you* who is allowing this to happen. You give too much . . . of *you*.

The Purpose in the Tenth Room

Replenishing your inner energy is critical to maintaining your sense of self. It's an essential part of your well-being. Only by taking time to think can you possibly figure out what matters most to you. Once you find that answer you'll be able to reemerge with a direction, with your inner compass reset. Then it's possible to be happy no matter where you are and what you're doing, since you can keep the perspective of that bigger picture in mind even doing the little have-tos that exist in every room.

That is the true activity in the Tenth Room: the *thinking* you do there, about your life and your role in the universe. Of course we often find ourselves ruminating about the people, the problems, or the things that are bugging us. A boyfriend who hasn't called, a child not behaving the way you'd like, a checking account without enough money in it. And while each of these is a valid concern, and crucial to resolve, so is the following series of questions, which often gets pushed off the to-do list altogether:

What about you?

What makes you happy?

What do you love and how can you do more of it?

What is it you want out of your life?

What does it all mean for you?

These are the questions you address in the Tenth Room. So it's not only a "time-out" from the hustle and bustle of the house, or the problems in other rooms. Assume all your other problems are out of mind for one moment (the psychic equivalent of having all the other rooms neat, or at least taken care of, as improbable as that sounds): Now what? What is your purpose?

We know how daunting this question sounds. And how difficult it is to find the space to ponder it. Sometimes it can take years to get to the point where you are ready. And even then it takes enormous discipline to shut out the noise from the other nine rooms.

Other people and problems tend to follow you into this space. But your job is to shut the door on them and keep them out. This is about you and you alone. Don't allow the people you love, or anything else, to crash through into your Tenth Room. In other words, don't give the key to the Tenth Room away. Don't invite them in, emotionally speaking. This is your space alone! And now that you are there, you have the opportunity to ponder your purpose. But how? How do you get to this enormous question? The first step is to start by figuring out what your passion is, or just what it is that makes your heart sing. Because your passion (any activity you adore, or that sustains you) is what leads to purpose, and ultimately to meaning.

The meaningful life.

You want to figure that out, and it's never too late. Like Abby, who went back to med school in her forties after having a career and three kids, you can make a change if it's your passion and your purpose.

Your passions will change and evolve, especially with babies and little children, who are likely to fill your every free minute during those early, precious child-rearing years. But we are here to tell you that they grow up and move out, and that's a good thing. You'll always love them, to the point of aching at times, your heart will feel so full. But you won't always fill your day with the "Mommy needs" and then . . . what? That's your job to figure out. Get to the Tenth Room, take a seat (or do whatever it is that helps quiet your mind), and think, just think, *What is it I want to do?*

For me, the Tenth Room is when I bike or swim or jog, and the thinking I do during these long relaxing exertions is what led to writing this book. I joke that I was "writing while riding" and then I would come home and let the words and thoughts exit through my fingers onto the keyboard. But the thinking was done on the open road, when my mind was free of clutter. So I do my thinking while moving through space, on a bike, or jogging or swimming. For me the passion is both the physical act of moving and the intellectual act of writing. The purpose is to help women feel empowered. That gives meaning to my life. Catherine adds that her work, helping women make choices they didn't think they had, is another way of empowering women and adding meaning to her life.

Think about it: your life, and what *you* want it to be all about. Is it your role in helping others? That can mean your children, your husband, your extended family, other people in your community, your church, your god—whoever or whatever it is that brings you a sense of purpose. Or it may be some other way of having an impact on your world or being a catalyst for social change. No one is here to tell you. Only you can answer that question, and whatever it is, it's valid. Then the purpose of your actions, big and small, will be clear and become meaningful. And that leads to a happier you, in every room of your house.

Edith's Excellent Adventure
. . . and Yours

Most people know Edith Wharton's *The House of Mirth* as well as her best-known book, *The Age of Innocence*, for which she won the Pulitzer Prize in 1921. There's a lesser-known short story by Edith Wharton that was the source of the quote at the front of this book, called "The Fulness of Life."

The story itself is significant because it talks about what a woman might feel like and think about right as she is dying and enters eternity. The lessons from the story are both profound and disturbing, first because we rarely ever want to think about what it might be like to look back on our lives and assess whether or not we found true love, happiness, and lived every day to its fullest. The upsetting part for us is that Wharton's message (that she waited for footsteps that never came) could be interpreted as a woman deciding to settle, by staying with a man despite the fact that he would never know her fully. In other words, they were not soul mates. Our point is that no one *can* ever know you fully. You're lucky if you ever get to know yourself fully, and that brings us to the other half of the story: about the rooms not yet discovered. Wharton says the woman in the story wished someone would find those unexplored rooms. We would say that is your job, to explore and discover all aspects of your own potential, and that if you don't, you may be missing out on the fullness of life.

Let's Revisit the Story Together . . .

In "The Fulness of Life," a dying woman reflects on the "fragmentary images of the life that she was leaving." She has mostly mundane thoughts of a to-do list left undone, the verse not written and the bills not paid, and a flash of gratitude that no one will ever ask her again "What's for dinner tonight?" She thinks of her spouse not in terms of what she'll miss but in terms of what she won't: "She should never again hear the creaking of her husband's boots—those horrible boots."

When the nurse pronounces her dead, she enters a valley with a serpentine river and a gorgeous landscape, and she suddenly realizes, "And so death is not the end after all . . ." As she gazes out onto the vastness of eternity, the Spirit of Life appears before her and says: "Have you never really known what it is to live?"

She answers, "I have never known that fulness of life which we all feel ourselves capable of knowing; though my life has not been without scattered hints of it, like the scent of earth which comes to one sometimes far out at sea."

They discuss what the fullness of life means, and she admits how difficult it is to put into words: "Love and sympathy are those in commonest use, but I am not even sure those are the right ones, and so few people really know what they mean."

The Spirit asks about her marriage, and she says she was "fond" of her husband, "just as I was fond of my grandmother," and adds that it was a very "incomplete affair," though their friends thought of them as a "very happy couple." Then she explains: "I have sometimes thought that a woman's nature is like a great house full of rooms: There is the hall, through which everyone passes in going in and out; the drawing-room, where one receives formal visits; the sitting-room, where the members of the family come and go as they list; but beyond that, far beyond, are other rooms, the handles of whose doors perhaps are never turned; no one knows the way to them, no one knows whither they lead; and in the innermost room, the holy of holies, the soul sits alone and waits for a footstep that never comes."

Our Eureka! Moment

I found this quote after Catherine and I finished writing the proposal for this book and had a "Eureka!" moment. I immediately called Catherine and said, "Read this! Turns out we're on to something—no less a literary light than Edith Wharton agrees with our depiction of a woman's inner emotional life as rooms in a house!"

When Catherine first read the story, she felt sad for the narrator, because the ending appears to have an unhappy twist. The Spirit of Life asks the woman if her husband ever got beyond the family sitting-room, and she says, "Never . . . and the worst of it was that he was quite content to remain there." He thought it "perfectly beautiful," she says, "and sometimes when he was admiring its commonplace furniture . . . I felt like crying out to him: 'Fool, will you never guess that close at hand are rooms full of treasures and wonders such as the eye of man hath not seen, rooms that no step has crossed but that might be yours to live in, could you but find the handle of the door?'"

The Spirit asks if she shared her "scattered hints" of the fullness of life with her husband, and she says, no, never, since he had little sophistication, while her best moments were found in the subtler things: the perfume of a flower, the verse of Dante and Shakespeare, the beauty of a sunset, a calm day at sea. In fact, she tells the Spirit, no one ever touched "a single note of that strange melody which seemed sleeping in my soul."

She is then offered a "soul mate" to share eternity with, someone who will finish her sentences, read her thoughts, appreciate all the same things. But she decides that she must wait for her husband instead. The Spirit of Life tells her that her husband will not understand her any better in eternity than he did on earth, and she protests that it doesn't matter, since "he always thought that he understood me," and in that moment she realizes that understanding *him* and being needed by him was enough for her. And will be, forever.

The Spirit asks her to "consider that you are now choosing for eternity" to be with her husband. She scoffs, "Choosing! I should have thought that *you* knew better than that. How can I help myself? He will expect to find me here when he comes, and he would never believe you if you told him that I had gone away with someone else." And so she sits down and waits for the creaking of his boots.

The story appears on first read to be about the main character resigning herself to a "helpmate" vision of a woman's life, but the ending isn't as much about her lack of choice (the Spirit did give her a choice) as it is about her deciding that she did truly love her husband, despite all his shortcomings. And she loved being needed, being *his* soul mate.

Catherine says that while this story was written more than a century ago, it's as relevant as if it were written today. In fact Wharton's character could easily have been a patient of Catherine's any given morning, recounting a dream. It's the topic women want to discuss most, this question of what they can expect from a partner, how do we really connect with somebody else, and even, what is love? Catherine explains, "People think the idea of a soul mate or the perfect partner will solve all their problems and make them happy and fulfilled for life." But though someone else can complement you, they can't complete you. You have to complete yourself.

We believe that Wharton's story is about realizing you always have a choice, about how you act or react to the events in your life. Your life is what it is, and it's never going to be perfect. Her narrator gets to decide how to define her role within her life, and even her afterlife. Choice is the key here. Do you want to clean a room? Close that door? Live with a mess? The choice is yours.

What "Handle" Have You Not Yet Turned?

In Wharton's view of a woman's life, the house has rooms not yet explored, and we'd say those aren't for others to find or explore, but for *you* to do so. The room in your house where no one has gone could be a new interest, passion, or relationship—some part of your life or yourself not yet tapped or discovered. The narrator is implying she is disappointed that her husband never went into those inner chambers. But in our version of the house, it's not his job; it's for *you* to discover, and it's your life's journey to do so.

In that Tenth Room, you need space to be quiet and peaceful enough to ask yourself, *When everyone else is taken care of and every other detail has been attended to, what do I want? What do I reach for?* Once you answer that question—and have the time to devote to "the answer"—then you can discover your passion, lead your authentic life, and find meaning beyond the day-to-day details. The fullness of life can be yours, but you need to be the one to reach for it. Even make it a priority.

How Do You Live Life to the "Fullest"?

Imagine you are Wharton's character and life is leaving your body . . . What would you miss? What would you look back on and think: Those were my "perfect moments." How could you have experienced more of them? And what could you have given up? What time wasters should you have skipped to fit in more fullness-of-life moments?

Imagine you are on your deathbed. It may sound like a morbid exercise, but it's meant to be a life-affirming one, since it allows you to think about the big picture and what matters most. I find the chance to think this way whenever I take a yoga class, since the final pose is called the corpse pose, or Savasana. True yogis will say this is the hardest pose, since although it simply involves lying down on your back, the challenging part is clearing your head and chasing away all the to-dos and random thoughts that try to find a place there, since you are supposed to be cleansing your mind completely and preparing for a rebirth. For me, the "I regret" list is hardest to turn off, as in "I regret that brownie! I regret that dumb comment I made! I regret rushing through a meeting or not walking my daughter to school more often."

This is usually chased by my "I wish I'd . . ." list, as in I wish I were a better person, a nicer wife, a more patient mother, a more creative editor and writer, a more empathetic friend, and a more visionary leader. These thoughts are equally noisy and hard to quiet, but they also remind me of how I want to lead my life; and when I finally do walk out of yoga class and back to my busy life I am determined not to allow the petty annoyances to get me down and to try to be a better person.

Catherine would say, think about it in reverse: If you were to look back on your life, what would you regret *not* doing or *not* saying? Make that a priority today.

One Final Pearl: It's All in You!

Now that you've completed the rehab of your emotional house—Tenth Room included—you get the final pearl, the one that is truly the most treasured, and it's this: *It's all in you.*

You have the power to change your patterns of behavior, appreciate your happiest moments, and find *your* fullness of life. That leaves one remaining question about the idea of *It's all in you* and that question is: What is *It*?

Answer: You are the only one who gets to decide that.

The story about a woman waiting for footsteps that never come is both sad and hopeful. Think about it this way: You can get up and take the first steps—make them your *own* footsteps—toward your vision of a happy inner self, to find your passion and your purpose. And if you catch yourself waiting for others to make you happy—waiting for those footsteps—you could spend a very long time waiting.

Instead, remind yourself: *It's all in you.* All you have to do is take the first step, and then another, and another and see where they lead.

Readers' Guide

A *Nine Rooms* Book Club

The Nine Rooms of Happiness is a great selection for any book club (or group) where the members want not only to share a good read, but also to help one another explore and solve the little problems that are bringing them down and stealing their day-to-day happiness. Our objective here is to allow the group to improve the lives of its members by helping them learn to help themselves.

What is a *Nine Rooms* Book Club? It can be a group of friends, neighbors, or acquaintances interested in improving their lives. (It can even be a community online.) It doesn't have to be a book club per se, since any group can use this guide: at a dinner party, on a long car ride, or at a girls' night out—any gathering where sharing stories and listening to others is the point. We've created this guide to structure the discussion in a way that will lead to self-exploration and a new understanding of how to deal with those nagging little problems of daily life.

The only requirement is that you be willing to open up to those assembled about your "Mess of the Day" and know the *key processes* that are offered in the book in Chapter 5. The discussion of these key processes will help you solve your problems and suggest new ways to think about your personal patterns of behavior that are keeping you stuck. In the group, depending on your preference, you may choose to appoint a facilitator or just pass the role from one person to the next around the table. Hold a "pearl" or other token to remind everyone who is leading the discussion at that moment.

The first step is to familiarize yourself with the chart of nine key processes (pp. 38–39), though of course it helps to have read the entire book! Next, each person has to think of what their own personal Mess of the Day is, which is basically the one conflict in your messy room that makes you unhappy, even if all the other rooms of your emotional house are neat and tidy (i.e., happy). You figure this out by asking yourself: "What is bringing me down?" even when everything else may be going smoothly, and you should be feeling happy.

Next, start with one person who is willing to share their Mess of the Day. Once they do this, the others gathered should be able to identify the answer to the question: *What room are you in?* Whether your issue is that a child isn't listening, or a friend is upset with you, or your work isn't going well, or whatever the case may be—this is the starting point. The facilitator can then ask: Are you really there in that room, or does this relate to something else? Where did the problem originate? You may need to shift rooms to get to the source.

Now the discussion moves to the Five Steps:

1.   Identify the problem . . . You've already done this; it's your Mess of the Day. (You may have more than one, but start with the biggest!)

2.   Figure out the source of the mess. The question is: What pattern are you repeating that is keeping you stuck? You may or may not already be aware of your own role in the conflict.

3.   Are you in the wrong room? What room should you be in? Are you screening (replaying events from your past) and therefore actually in the basement? Are you possibly reacting to your ancestors' expectations, in which case you are in the attic? If you are thinking about your body during sex, you're not in the bedroom but the bathroom, the source of well-being and self-care.

4.   Break the pattern and help clean up the room by identifying a key process that will allow you to approach it with a new strategy. Here, we ask the discussion group to look at possible solutions from the key process cheat sheet, which helps us to think anew about an old or recurring problem. Allow for disagreement and expect to hear the words "That will never work," since it may take time for group members to absorb and fully integrate new thinking into an old and familiar pattern. It's also possible

that a member will need to try more than one key process to find the one that works for her.

5. Come up with a "pearl," or saying, to help remind the individual what she needs to think about the next time she finds herself in the same situation. This should be a useful shorthand way to remind her to stop and think about how she's participating in the dynamic, and what she can do to change it, now and in the future.

The entire discussion may be focused on one person's mess or more than one person's, depending on how deep the group chooses to go or how much ground you want to cover. We recommend trying to keep each scenario short, concise, and to the point, so that more problems get addressed and more group members feel served. This way, you can try again the following week with the same people all bringing new messes and trying new key processes. How often you meet is up to you, but the more frequently you meet, the more key processes you'll get to, giving everyone the chance to feel heard.

Finally, a higher and more important piece of work awaits: This last exercise is crucial because it focuses on the positive and shifts away from negative messes to allow those gathered to address the larger question of finding their personal passion, feeling more meaning in the day-to-day events of their lives, and experiencing a sense of purpose.

We suggest that you leave at least the last 10 percent of the meeting time for a discussion about the Tenth Room, with the facilitator now asking: Let's all close the door on the messy rooms and enter our Tenth Room, the space away from the rest of the house, where you can forget your troubles and concentrate on the inner you, the personal pursuits that have nothing to do with tasks and work, chores and "shoulds," but simply with what makes you tick. Take a quiet moment to think: Where is that safe place for you? It can be anywhere you find peace, such as in your car, driving, or in your garden, weeding, or just walking down the street in no big hurry. It doesn't matter, so long as you can get to your Tenth Room regularly and spend time there.

You will then be asked to metaphorically enter your Tenth Room, to think about what it is that makes you happy and how to get more of that into your life. The facilitator may ask people to momentarily close their eyes or otherwise relax into this exercise and imagine themselves in a quiet space where they can think and ask themselves: *What is it that makes me most happy?* Or: *Where do I feel most passion? What gives me a sense of meaning? A feeling of being fulfilled?* For some, this is a place where they find peace, such as while reading or cooking or gardening, or even just walking and thinking (especially if your life is stressed, fast paced, and hectic), while for others it's where they feel most energized and challenged (perhaps doing a favorite activity or sport, such as skiing or biking, or taking physical risks, especially if they want more excitement and a feeling of being engaged). The passion comes from within; it emanates from a sense of being focused and in the moment, a sense that this is where you want to be, aware of living your life to the fullest.

In the Epilogue of *The Nine Rooms of Happiness*, we ask readers to identify the above feeling before they leave their Tenth Room and return to their often messy lives, taking with them this realization of what it is that brings them happiness, so they can reenter the fray in a more meaningful way. For each of us it's different. But know this: It is the thing that you would regret not doing more of if you were to die tomorrow. This is the work of the Tenth Room: to think about what that is for you. Find your passion—the one thing that gives you meaning beyond taking care of the little endless messes of the day.

The work of the *Nine Rooms* Book Club is to help each member understand what it is that most makes her feel her life is meaningful, and to make time for that on a regular basis. So not only should the club help minimize the little things that fall under the category of "What brings you down?" and help clean up those messes, but it should help maximize those meaningful moments in life that would be the answer to the question "What brings you up?" when everything else is out of whack or making you unhappy. The ultimate goal: to find more time for those positive moments in your daily life.

Questions and Topics for Discussion

Use these guided topics, alongside the chart of key processes, to rethink new approaches to situations that create conflict, unhappiness, or stress. In each case, you can choose different "keys" to unlock the door and enjoy a more satisfying experience in each room of your emotional house.

Again, you may want to appoint one facilitator or moderator, or go around the circle and allow each person to talk freely or share a story, a key process, or a pearl. Ask the entire group to think of the answers to these questions in advance and hopefully be willing to share a Mess of the Day or perhaps a *screen memory*, a point of conflict or seed of discontent. Then one or more persons may offer a helpful suggestion of a key process and an explanation of how it could work as a new approach. Perhaps you can also ask each member to offer up their favorite pearl or takeaway thought, or the one saying that helps them remember to be happy and grateful, and content in the moment, and not to let the little things get them down.

To get to the Mess of the Day, the first question is always the one we asked women when we were interviewing them for the stories in the book. It is:

1. What brings you down when everything else is going well? What is the "Mess of the Day" that can distract you from your life, strip your buzz, and steal your joy? (It could be your unruly To Do list, your child's report card, an unpaid bill, a long overdue return phone call to a friend, etc.)

2. When you are in the basement, what is your screen memory, meaning the scene from your past you will never forget, which you can conjure up as if it happened yesterday? It defines who you are, even now. (It can be a negative comment from a parent, a mean-girl incident back in school, or a teacher who made you feel as if you'd never amount to anything.) How can you stop reacting to this fossilized scene, now that you are thinking about it as an adult?

3. In the family room, what is the one single relationship that can drive you crazy? Your critical or controlling mother? A grown sibling who still treats you as if you were both teenagers? A tough or judgmental father? When they do push your buttons, can you use the relationship equation to change the dynamic and make the outcome of your interaction better and less stressful?

4. The living room is a place where friendships and comparison both come into play. How are your relationships? Friendships change over time; consider the quality of your interactions now, not as they once were. Ask yourself: Are you fulfilled with your current circle? If an important friendship is in flux, it may be you who's in transition. What does it say about your life that an old friend no longer satisfies your emotional needs? How are you evolving, and can you explain to her what you're feeling these days and share the new you?

5. The office is the place to ask how it's going, in terms of your work or job and your long-term financial outlook. How do you feel about the choices you have made (perhaps not to work while raising a family)? What are your goals? Are you where you hoped to be by now? If not, why not, and how can you remedy the situation? (Own up to your participation in the situation. Of course there is an economic crisis, but there are things you *can* do to move closer to your goals, at work and in your off hours.) Ask yourself: What's keeping me back? And finally: Am I doing something rewarding? Is this work meaningful? Am I finding purpose in my day? If you want to make a change, there are ways to do it, as you'll see in the Readers' Feedback section.

6. In the bathroom, how is your health, your well-being, your stress management and overall self-care? Are you sleeping enough, trying to eat right? Making time to exercise regularly and concentrating on taking care of your body and being smart about prevention? (It can be hard to do it when you have a family and a job, but you need to make time for yourself, even if it's just an hour a day.) Next, how do you feel about your body, your looks and shape or weight? Body image—what you see in the mirror and what number you read on the scale—is a bathroom issue, as is treating yourself

right. You need to take care of yourself, and if you aren't, why not? We say, concentrate on the floss, not the flaws. If you need to take better care of yourself (you're tired all the time, never get to exercise, don't feel physically at your best), then what can you do to make the changes that will lead you to feel better and healthier too? It's not selfish; it's self-preservation.

7. How is it going in the bedroom? Are you satisfied with the sex you're having (or fine with not having), or are there things you want to change and improve? When you think about the sex you wish you were having, what holds you back? Communicating with your significant other? Upset at him for not helping or supporting you enough? The bedroom can also be a good place to discuss all kinds of affection, physical intimacy, flirtation, a wandering eye, or lack of loving connection in your relationship. What is it that you feel is missing in this room and how can you rethink your approach and start to remedy the situation? The Venn diagram of your lives is an apt place to start. Are you overlapping to your own liking? How can you overcome romantic obstacles in order to enjoy a healthier and more fulfilling love life?

8. The kitchen, where the table serves well for discussing the business of the household, is the place to ask: How are you feeling about the chores of your daily life? If and when you get overwhelmed, do you ask for help? Are you engaged in a constructive dialogue with other members of the household? Are you feeling heard? Supported? If the scripts need to change, are you able to initiate a new conversation in order to come to an understanding with your family/roommates/spouse to find a more satisfying balance? Are you getting your emotional needs met, feeling nourished, emotionally speaking, and feeling a sense of accomplishment in getting things done? (Not every moment has to be blissful—emptying the dishwasher will never be an inspired act—but you should see the bigger goal in the day-to-day tasks that need doing.) If not, how can you change that and find more joy in your daily life?

9. The kid's room is less about whether or not you have kids but how you feel about your personal situation. If you don't have kids, how did you

come to this decision and how do you feel about it? If you do have kids, are you enjoying parenting? Chances are, not every moment is easy, joy-filled, and a scrapbook photograph of family harmony. When you have little ones, you may feel exhausted most of the time. Are your standards out of reach? As a parent, you may want to ask: How can I be a good enough parent without trying or needing to be a perfect one? Perhaps one problem is your own unrealistic expectations. What are your common frustrations with your kids? How can you shift that dynamic? How can you be a happier parent, feel you are doing well enough, and also have time to be the person *you* want to be?

10.   In the attic, are your family expectations weighing you down, pressuring you to be someone you don't want to be? Are you living the life you want to live? Or are you living the dream that belonged to someone else: the one that a grandparent or other relative had in mind for you? How can you turn around and explain to family members that you need to be the version of you that *you* like, not the one that they are imposing on you from above?

11.   Where is your Tenth Room? Where do you go to think and get away from all the other rooms, the messes and the tidy ones as well? Where is your mouse hole? Where do you find peace? How often do you get there? Don't wait until every other room is neat and tidy, since they never all will be. Instead, close some doors and walk away to your own little space or place to think. Get there often enough (daily is optimal) to do the important work of thinking about what makes you happy. Ask yourself what brings you "up" and is something you truly love to do. Then figure out how to do it more often. It's the first step to becoming a happier person, right now and every day.

12.   Finally, if you were to die tomorrow, what would you regret *not* doing? What would you wish you had made more time for? How can you fit that into your day, right now? This is not a morbid exercise but a life-affirming one. It's your responsibility to know what brings you joy, or calm, and how you can pursue it and make it a bigger part of your life. You need to identify your passion, find your purpose, the thing that brings you a sense of meaning and makes you happy, in every room of your emotional house.

Readers' Feedback and Frequently Asked Questions

"What's the biggest room in your house?"

We can't tell you how often we've heard this. Everywhere we spoke and met with readers, from San Francisco to New York City, Toledo to Tampa, on talk-radio shows and national television such as the *Today* show, everyone wanted to know: What is the biggest room in your emotional house? The question could also be interpreted as: Am I normal? Something women ask *Self* all the time. In Catherine's practice, the same question gets framed as: Have you seen this before? Am I the only one? The answer, of course, is it's normal to wonder if your problems are universal, or are they unique? And is your own strain of zaniness normal?

Everyone wants to know they're not alone, not crazy, not off the charts or abnormal. We would say: What is normal for *you* is what matters, and what makes *you* happy is something only you can determine. We answered the question this way: There is one room we all share, and it is usually (though not always) the biggest room of all. Technically, it's not even a room—it's the basement, the blueprint, the entire footprint of the house. It is our past, and we all have one.

How your childhood went, what influences you felt both within your family and beyond (teachers and coaches and the like), and whether you were a great student or a terrible one, an athlete or a nerd, an actress or an artist, or all of the above, chances are you still react to memorable experiences from those formative years, and will continue to do so for the rest of your life. The events and circumstances of your past affect you daily, and influence you even now, as an adult. How could they not?

The second part of the answer is that the biggest room changes. Rooms get smaller and bigger, doors open and close, messes come and go, and this is perfectly normal as you move through different stages of your life. Your priorities shift. And while it's easy to generalize, the truth is that we all arrive at different stages at different ages, and it depends on where you are emotionally, professionally, romantically—in every area of your house. Generally in your twenties, friends are the family you choose; your living room is large, crowded, and complicated. In your thirties, you may be still seeking a mate, or in a relationship, and the bedroom looms large. These walls shift again if and when you settle down and have kids. In your forties, you may be balancing work and family, saving for college, retirement, or having to take care of aging parents.

Each stage of your life finds a new room becoming more prominent, and there are few constants, aside from what they say about death and taxes! So when you ask, "What is the most significant room in my house?" only you know the answer to that question. It's wherever you spend the most time, emotionally speaking.

Yet another source of content has been our Web site, NineRooms.com, where we blog, and readers comment or post responses on their own blogs and link back. Some of the most interesting blog posts have taught us how readers are using *The Nine Rooms of Happiness*, and specifically the key processes, to become happier in unexpected ways. One blogger writing under the title BikiniBy30 explained she relates to Lucy's confessions about her tendency to stress-eat, and this writer used the book to help her figure out why. Once she realized the source of her problem, she brilliantly hatched a plan to see if she could change her life and become happier and healthier too. The book and blog at NineRooms.com offered the clarity she needed to think differently and approach her problem from an entirely new angle.

BikiniBy30's job was making her stressed and miserable, so she decided to see if she could afford to live on just half her income, as a way of giving herself permission to quit and get a lower-paying job she would love. She started off thinking she was in one room, the bathroom, worried about her body (and wanting to sport a bikini by the time she turned thirty). Then she turned her attention to the source of the problem, which brought her to the office, where she was stressing over her lack of inspiration on the job. There is a saying Lucy likes to use almost as much as "Suck it up, buttercup!," which is that every time the urge to stress-eat comes along, instead of asking herself, "What should I eat?" she levels the better, more apt, question at herself: *"What's eating me?"*

Usually it's a problem you can solve, if you can figure out the answer.

And it's almost always unrelated to food or hunger or the need for sustenance. Stress-eating is a way of comforting yourself, or smothering your stress with a rich blanket of carbs, in the form of ice cream or cookies or chocolate, or something equally high in calories and fat. For Lucy, the editor of a magazine about health and well-being, knowing what to eat is only part of the problem; actually following your own best advice is the tougher part. Especially when stressing. The book helped BikiniBy30. And now others. She got the gist of the book, figured out her negative pattern, and at first replaced it with a new one, which was: Not to decide is to decide. She was going along with the situation. Finally, though, BikiniBy30 decided to try out the pearl "Go or grow." Meaning, go along with the status quo and be unhappy, or be willing to take a risk and grow. She put it to work so well, she's now taking the financial steps she needs to be free of the stressful job and at liberty to pursue a new career. Oh, and this process has helped her stop stress-eating in the meantime. Lucy wrote to tell her that once she was well into a wardrobe of skimpy bikinis, she should start a new blog about how to live on half your salary!

Other great content came not from responses to our blogs, or posts from other bloggers, but from the dozens of "Messes of the Day" posted on our Web site, NineRooms.com. We shared some of them in the Q&A portion of our talks during our book tour and radio appearances. And we'd like to share a couple here as a way of prompting discussion in your own *Nine Rooms* Book Club.

Technology Takes Over, Never Alone! This makes us think about the idea that "Even my BlackBerry gets to recharge," presented in the Tenth Room chapter of the book. The fact that you can be in touch and communicating at all times means you have little time to think or just be. You need to get away from the smart phone and screens of all kinds and retreat into the Tenth Room daily or as regularly as possible, so you can think about what makes you happy. Technology takes over your life and people can find you at all times—at the beach, on the ski mountain, on the golf course, on a hike, wherever we used to be able to get away and truly think and breathe without hearing that little chime in our pocket, beckoning us back to the office or the problem at hand. There is no chance for spending undivided attention on those present. When was the last time you had an uninterrupted conversation? We say: You can take back the power. You own the technology. Unplug it. Unplug *yourself*. Then go off and do something fun and joyful. You can always plug back in whenever you choose.

Here an unlikely key process comes into play: the relationship equation, or $A + B = C$. But this time, B is not a person, but your handheld device. It's controlling you, just like a nagging mother. Change A, yourself, and C, the relationship you have with B, will change. Unplug that thing. Put it in a drawer when you get home and don't take it out till after your critical personal time. Show it who's boss. Put it away when you're at the dinner table or doing something fun with your family. Technology may try to take over, but until it grows legs, you get to throw it in a drawer and ignore it any time you like.

I Feel Squeezed, Like I'm Part of a "Sandwich" Generation. The kids need me, but so do my aging and ailing parents. Between the teenagers whom I am still fully responsible for, and the eightysomethings whom I now have to worry about, I have no time, money, or fun left over for me.

We hear this a lot, especially from women in their late forties and early fifties who thought they'd be "done" parenting twenty years after giving birth to their children, but are now having to parent the parents who raised them. Now that the generation ahead of us is living longer (and we feel grateful for their presence in our lives), they also require more care and attention, and often as they age they have health issues that may even require them to move back in with us. Suddenly, the dinner table is your kids, your spouse, and one of his parents or yours. What could have been an easy time is now triply complicated by the emotional, physical, and financial needs of all three generations. College tuition competes in your savings account with nursing care. Who has anything left over for vacation? It's not only the monetary load, but the psychic cost that gets to you, since every waking minute you are concerned with the needs of others. What about the need to enjoy and take care of yourself?

A recent statistic that made us think of the need to get to the Tenth Room: Women spend just fifteen minutes of "me time" daily, as opposed to several hours on housework, plus hours with children, another 7.5 hours working and generally "being there" for everyone else who needs them. What about *themselves*?

On the tour, we gently reminded these generous women to be generous to themselves as well. We would explain, again, that you're no good to anyone if you are so worn out and depleted that you can't function, or do so joyfully. You need to take time and space away, to nurture yourself, to do what makes you laugh and feel happy and healthy, and to replenish the energy you feel is sapped by everyone and everything around you. The key process: Know your limits. You have to create boundaries. Be strong to help others. Put yourself on your to-do list, sometimes at the top.

This may sound selfish, but it's not. In fact, it's self-preservation. If your kids and parents love you, they will not only make it possible, they will insist that you do it. (If they don't, remember that even when there is conflict, such as when one of them squawks, "Wait, I need you here!," you can explain that you need to get away for a while. There's another key process: Conflict is okay. It's part of life. Be willing to say "Good-bye!" for an evening out with your friends and remind them that you love them. It's as easy as: "Dinner's in the freezer. See ya when I get home!" Then walk out the door with a wave good-bye!)

The dialogue with readers continues online, at NineRooms.com, where readers post comments and Lucy and Catherine blog regularly and offer advice, and visitors continue to help each other solve their Messes of the Day.

Do you have a book club that wants us to join in, to discuss the important issues in this book? Contact us at NineRooms.com and we will do our best to be present, one way or another, to say: Thank you for reading!

Robert Erdmann

Todd Plitt

LUCY DANZIGER has been editor in chief of *Self* magazine for more than nine years and grown the circulation to nearly seven million monthly readers. As a blogger on Self.com and also for Yahoo Health, writing about how to be healthier and happier in stressful, overly busy times, Danziger has grown a following of hundreds of thousands of online viewers each month. CATHERINE BIRNDORF, M.D., is a psychiatrist and the founding director of the Payne Whitney Women's Program at New York-Presbyterian Hospital/Weill Cornell Medical Center. She is also a contributing columnist for *Self*. Both women live and work in New York City.